Palgrave Studies in Equity, Diversity, Inclusion, and Indigenization in Business

Series Editor
Eddy S. Ng, Queen's University, Kingston, ON, Canada

This series seeks to assemble scholarly research around equity, diversity, inclusion, and indigenization in the business world. The books in this series will explore contemporary diversity topics such as gender and corporate governance, sexuality and career development, social justice in the workplace, race and marketing, Indigenous inclusion, supplier diversity, mental health and neurodiversity at work, and more.

Through rigorous, disciplinary and interdisciplinary research and contributions from leading scholars, this series will provide an in-depth exploration of each topic and challenge scholars and practitioners to consider expanding their own awareness while addressing ways to make business (and society) more inclusive. The series speaks on behalf of anyone who has ever been affected–directly or indirectly–by discrimination or exclusion.

Emiel L. Eijdenberg · Thirumaran K ·
Pengji Wang · Caroline Wong
Editors

Indigenous Entrepreneurship in Southeast Asia

Theoretical and Practical Implications

palgrave
macmillan

Editors
Emiel L. Eijdenberg
JCU Singapore Business School
James Cook University
Singapore, Singapore

Thirumaran K
JCU Singapore Business School
James Cook University
Singapore, Singapore

Pengji Wang
JCU Singapore Business School
James Cook University
Singapore, Singapore

Caroline Wong
JCU Singapore Business School
James Cook University
Singapore, Singapore

ISSN 2731-7307 ISSN 2731-7315 (electronic)
Palgrave Studies in Equity, Diversity, Inclusion, and Indigenization in Business
ISBN 978-3-031-54456-9 ISBN 978-3-031-54457-6 (eBook)
https://doi.org/10.1007/978-3-031-54457-6

This Palgrave Macmillan imprint is published by the registered company Springer Nature Switzerland AG
The registered company address is: Gewerbestrasse 11, 6330 Cham, Switzerland

Paper in this product is recyclable.

Foreword

It is estimated that two-thirds of the world's Indigenous peoples live in Asia, of which between 90 and 125 million reside in South East Asia (SEA). The discourse on these populations tend to focus on the politicization of their history; their displacement as a result of economic development; and their lack of voice and representation. And not enough of the support and policies that would enable them to increase their contribution to the economic wellbeing of their communities, societies and countries.

The good news is that change is happening. The increasing focus on inclusive and sustainable economic growth is drawing attention to, and appreciation of, the role and contribution of Indigenous peoples and entrepreneurship.

The challenge lies in the varying definition of Indigenous populations, Indigenous economy and Indigenous entrepreneurship. This is in turn compounded by the paucity of quality data, specifically the disaggregation of data on the basis of Indigenous identifiers, and, or ethnicity. This publication serves to meet a significant part of this challenge.

Despite being home to sizable Indigenous peoples, there are some countries in SEA where there have been no studies on Indigenous entrepreneurship. Greeni Maheshwari and Chi Tran Mai argue that this research gap is a missed opportunity for policy-makers to support Indigenous Entrepreneurs' (IE) growth and contribution to their respective communities and countries. These researchers' work fills this gap and provides directions for future research in this area.

Entrepreneurs of micro, small and medium-sized enterprises face the common challenges of access to credit, capital and markets; they require skills and capacity building; they need to harness their leadership potential; and manage the advancement of digitalization. IEs must not only deal with this list of challenges, but also the effective commercial use and protection of local and traditional knowledge. Herein is the role of scholarship. Each of the contributors to this publication address these challenges in turn.

Chung Thanh Phan, Diem Thi Hong Vo, Daniel Borer and Thuy Minh To share the successes of microcredit programs implemented in Vietnam and Thailand to support vulnerable populations, specifically women-managed businesses and businesses of rural households. Their analysis provides important policy implications for improving access to finance for IEs in developing countries.

Policies to facilitate Indigenous entrepreneurship must consider cultural heritage, traditional occupations, crafts and knowledge. Sharon G. M. Koh, Audrey K. L. Siah and Andrei O. J. Kwok explore the critical factors that serve as barriers to adopting Indigenous entrepreneurship practices among the Mah Meri community of Malaysia. They highlight the "way of life" which has implications on the nexus of mainstreaming entrepreneurship, and traditional knowledge and customary lifestyle. Likewise, Naida Culshaw, Natalie Limwatana and Thao Ngo explore how the aspect of community and intergenerational knowledge shaped the business strategy of a Thai IE.

Kathleen M. Adams and Dirk Sandarupa further this discussion with the case of a small-scale IE whose resilient business strategy for managing a restaurant-hotel in South Sulawesi is based on local wisdom.

Digitalization can be used to extend the reach and capacity of IEs. Stavros Sindakis and Sakshi Aggarwal studied the importance of digital technology in the growth of Indigenous entrepreneurship in Southeast Asia, while exploring how family, community and business partners can support one another to fill institutional gaps and promote Indigenous entrepreneurship.

Leadership, voice and agency are necessary to further our appreciation of Indigenous peoples, and by extension Indigenous entrepreneurship.

Endro Puspo Wiroko and Ade Iva Murty share the uniquely Javanese–Indonesian concept of "diuwongke," which describes employees' perception of their leaders treating them with dignity and respect at work. "Diuwongke" helps in the understanding and shaping of servant leadership among the Javanese.

In his study of the Iu Mien community of Northern Thailand, Urai Yangcheepsutjarit demonstrates how these IEs use their craft to "reshape their community's power in Thai society." In so doing, he argues, these IEs are not just making a living but are community leaders and social activists.

Oliver S. Crocco, Omaima Hajjami and Bethany Hager highlight that in Myanmar the lack of government support for health, education and business in ethnic minority areas, coupled with the ongoing conflict, has necessitated the rise and importance of community-based Indigenous enterprises, which have the additional impact of promoting human development.

Aida Idris, Siti Nur Husna Tukiran, Nazzatush Shimar Jamaludin, Nurhidayah Bahar and Shaiful Azlan Abdul describe the impact of the pandemic on the entrepreneurs involved in the "halal" herbs sector in Malaysia. Post-pandemic, the government introduced a slew of economic stimulus packages to support these entrepreneurs. However, there is no comprehensive framework to gauge the impact of such programs, a gap which they hope to fill with their work, thus contributing to impact analyses of such policy measures.

The contributors to this publication reinforce the role of the researcher in providing voice and agency in support of a community deprived of such either by circumstance, or where research and policy gaps exist.

Dr. Rebecca Fatima Sta Maria
Executive Director
APEC Secretariat

Rebecca Fatima Sta Maria is Executive Director at the Asia-Pacific Economic Cooperation (APEC) Secretariat in Singapore.

Contents

Notes on Contributors

Shaiful Azlan Abdul began his academic career in 1997 and is now a Lecturer at Universiti Teknologi MARA (UiTM).

Kathleen M. Adams is a Professorial Research Associate in Anthropology at SOAS University of London, Professor Emerita at Loyola University Chicago, and Adjunct Curator at the Field Museum of Natural History.

Sakshi Aggarwal is an avid Research Associate at Innolab Research with more than eight years of academic research experience.

Nurhidayah Bahar holds a Senior Lecturership at the National University of Malaysia, where she contributes significantly to the field of information systems.

Daniel Borer is a Swiss economics and business graduate from Basel University, Switzerland, and the London School of Economics, United Kingdom.

Oliver S. Crocco is an Assistant Professor of Leadership and Human Resource Development at Louisiana State University, USA.

Naida Culshaw is a weaver and community alchemist, Lecturer, and Doctorate of Business Administration candidate at Grenoble Ecole de Management, France, as well as a coach and consultant.

Emiel L. Eijdenberg is an Associate Professor and the Singapore Director of the Centre for International Trade and Business in Asia (CITBA) at

James Cook University, Singapore. Dr. Eijdenberg's research interests are about entrepreneurs(hip) and tourism in emerging countries. Dr. Eijdenberg's work is published in journals such as *Journal of African Business*, *International Journal of Entrepreneurial Behavior and Research*, *International Journal of Market Research* and *Journal of Heritage Tourism*, and in several books, conference proceedings and edited volumes published by Edward Elgar Publishing, Emerald Publishing, Palgrave Macmillan, Routledge and Springer.

Bethany A. Hager is a Ph.D. student in the School of Leadership and Human Resource Development at Louisiana State University, USA.

Omaima Hajjami is a Ph.D. student in the School of Leadership and Human Resource Development at Louisiana State University, USA.

Aida Idris currently serves as a Professor of Entrepreneurship at the Faculty of Business and Economics, Universiti Malaya (UM).

Nazzatush Shimar Jamaludin is an inorganic chemist who specializes in coordination chemistry, synthesis and characterization of metal complexes, involving d-block elements, sulfur-based and naturally occurring ligands.

Thirumaran K is an Associate Professor and the Academic Head of JCU Singapore Business School at James Cook University, Singapore. Dr. Thiru's research is varied but is developing specializations in cultural and luxury tourism. Thiru coined the term "affinity tourism." Affinity tourism refers to the propensity of guests to partake in the "familiar" and "similar" cultural experiences while at a destination. Dr. Thiru's work is published in journals such as *Sustainable Production and Consumption* and *Tourism Management Perspectives*, and in several books and edited volumes published by Edward Elgar, Routledge and Springer.

Sharon Koh is the Director of Graduate Research Programs and a Senior Lecturer at the School of Business, Monash University Malaysia.

Andrei Kwok serves as the Director of Graduate Coursework Studies and is a Senior Lecturer at the School of Business, Monash University Malaysia.

Audrey Siah Kim Lan is a Senior Lecturer of economics and Coordinator of the Department of Economics with Monash University Malaysia.

Natalie Limwatana is a regenerative designer, mud builder, artist and facilitator in North Thailand. She is an ambassador for Global Ecovillage Network Oceania (GENOA) and Asia in Thailand.

Greeni Maheshwari currently works as a Senior Lecturer within the Department of Management at RMIT Vietnam and has earned her Doctorate in Business Administration degree (DBA) in Global Business and Leadership from California, USA.

Chi Nguyen Tran Mai is a Research Assistant in the School of Communication & Design at RMIT University Vietnam where she completed her Bachelor's degree in Communication with Distinction.

Ade Iva Murty is a Lecturer and researcher at the Faculty of Arts & Sciences, Sampoerna University, Jakarta.

Emmanuel Mushimiyimana is a Lecturer at the University of Rwanda and received his Ph.D. from University of Leipzig.

Thao Ngo is a learner and educator from Vietnam. Kin has been a member of NextGENOA (The youth network of Global Ecovillage Network Oceania and Asia) since 2016 and joined the GENOA Operations team in mid-2020 as the network coordinator.

Chung Thanh Phan currently works at RMIT University, Vietnam campus, as a Lecturer and active researcher.

Dirk Sandarupa is an Assistant Professor at the Department of Tourism at Hasanuddin University in Makassar, Indonesia, and an entrepreneur.

Stavros Sindakis holds the position of Professor of Entrepreneurship and Innovation Management at Chongqing Technology and Business University and is a Visiting Professor at the Hellenic Open University.

Thuy Minh To is an assistant at RMIT University's Vietnam campus, where she researches in economics-related fields.

Siti Nur Husna Tukiran is a Master of Philosophy student at the Institute for Advanced Studies, Universiti Malaya (UM), with a Bachelor's degree in Islamic Studies and Science also from UM.

Diem Thi Hong Vo is a Lecturer in economics/Blockchain Enabled Business at RMIT Vietnam.

Pengji Wang is an active researcher at James Cook University, Singapore. Associate Professor Wang's research interests are in the areas of corporate governance, international business and sustainable business practice. Much of her research aims to bridge the understanding between East and West, through refining theories to Eastern contexts and/or comparing firms' and individuals' behaviors between East and West.

Endro Puspo Wiroko is a Lecturer and researcher at the Faculty of Psychology, Universitas Pancasila, Jakarta.

Caroline Wong is the Associate Dean of Learning and Teaching and an Associate Professor at James Cook University, Singapore. Dr. Wong's research in knowledge management takes on a multidisciplinary approach that extends into knowledge-based cities, smart cities, creative cities and creative industries with special focus on Singapore. Dr. Wong's work is published in journals such as *Journal of Knowledge Management, Journal of Knowledge, Culture and Change Management, Journal of Brand Management* and *International Journal of Architectural Research*, and in several books and edited volumes published by Palgrave Macmillan and Springer.

Urai Yangcheepsutjarit is currently a Ph.D. candidate in the International Social Sciences Programme at the Faculty of Social Sciences, Chiang Mai University, Thailand.

List of Figures

List of Tables

CHAPTER 1

A Brief Introduction to Indigenous Entrepreneurship and Its Relevance in Southeast Asia

Emiel L. Eijdenberg, Thirumaran K, Pengji Wang, and Caroline Wong

Taking Stock of the Terms and Definitions

While indigenous peoples and entrepreneurship have long existed at the beginning of times, *indigenous entrepreneurship* has been viewed as an emerging research discipline as there was no definitive concept prior to 2001 of the term in management and entrepreneurship literature (Dana, 2015; Hindle and Moroz, 2007). Before diving deeper in indigenous entrepreneurship as a research field (Hindle & Moroz, 2010; Padilla-Meléndez et al., 2022; Salmon et al., 2022), especially in the relatively unexplored context of Southeast Asia, we take one step back by untying the definition.

E. L. Eijdenberg · T. K · P. Wang (✉) · C. Wong
James Cook University, Singapore, Singapore
e-mail: pengji.wang@jcu.edu.au

E. L. Eijdenberg et al. (eds.), *Indigenous Entrepreneurship in Southeast Asia*, Palgrave Studies in Equity, Diversity, Inclusion, and Indigenization in Business, https://doi.org/10.1007/978-3-031-54457-6_1

An understanding of the word "indigenous" sheds great insights into place (their land, location), the people (their cultural values and traditions), and their understanding of business that focus on both economic and non-economic objectives (Dana, 2015). The word "indigenous" refers to two different meanings that are not mutually exclusive. First, the term refers to "the people who originally lived in a place, rather than people who moved there from somewhere else" (Cambridge Dictionary, 2022). In this context, "indigenous" refers to the location of the *place* or *land* and the native people ("Sons of the Soil") who have been living there besides (dominant) outsiders or foreigners who have started to populate the place or land throughout time (Banerjee, 2022). Examples are the Aboriginals and Torre Straits Islanders in Australia, the Māoris in New Zealand and the Inuits in Canada. "Indigenous," therefore, often refers to a specific ethnic group, for example, a tribe, a clan or a kinship community. In light of this understanding, approximately 476 million people, which represents between 5 and 6% of the world's population spread over 90 countries are considered indigenous (Food & Agriculture Organization, 2021; World Bank, 2021).

The second understanding of "indigenous" is more holistic and relates to the identity of indigenous people who practice and uphold the unique traditions of their culture. The United Nations' Department of Economic and Social Affairs describes indigenous peoples as inheritors and practitioners of unique cultures and ways relating to people and the environment (UNDESA, 2003). More specifically, the following characteristics of indigenous peoples as proposed by the United Nation's Permanent Forum on Indigenous Issues (2023, p. 1):

1. *Self-identification as indigenous peoples at the individual level and accepted by the community as their member*
2. *Historical continuity with pre-colonial and/or pre-settler societies*
3. *Strong link to territories and surrounding natural resources*
4. *Distinct social, economic, or political systems*
5. *Distinct language, culture, and beliefs*
6. *Form non-dominant groups of society*
7. *Resolve to maintain and reproduce their ancestral environments and systems as distinctive peoples and communities.*

Following the two understandings of "indigenous," ***indigenous entrepreneurship*** involves "the creation, management, and development of new ventures by indigenous people for the benefit of indigenous people" (Hindle & Lansdowne, 2005, p. 9). Indigenous entrepreneurship has been shown to promote self-determination, economic independence, and traditions in indigenous communities (Henry et al., 2018).

Why Focus on Indigenous Entrepreneurship?

The topic of indigenous entrepreneurship has affirmed itself as an independent field of research from the mainstream entrepreneurial literature (Croce, 2017). Mainstream entrepreneurship research based on Western economic thoughts suggests that rationally one would choose to maximize profits (Dana, 2015). Hence entrepreneurship from a non-indigenous perspective mainly focuses upon the identification of opportunities (Santamaria et al., 2023; Shane & Venkataraman, 2000) and commercialization of innovation (Lindsay, 2005), takes shape with the creation of formal businesses (Croce, 2017), and gives paramount importance to economic performance, such as growth in sales, productivity, profit, share value, and market share (Dana, 2015).

In contrast, studies have indicated that indigenous peoples have rich and heterogeneous cultural values often incompatible with mainstream theories' basic assumptions (Banerjee, 2022; Boussebaa, 2022, 2023; Dana, 2015). Driven by distinct indigenous values, indigenous entrepreneurs see entrepreneurship differently from the classic individualistic perspective that has emerged in the mainstream literature on entrepreneurship (Anderson, ; Lindsay, 2005). Indigenous people seem to be more influenced by non-economic causal variables in pursuing entrepreneurship opportunities (Bastien et al., 2023; Bruton et al., 2022). For example, Ndemo (2007) reported that if the Maasai people of Kenya had a choice, they would rather retain their traditional economic system instead of integrating themselves with the rest of Kenya in a market economy. Moreover, Degen (2007) noted that Bedouins persisted in raising sheep, even at an economic loss to maintain their traditional lifestyle. Dana and Light (2011) showed that entrepreneurship among the Sámi is different in form and substance from the commonly accepted Western model and so Light and Dana (2013) revealed similar findings in their study about indigenous people in Alaska.

However, indigenous entrepreneurship as a separate field is rather premature. As a result, it is worthwhile to move away from the mainstream entrepreneurship and management literature developed mainly in the Western ("Euro-American") context (Banerjee, 2022; Boussebaa, 2022, 2023) to one taking on a more insider view from individuals on the ground (e.g., qualitative studies and case studies) to deepen the understanding of indigenous entrepreneurship.

The Need for More Indigenous Entrepreneurship Research in Southeast Asia

A literature review by Croce (2017) showed that indigenous entrepreneurship research has been committed to understanding the driving force behind entrepreneurial activities (e.g., Lindsay, 2005; Peredo et al., 2004), the different indigenous contexts and their indigenous entrepreneurial outcomes (e.g., Hindle & Moroz, 2010), their growth trajectory or models (Hindle & Moroz, 2010; Peredo et al., 2004), and government policies (Shoebridge et al., 2012). Research has also revealed rich heterogeneity among indigenous peoples in that their respective values are far from identical (Dana & Anderson, 2007). The context, history, and place are seen as inseparable from indigenous entrepreneurship (Dana, 2015). Consequently, theories developed and evidence found from indigenous entrepreneurship in one group or region may not readily apply to another.

According to the United Nations, two-thirds of the world's indigenous peoples live in Asia (United Nations, 2014), including Southeast Asia that comprises 11 countries (i.e., Brunei, Cambodia, Indonesia, Laos, Malaysia, Myanmar, Philippines, Singapore, Thailand, Timor-Leste, and Vietnam) of which ten (Timor-Leste excluded) belong to the Association of Southeast Asian Nations (ASEAN, 2023), see Figs. 1.1 and 1.2.

Southeast Asia has a population of more than 689 million people as of Nov 2023 (Worldometers, n.d.) with an average gross domestic product (GDP) per capita of US$ 5.69 thousand (International Monetary Fund, n.d.). These countries have a high diversity of ethnic groups (ranging from Lolo, Malayic, and Tai peoples), religions (such as Animism, Buddhism, Christianity, Confucianism, Hinduism, Islam, Taoism), hundreds of languages and dialects (such as Burmese, English, Filipino, Khmer, Malay, Thai), and different socio-economic systems and institutional contexts (e.g., Cambodia as a constitutional monarchy

Fig. 1.1 Map of ASEAN. *Source* Freepik: https://www.freepik.com/free-vector/asean-map-illustration_10781593.htm#query=south%20east%20asia%20map&position=4&from_view=keyword&track=ais&uuid=f23d9e16-7f34-4955-a99a-236dc4489960">Freepik</a>

and emerging economy, and Singapore as a parliamentary republic and advanced high-income economy) (Coedès, 1975; SarDesai, 2018; Steinberg, 1985). Table 1.1 shows several key statistics of the Southeast Asian countries. Many of the Southeast Asian nations have diverse indigenous population groups with an estimation of 150 million (Salamanca, 2019), as shown in Table 1.2.

Those indigenous people are involved in various entrepreneurial activities. As a way of illustration, in Indonesia, 97.2% of the country's workforce is employed in micro, small, and medium-sized enterprises (MSMEs), contributing close to 60% of the US$ 1.2 trillion economy

Fig. 1.2 ASEAN flags. *Source* Pixabay: https://pixabay.com/vi/photos/asean-indo-vietnam-ensign-federal-4692563/

Table 1.1 Key statistics of Southeast Asia

	Average GDP growth rate (1980–2022)[1]	*GDP per capita in US$ in 2022 (current price)*[2]	*Population (2023)*[3]	*Land area (square kilometer) as of 2020*[4]
Brunei Darussalam	1.01	27,255.90	452,524	5270
Cambodia	6.69	668.46	16,944,826	176,520
Indonesia	5.29	1903.72	277,534,122	1,877,519
Laos	6.21	1012.59	7,633,779	230,800
Malaysia	5.54	5968.83	34,308,525	328,550
Myanmar	7.36	746.05	54,577,997	652,670
Philippines	3.75	1666.42	117,337,368	298,170
Singapore	6.11	32,028.35	6,014,723	718
Thailand	4.73	3376.49	71,801,279	510,890
Timor-Leste	3.12	1049.40	1,360,596	15,006
Vietnam	6.33	1267.61	98,858,950	313,429

Sources
[1] International Monetary Fund: https://www.imf.org/external/datamapper/NGDP_RPCH@WEO/THA/IDN/PHL/VNM/MYS/SGP/BRN/KHM/LAO/MMR/TLS
[2] International Monetary Fund: https://www.imf.org/external/datamapper/PPPPC@WEO/THA/IDN/PHL/VNM/MYS/SGP/BRN/KHM/LAO/MMR/TLS
[3] Worldometers: https://www.worldometers.info/world-population/south-eastern-asia-population/#:~:text=South%2DEastern%20Asia%20Population%20(LIVE)&text=The%20current%20population%20of%20South,of%20the%20total%20world%20population
[4] The Global Economy: https://www.theglobaleconomy.com/rankings/land_area/South-East-Asia/

Table 1.2 Estimated indigenous populations in a selection of Southeast Asia countries

	Estimated indigenous population	*Percentage (%) of total population*	*Number of indigenous groups*
Brunei Darussalam	71,000	16.7	7–11
Cambodia	197,000	1.34	24
Indonesia	50–70 million	20–29	More than 700, but the government recognizes 365 ethnics and sub-ethnics as "Isolated Adat Communities"
Laos	2.4–4.8 millions	35–70	49
Malaysia	3.4 million	12	97
Myanmar	14.1–19.2 millions	30–40	135
Philippines	12–15 million	10–15	110
Thailand	1.1 million	1.5	34
Vietnam	10 millions	13.8	54 (including the majority Kinh)

Source International Work Group of Indigenous Affairs, https://www.iwgia.org/images/publications/0511_ASEAN_BRIEFING_PAPER_eb.pdf

(Tanuwidjaja, 2021). Among those MSMEs, there is a rise of a new generation of successful indigenous entrepreneurs, i.e., *Pribumi*, which consists of many ethnic groups—e.g., Batak, Bugis, Javanese, and Sundanese, excluding "Foreign Orientals" (including Chinese, Arab, and Indian descent) (Njoto-Feillard & Azali, 2016). In Malaysia, the Orang Asli, an indigenous community, sees the importance of developing infrastructure such as roads and the economy and making ends meet (Seow et. al., 2013). As a consequence, the Orang Asli community is increasingly involved in entrepreneurial activities by mainly selling forest products and produces (e.g., herbs, tripolis, and wooden products) (Keat et al., 2018).

At the same time, these thriving indigenous entrepreneurs face various challenges in their business circles, including poor health, discrimination, suboptimal education (Colbourne, 2017), improved access to markets locally, nationally, and even internationally (Kristiansen, 2002), and systematic discrimination and deep-seated societal bias from their local context (Isabella, 2020). Despite the valuable work carried out by these indigenous populations in Southeast Asia, much remains unknown about indigenous entrepreneurial activities on the ground and their pressing challenges such as access to resources and markets, and societal acceptance and appreciation in Southeast Asia.

One would assume that with the sheer size and great diversity of the indigenous populations, as well as the thriving entrepreneurial activities in Southeast Asia, it would enable us to paint a rich tapestry of indigenous entrepreneurship in this region. Yet, Southeast Asia remains one of the largely unexplored sub-regions in the world. In the literature review conducted based on 264 scholarly articles published from 1992 to 2020 (Padilla-Meléndez et al., 2022), it is found that indigenous entrepreneurship research is mostly conducted in Australia, Canada, New Zealand, United States, Mexico, Peru, and India. With regard to Southeast Asia, the indigenous entrepreneurship in Indonesia and Malaysia has received some attention, with eight and six studies being published, respectively; whereas the indigenous entrepreneurship in other Southeast Asia regions barely has been investigated.

Against this background, this book includes a collection of contributions addressing the multivariate issues related to indigenous entrepreneurship in Southeast Asian countries such as Malaysia, Myanmar, Vietnam, and Thailand. The collection of contributions in this book employs multiple methods, including conceptual analysis, literature review, qualitative approaches such as field work interviews and observations, document and discourse analysis, ethnographic, and case studies, and quantitative approaches such as regression based on archival data. The chapters demonstrate prototypical examples of indigenous entrepreneurship in Southeast Asia, showcasing these enterprising individuals' everyday entrepreneurial practices as well as their strategies to cope with the ever-changing external environment and the associated challenges. The book thereby offers scholars, students, and practitioners a closer look inside this unique socio-economic activity in this emerging geographic region.

The insightful findings on the one hand could benefit indigenous population by revealing the current status of the best practices adopted by and unique challenges faced by the indigenous entrepreneurs in Southeast Asia. These insights not only help indigenous entrepreneurs in Southeast Asian region reflect their own practices, but also facilitate other business practitioners and policy-makers to develop a deeper understanding about the indigenous entrepreneurs, which will help navigate their effort in collaborating or helping the indigenous peoples for growth. In terms of generalization, the findings could also shed light to the indigenous entrepreneurship in other regions in the world, such as the Americas or Africa, where economic development levels and institutional environments share some similarities as some of those in Southeast Asia.

Lastly, this book's fresh perspectives could equally contribute to the broader societies, influencing dominant societies and theories significantly. While indigenous communities investigate the financial viability of their entrepreneurial ventures, that is not the end in itself. It is rather a precondition necessary for the achievement of multi-dimensional successes, e.g., protection of ecological balance, solidarity, respect for and preservation of traditional values and cultural practices, reduction of poverty, and social-economic equity and a holistic view of growth, and so on. With a focus on social, environmental, and business value, insights gained from indigenous entrepreneurship could inform mainstream society. In the mainstream Western-style vision on corporations, Corporate Social Responsibility (CSR) and sustainable development have become important themes (Carroll, 1999), which share similar concerns as indigenous entrepreneurs. One way to develop such responsible and sustainable business models could be incorporating indigenous entrepreneurs into corporates' strategies, such as supply chain strategies and marketing strategies. Indigenous entrepreneurial activities leveraging the locally available resources and incorporating the socio-cultural values and interests of the local population provide home-grown solutions and tend to be more sustainable and readily acceptable. Grassroots innovations from the indigenous entrepreneurial efforts constitute a more collaborative bottom-up engagements and have been known to deliver sustainability benefits in areas where the prevailing top-down measures wrestle. Thus, understanding the development models and challenges of indigenous entrepreneurship could inform the adoption of such bottom-up approach for sustainable business model innovation.

Summarized Overview of Chapters

Maheshwari and Nguyen's literature review opens this book's collection. Based on review of 171 articles published from 2006 to 2022 on indigenous entrepreneurship worldwide, particularly in Southeast Asia, the authors highlight that research efforts on Southeast Asia indigenous entrepreneurship are not gaining much ground as global indigenous entrepreneurship and little or no study has been done on indigenous entrepreneurship in a few Southeast Asian countries particularly Laos,

Vietnam, Philippines, Thailand, and Brunei. Their chapter pinpoints the theoretical and empirical gaps in understanding indigenous entrepreneurship in Southeast Asia and calls for more research efforts to be devoted to this field.

Several chapters have been devoted to issues pertaining to disadvantaged, socio-economic factors such as macro-economic developments on indigenous entrepreneurship. In Chap. 3, Koh et al., offer an overview of the main inhibitors preventing indigenous groups in the Mah Meri village in Malaysia from embarking on indigenous entrepreneurship to improve their livelihood. In Chap. 4, Idris et al. focus on the entrepreneurial activities by the Bumiputera SMEs in the Malay-Bumiputera halal herbs industry. The authors reviewed their supply chain and identified the challenges and barriers faced, particularly due to the COVID-19 pandemic, based on which they recommended a framework from the point of resource-based view to guide government policy initiatives. In Chap. 5, Mushimiyimana pays particular attention to the marginalization, rejection, and impoverishment that indigenous people experienced. The author examines how the Philippines government treated Lumad people of Mindanao with the aim of assimilating them and the effects on their livelihood and entrepreneurship and calls for use of modern way of governing indigenous peoples such as adoption of multiculturalism and inclusive governance.

In addition, a few chapters showcase the best practices of indigenous entrepreneurs in Southeast Asia in improving indigenous people's livelihood and wellbeing. In Chap. 6, Yangcheepsutjarit reports their field work research based on the indigenous group of the Iu Mien or Yao in Thailand and shows how they utilized their family-owned silver crafts businesses as a gentle form of social activism to non-aggressively reach out to, connect, and communicate with, and influence diverse groups of people in mainstream Thai society, as well as to support their livelihoods. In Chap. 7, Adams and Sandarupa share an interesting micro-case study of a successful indigenous entrepreneur whose local cultural insights enabled him to cultivate relationships and engagements with local community partners and grow a thriving business in an unlikely location in Indonesia. This highlights the role of indigenous wisdom and local knowledge in fostering business resilience and entails a distinctly different path than those commonly advocated by Western tourism and business schools. In Chap. 8, Culshaw et al. present the journeys of two indigenous entrepreneurs based in Thailand and reveal some success factors such as access to transformational educational opportunities, being embedded in local culture, and embracing an indigenous innovative approach to project design and implementation. In Chap. 9, Crocco et al., concentrate on Community-Based Enterprise (CBE) as a form of indigenous entrepreneurship in promoting human development in Myanmar. They present compelling examples in which CBE provides training and education to support various segments of Myanmar's population such as those in the agriculture and tourism sectors.

In terms of deficient socio-economic development, indigenous women entrepreneurs deserve special attention. Indigenous women still constitute one of the most socially disadvantaged groups in the world. Despite literature highlighting the many benefits of indigenous women entrepreneurship, including empowerment and elevating their socio-economic status (e.g., Minniti, 2010; Shah & Saurabh, 2015; Williams & Martinez, 2014), limited attention is given to exploring indigenous women entrepreneurship as a research topic. In Chap. 10, Phan et al. investigate indigenous entrepreneurship from a gender perspective by focusing on Vietnam and Thailand—two emerging countries in Southeast Asia. The chapter examines if there is any gender-based discrimination in accessing financial services for rural household indigenous entrepreneurs. The chapter has not found evidence of gender discrimination in credit access, giving us a promising picture of indigenous women entrepreneurs being empowered in handling their households and their businesses in those two countries.

Wiroko and Murty take on a more micro-level approach and examine the "diuwongke" practice in entrepreneurship, that refers to an indigenous psychological phenomenon in Indonesia whereby people are treated with dignity and respect and that mediates the relationship between the perceived leader's servant leadership and work engagement. Their findings highlight the importance of employee-centric leadership in the indigenous culture in Indonesia.

Finally, Sindakis and Aggarwal take on a digital perspective to entrepreneurship. The authors study the persistent problem of rural poverty in emerging nations of Southeast Asia and examine how family, community, and business partners can support one another to fill institutional gaps and promote entrepreneurship in enterprises. They recognize that the most significant barriers to entrepreneurship, particularly for newcomers, are connected to time and space constraints, a need for more networks, and restricted marketing mobility. Digital entrepreneurship can help with some of these issues by examining how digital technology, such as smartphone apps, can assist in improving these interactions.

References

Amofah, S. (2021). Indigenous women social entrepreneurship; Poverty alleviation tool used by development NGOs in Ghana. *Athens Journal of Social Sciences, 8*(2), 151–168.

Anderson, R. B. (2002). Entrepreneurship and Aboriginal Canadians: A case study in economic development. *Journal of Developmental Entrepreneurship, 7*(1), 45.

Anderson, R. B. (1999). *Economic development among the aboriginal peoples of Canada: The hope for the future*. Captus Press.

ASEAN (2023). About ASEAN. https://asean.org/about-asean.

Banerjee, S. B. (2022). Decolonizing management theory: A critical perspective. *Journal of Management Studies, 59*(4), 1074–1087.

Bastien, F., Coraiola, D. M., & Foster, W. M. (2023). Indigenous peoples and organization studies. *Organization Studies, 44*(4), 659–675.

Boussebaa, M. (2022). Unsettling West-centrism in the study of professional service firms. *Human Relations,* Early Cite. https://doi.org/10.1177/00187267221128262

Boussebaa, M. (2023). Decolonizing international business. *Critical Perspectives on International Business,* Early Cite. https://doi.org/10.1108/cpoib-12-2022-0121

Bruton, G. D., Zahra, S. A., Van de Ven, A. H., & Hitt, M. A. (2022). Indigenous theory uses, abuses, and future. *Journal of Management Studies, 59*(4), 1057–1073.

Carroll, A. B. (1999). Corporate social responsibility: Evolution of a definitional construct. *Business and Society, 38*(3), 268–295.

Coedes, G. (1975). The Indianized states of Southeast Asia. University of Hawaii Press.

Colbourne, R. (2017). Indigenous entrepreneurship and hybrid ventures. In *Hybrid ventures* (Vol. 19, pp. 93–149). Emerald Publishing Limited.

Croce, F. (2017). Contextualized indigenous entrepreneurial models: A systematic review of indigenous entrepreneurship literature. *Journal of Management and Organization, 23*(6), 886–906.

Croce, F. (2020). Indigenous women entrepreneurship: Analysis of a promising research theme at the intersection of indigenous entrepreneurship and women entrepreneurship. *Ethnic and Racial Studies, 43*(6), 1013–1031.

Dana, L. P. (2015). Indigenous entrepreneurship: An emerging field of research. *International Journal of Business and Globalisation, 14*(2), 158–169.

Dana, L. P., & Anderson, R. B. (2007). *International handbook of research on indigenous entrepreneurship*. Edward Elgar.

Dana, L. P., & Light, I. (2011). Two forms of community entrepreneurship in Finland: Are there differences between Finnish and Sámi reindeer husbandry entrepreneurs? *Entrepreneurship and Regional Development, 23*(5–6), 331–352.

Degen, A.A. (2007) 'Traditional livestock production among Bedouin in the Negev Desert', in L. –P. Dana, & R. B. Anderson (Eds.) *International handbook of research on indigenous entrepreneurship*. Edward Elgar, Cheltenham.

Cambridge Dictionary (2023). Indigenous. https://dictionary.cambridge.org/dictionary/english/indigenous.

Filatotchev, I., Ireland, R. D., & Stahl, G. K. (2022). Contextualizing management research: An open systems perspective. *Journal of Management Studies, 59*(4), 1036–1056.

Food and Agriculture Organization. (2021). Indigenous Peoples. https://www.fao.org/indigenous-peoples/en/.

Global Entrepreneurship Monitor. (2023). GEM's 2022/2023 Global Report: Adapting to a "New Normal". https://gemconsortium.org/report/20222023-global-entrepreneurship-monitor-global-report-adapting-to-a-new-normal-2.

Henry, E. Y., Dana, L. P., & Murphy, P. J. (2018). Telling their own stories: Māori entrepreneurship in the mainstream screen industry. *Entrepreneurship and Regional Development, 30*(1–2), 118–145.

Hindle, K., & Moroz, P. (2010). Indigenous entrepreneurship as a research field: Developing a definitional framework from the emerging canon. *International Entrepreneurship and Management Journal, 6*, 357–385.

International Monetary Fund. (n.d.). GDP per capita, current prices. https://www.imf.org/external/datamapper/NGDPDPC@WEO/SEQ?year=2023.

Isabella, K. (2020, September 21). Barriers and hurdles: Indigenous entrepreneurship in Canada. IT World Canada. https://www.itworldcanada.com/blog/barriers-and-hurdles-indigenous-entrepreneurship-in-canada/436007.

Keat, N. J., Nath, T. K., & Jose, S. (2018). Indigenous agroforestry practices by Orang Asli in peninsular Malaysia: Management, sustainability and contribution to household economy. *Indian Journal of Traditional Knowledge, 17*(3), 542–549.

Kristiansen, S. (2002). Competition and knowledge in Javanese rural business. *Singapore Journal of Tropical Geography, 23*(1), 52–69.

Light, I., & Dana, L. P. (2013). Boundaries of social capital in entrepreneurship. *Entrepreneurship Theory and Practice, 37*(3), 603–624.

Lindsay, N. J. (2005). Toward a cultural model of indigenous entrepreneurial attitude. *Academy of Marketing Science Review, 5*(5), 1–17.

Minniti, M. (2010). Female entrepreneurship and economic activity. *European Journal of Development Research, 22*, 294–312.

Naveen, S., Parida, J. K., & Panda, I. (2023). Tribal women empowerment through entrepreneurship: Evidence from Mayurbhanj District, Odisha. *Frontiers in Sociology, 8*.

Ndemo, B. (2007) 'The Maasai: entrepreneurship and change', in L.-P. Dana, & R. B. Anderson (Eds.) International handbook of research on indigenous entrepreneurship, Edward Elgar, Cheltenham.

Njoto-Feillard, G., & Azali, K. (2016). Is a new entrepreneurial generation emerging in Indonesia? https://www.iseas.edu.sg/images/pdf/TRS13_16.pdf.

Padilla-Meléndez, A., Plaza-Angulo, J. J., Del-Aguila-Obra, A. R., & Ciruela-Lorenzo, A. M. (2022). Indigenous entrepreneurship. Current issues and future lines. *Entrepreneurship and Regional Development, 34*(1–2), 6–31.

Peredo, A. M., Anderson, R. B., Galbraith, C. S., Honig, B., & Dana, L. P. (2004). Towards a theory of indigenous entrepreneurship. *International Journal of Entrepreneurship and Small Business, 1*(1–2), 1–20.

Salamanca, A. (2023). Indigenous peoples of Southeast Asia reaffirm their rights. https://www.sei.org/perspectives/indigenous-peoples-of-southeast-asia-reaffirm-their-rights/.

Salmon, E., Chavez, J. F., & Murphy, M. (2022). New perspectives and critical insights from Indigenous peoples' research: A systematic review of indigenous management and organization literature. *Academy of Management Annals*, Early Cite. https://doi.org/10.5465/annals.2021.0132.

Santamaria, S., Abolfathi, N., & Mahmood, I. P. (2023). Demand pull versus resource push training approaches to entrepreneurship: A field experiment. *Strategic Management Journal*, Early Cite. https://doi.org/10.1002/smj.3560.

SarDesai, D. R. (2018). Southeast Asia, student economy edition: Past and present. Routledge

Seow, T. W., Mohamed, M., Jamiran, M. N. S., Abidin, Z., Zulhilmi, Z., Sam, M., & Aminah, S. (2013). Pembangunan sosioekonomi komuniti orang Asli di Malaysia.

Shah, H., & Saurabh, P. (2015). Women entrepreneurs in developing nations: Growth and replication strategies and their impact on poverty alleviation. *Technology Innovation Management Review, 5*(8), 34–43.

Shane, S., & Venkataraman, S. (2000). The promise of entrepreneurship as a field of research. *Academy of Management Review, 25*(1), 217–226.

Shoebridge, A., Buultjens, J., & Peterson, L. S. (2012). Indigenous entrepreneurship in northern NSW, Australia. *Journal of Developmental Entrepreneurship, 17*(03), 1250017.

South-Eastern Asia Population. Worldometers. (n.d.). https://www.worldometers.info/world-population/south-eastern-asia-population/.

Steinberg, D. I. (1985). BURMA IN 1984: Unasked Questions, Unanswered Issues. *Southeast Asian Affairs*, 111–130.

Tanuwidjaja, E. (2021). *Strategic reforms key to Indonesian MSMEs' greater contribution to the economy*. The Business Times. https://www.businesstimes.com.sg/asean-business/strategic-reforms-key-to-indonesian-msmes%E2%80%99-greater-contribution-to-the-economy.

United Nations Department of Economic and Social Affairs (UNDESA) (2023). Indigenous Peoples. https://www.un.org/development/desa/indigenouspeoples/about-us.html.

United Nations (2014). *Indigenous Peoples in the Asian region*. https://www.un.org/esa/socdev/unpfii/documents/2014/press/asia.pdf.

United Nations Permanent Forum on Indigenous Peoples (2023). Who are indigenous peoples? https://www.un.org/esa/socdev/unpfii/documents/5session_factsheet1.pdf.

World Bank (2021). Indigenous Peoples. https://www.worldbank.org/en/topic/indigenouspeoples.

CHAPTER 2

A Systematic Review of Literature (2006–2022) on Indigenous Entrepreneurship in Southeast Asia and the World

Greeni Maheshwari and Chi T. M. Nguyen

Introduction

Entrepreneurship is the creative process of establishing a new business that normally engages with cooperative networks and financial assistance from institutions and governments. It includes interpersonal, organisational, environmental, and process components (Frederick et al., 2006). Two derivatives of entrepreneurship are entrepreneurs and enterprises. While an entrepreneur is an individual or group of people who integrate resources based on original ideas in order to either enhance the value of the new/existing products or provide innovative solutions in rendered services, an enterprise is an outcome of the entrepreneurial process in

G. Maheshwari (✉) · C. T. M. Nguyen
RMIT University, Ho Chi Minh City, Vietnam
e-mail: greeni.maheshwari@rmit.edu.vn

E. L. Eijdenberg et al. (eds.), *Indigenous Entrepreneurship in Southeast Asia*, Palgrave Studies in Equity, Diversity, Inclusion, and Indigenization in Business, https://doi.org/10.1007/978-3-031-54457-6_2

operating to deliver the products or services to the society (Ayatse et al., 2013a, 2013b). Due to entrepreneurship's crucial role in the development of an economy, it has become a recognised phenomenon in research studies (Maheshwari & Maheshwari, 2021). Since entrepreneurial activities impact technological progress, increase industrial efficiency, and alter the market structure and the competitive environment, they are seen as crucial in defining modern market economies (Kuratko, 2011). Additionally, entrepreneurs play a crucial role in society by creating millions of jobs across the world and enabling access to the prosperity of a sizeable population, particularly minority populations (Kuratko, 2011).

However, in reality, not many entrepreneurs can sustain their business venture; despite growth in quantity, only a small proportion can grow to be successful, while the number of entrepreneurs who failed in business was remarkable (Zainol & Daud, 2011), especially for the Indigenous population in the Southeast Asian context. Applying the methodology from the publication "Standard Country or Area Codes for Statistical Use" by the Statistics Division of the Department of Economic and Social Affairs - United Nations (1999), this study covers 11 countries: Brunei Darussalam, Cambodia, Indonesia, Laos, Malaysia, Myanmar, the Philippines, Singapore, Thailand, Timor-Leste, and Vietnam. As defined by the International Labour Organisation, Indigenous people are defined as descended from the groups who lived in a nation or the region to which it belonged at the time of the country's conquest, colonisation, or the drawing of the current state boundaries (Agbim, Oriarewo, et al., 2013a, 2013b). Across 90 countries, the Indigenous population is estimated to be approximately 476 million people belonging to over 5,000 distinct groups, which comprises 6.2% of the global population, as reported by the United Nations (2021). In Southeast Asia, the term "Indigenous" has a long history of use. However, it is essential to recognise that historically, European colonisers employed this term for specific purposes. Initially, European colonisers used the term "Indigenous" as a means of distinguishing themselves from the colonised Asian populations. Later on, it served as a tool to differentiate between Europeans and Asians, with exceptions made for early twentieth-century immigration from other regions of Asia (Morton & Baird, 2019). This historical context highlights the complexity of terminologies used during colonial periods and underscores the evolving nature of language in describing Indigenous communities (Morton & Baird, 2019). However, with the dynamic complexity of the socio-political context during colonisation and immigration of various population, there have been conflicting approaches to categorise Indigenous people with ethnolinguistic and religious minorities (Clarke, 2001), leading to inconsistency in reporting the quantity of Indigenous Southeast Asians. The Stockholm Environment Institute reported that this number was approximately 150 million in 2019 (Salamanca, 2019), while a publication by the Asia Indigenous Peoples Pact (AIPP) Foundation in 2015 declared this population to be 93–124 million (Tessier, 2015). Against the total population of 657 million Southeast Asians (Patierno et al., 2019), this number remarkably equalled 14–23% of the population in 2019.

Indigenous entrepreneurship is the entrepreneurial process that encapsulates an Indigenous person's or people's aim to become self-reliant and socially integrated (Foley, 2008). The development, administration, and formation of new businesses by Indigenous people for the benefit of other Indigenous people are referred to as Indigenous entrepreneurship, in which the resulting organisations of this entrepreneurial process can be found in the public, private, or non-profit sectors (Hindle & Moroz, 2010). Creating businesses by Indigenous people based on their heritage of cultural activities, native endowment, and resources is an example of Indigenous entrepreneurship, which represents economic activities related to the culture of the indigenes of a region (Akpor-Robaro & Erigbe, 2019). Indigenous entrepreneurship in Southeast Asia was found to provide a wide range of benefits on many levels. At a micro level, Indigenous entrepreneurship provides a sustainable source of income for Indigenous individuals who directly participate in entrepreneurial activities (Wambrauw et al., 2019). At a local scale, job opportunities and fund generation are a few benefits of entrepreneurial activities in specific Indigenous communities (Cheng & Hong, 2021). As illustrated in Fig. 2.1 (Persoon et al., 2007), in a larger landscape, which is at a national and regional level, Indigenous entrepreneurship is associated with ambitious goals to reduce poverty, strengthen the marginalised community with financial power (Amofah, 2021), and reach the emerging vision for sustainability in the business landscape and society in general (Khanal & Babar, 2007; Mokhtar & Hanafi, 2020). However, Indigenous Southeast Asians, generally not identified as Chinese or Indian in ethnicity, had little entrepreneurial role in contemporary business, trade, and finance (Huff, 2011). For instance, small Indigenous enterprises in Indonesia have weaker competitiveness with large, modern enterprises with more prosperous and more accessible resources (Agustiono et al., 2020). Indigenous enterprises were found to be lacking behind the Chinese-rooted entrepreneurs whose entrepreneurial activities could scale up remarkably and dominate Southeast Asian countries' economic states (Zainol & Daud, 2011). Reports from historical records showed the dominance of Chinese enterprises across Southeast Asia, or even in the case of Thailand, a complete absence of Indigenous big enterprises compared with dominance from Chinese entrepreneurs (Tipton, 2009). Explaining this phenomenon, the majority of Southeast Asian countries were found to be in shortage of entrepreneurial initiatives rooted in indigeneity, and it can be argued that this resulted from the historical outcomes and institutional arrangements on the foundational background of colonisation (Tipton, 2009).

Regarding the importance of Indigenous entrepreneurship in Southeast Asia's regional landscape yet the phenomenon is underdeveloped and less able to compete with large enterprises and immigrant entrepreneurs, the need to thoroughly research and understand the needs and concerns of Southeast Asian Indigenous entrepreneurs is urgent for economic and sociocultural stability in the region. Even with this urgency, there is a noticeable gap in both the quantity and quality of research between Southeast Asian studies and studies from other areas across the globe. While examining Indigenous entrepreneurship in the Southeast Asian context, scholars found that research on the phenomenon had been predominantly investigated in particular regions but not Southeast Asia (Rembulan et al., 2022). Little understanding leading to insignificant support for Indigenous entrepreneurship in this region will waste the potential for Indigenous entrepreneurs to grow and contribute to their communities and society. Thus, there needs to be a raise for more attention towards the phenomenon in the region, leading to growing awareness of the need to nurture and support Indigenous entrepreneurship. Sub-Southeast Asian scholars in Indigenous entrepreneurship have emphasised the importance and urgency of researching and understanding entrepreneurship and the participation of the Indigenous group for future embedment and enhancement (Affizzah et al., 2016). To identify Indigenous entrepreneurship models and practices in various contexts and to make recommendations to policymakers and practitioners regarding Indigenous peoples' aspirations for entrepreneurial and economic development, a systematic review that gathers, evaluates, and synthesises all

Fig. 2.1 First workshop of The Regional Network for Indigenous Peoples in Southeast Asia (RNIP), part of the Cagayan Valley Programme on Environment and Development (CVPED), an academic partnership between the College of Forestry and Environmental Management of Isabela State University in the Philippines and the Institute of Environmental Sciences (CML) of Leiden University in the Netherlands. Note. First workshop of The Regional Network for Indigenous Peoples in Southeast Asia (RNIP), part of the Cagayan Valley Programme on Environment and Development (CVPED), an academic partnership between the College of Forestry and Environmental Management of Isabela State University in the Philippines and the Institute of Environmental Sciences (CML) of Leiden University in the Netherlands. Source: "*Indigenous peoples in Southeast Asia, sharing knowledge, building capacity, fighting poverty, saving diversity*" by Persoon et al. (2007). Copyright 2021 by Leiden/Cabagan: RNIP

of the studies on Indigenous entrepreneurship is crucial (Croce, 2017). Therefore, this study is motivated to respond to the call for more research and understanding of the phenomenon in the region by scholars to narrow the theoretical gap in Indigenous entrepreneurship research between Southeast Asia and global studies through an extensive literature review from 2006 to 2022. The following key parts form the structure of this study. In the next section, a brief literature review introduces the concept of Indigenous relationships and their relevant knowledge in the Southeast Asia region. The research methodology and findings of the study are reported in Sect. 3. The chapter concludes with the discussion and conclusion section discussing the theoretical and practical contributions, limitations, and suggestions for further research.

Background

Indigenous Entrepreneurship

Indigenous entrepreneurship is one of the more recent areas of academic research when it only first appeared in the 1990s in studies by Léo-Paul Dana (2015). However, it was not until 2004 that Peredo et al. (2004) pioneered making Indigenous entrepreneurship prominent in research as a separate category. Indigenous entrepreneurship literature is expanding from early pioneer work to theoretical development and more recent critical analysis, and it can be broadly divided into three categories: definitional clarity; empirical or theoretical data; and a supporting body of literature that, while not explicitly expressing Indigenous entrepreneurship, is tied to it by a common meta-narrative of independent Indigenous economic success (Evans & Williamson, 2017). Many definitions of the term "Indigenous" can be found in the currently existing literature that touches on social, geographical, political, or cultural perspectives, which range from the region before the subsequent inhabitants, locals' or immigrants' dominance in geography, politics, and the economy, to efforts to maintain certain distinctive social-cultural norms and institutions (Onwuegbuzie & Mafimisebi, 2021). It is not unexpected that there are differing views on the word "Indigenous entrepreneurship" given the disparities in opinion regarding both the essential characteristics of "entrepreneurship" and the mentioned crucial components that define the notion of "Indigenous" (Peredo & Anderson, 2006). A definition applied in many studies by Hindle and Lansdowne (2005, p. 132) defined Indigenous entrepreneurship as "the creation, management and development of new ventures by Indigenous people for the benefit of Indigenous people." Another early definition by Dana (2007, p. 4) identified Indigenous entrepreneurship as "self-employment based on

Indigenous knowledge." Indigenous entrepreneurs establish their enterprises from a perception rooted in their culture and traditions. This typically seeks to benefit the community by simultaneously producing economic, social, environmental, and spiritual value (Vázquez-Maguirre, 2020).

Growing along with the development of Indigenous entrepreneurship research, scholars have profoundly expressed the need to examine Indigenous entrepreneurship as a separate, distinguished phenomenon rather than placing it under the Western non-Indigenous concept of entrepreneurship (April & Itenge, 2020; Austin & Garnett, 2018; Baba & Fortin-Lefebvre, 2020; Bruton et al., 2018; Dana, 2015). Some cultural ideals have been found in opposition to the underlying assumptions of entrepreneurial ideas (Dana, 2015). Thus, theories created to describe entrepreneurial activities are insufficient to comprehend Indigenous entrepreneurship and lead to a limited number of studies being able to study characteristics of the formation of Indigenous businesses (Molina-Ramírez & Barba-Sánchez, 2021). Alleged similarities between social, ethnic, and Indigenous entrepreneurship were also another noteworthy concern of Indigenous entrepreneurship scholars (Hindle & Moroz, 2010). Even though there are similarities and differences between Indigenous entrepreneurship and the mentioned sub-categories of entrepreneurship that need to be further explored, this topic has established itself as a separate field of study from the mainstream entrepreneurial literature (Croce, 2017). Indigenous entrepreneurship distinguishes itself from other types of entrepreneurship in terms of the setting in which the business is operated, the kinds of objectives and results it aspires to achieve, and the structure and operation of the business, which is frequently focused on the community rather than the entrepreneurs themselves (Cahn, 2008).

Indigenous entrepreneurship can have a variety of economic to social advantages; given that many Indigenous people live in remote areas far from areas with work opportunities, entrepreneurship is vital to them based on the nature of their company activity and the function that it plays within a particular community (Ratten & Dana, 2017). The creation of Indigenous businesses that can employ Indigenous people is viewed as a way to increase employment in remote areas, mainly if the manufacturing of the commodities includes an export component rather than relying just on local markets (Furneaux & Brown, 2008). An essential component of any action plan to support the self-sustaining economic development of Indigenous peoples is entrepreneurial activity on various levels (De Bruin & Mataira, 2018). In both Indigenous communities and the larger society in which they are ingrained, Indigenous entrepreneurship—or entrepreneurial activities carried out by Indigenous people—promotes economic development and political stability (Macpherson et al., 2021). Indigenous entrepreneurship can also support broader emancipatory initiatives aimed at improving economic, social, and cultural well-being and self-governance (Henderson, 2018). Benefits for the environment and the Indigenous culture are also compelling factors alongside economic profit for Indigenous enterprises, entrepreneurs and the community (Brueckner et al., 2014). Additionally, Indigenous entrepreneurship can help preserve Indigenous culture, which can be seen as having intrinsic worth over the long run and playing a crucial role in a nation's identity (Macpherson et al., 2021).

The need and relevance of more Indigenous entrepreneurship scholarship from the geographical area of Southeast Asia is supported by recent literature that emphasises the importance of decolonising entrepreneurship and management research. With a wide acknowledgement of the challenging colonisation in management and organisational studies, it is prominently significant to incorporate Indigenous perspectives in organisation studies, challenging Western-centric assumptions in the field (Bastien et al., 2023). Banerjee (2022) argued for the decolonisation of management theory, highlighting the necessity of incorporating non-Western perspectives. This perspective was echoed by Salmon et al. (2023), who conducted a systematic review of Indigenous management and organisation literature and emphasised the unique perspectives, practices, and challenges faced by Indigenous entrepreneurs. As entrepreneurial activities have a foundation in a region or a country's culture, national cultures confine entrepreneurial enterprises' actions and traits, which differ greatly among countries and regions (Filatotchev et al., 2022). The systematic review by Padilla-Meléndez et al. (2022) highlighted that non-indigenous culture contributed remarkably to the clash between indigenous values and the broader business landscape dominated by non-indigenous cultures, and further led to marginalisation. Management and organisational studies, therefore, can set the foundational steps in fostering an entrepreneurial environment catering to Indigenous people based on Indigenous-based theories outside the Western context

(Bruton et al., 2022). This perspective is crucial for scholars seeking to engage with indigenous entrepreneurship in Southeast Asia in a respectful and meaningful way.

Indigenous Entrepreneurship in Southeast Asia

In Southeast Asia, Indigenous entrepreneurship faces various unresolved issues, ranging from the entrepreneurial capability of the Indigenous population to conflicting outcomes of governmental efforts to improve the effectiveness of Indigenous entrepreneurial activities. Tipton (2009) identified three main root problems inhibiting the growth of Indigenous entrepreneurship in the region under the umbrella context of capitalism and historical constraints from colonisation comprising: (1) a gap in reaching modern science and technology compared to other areas in the world due to low levels of investment from governments and private sectors; (2) poor efficiency of economic intervention by governments leading to the dominance of non-Indigenous Chinese enterprises and political allies; and (3) the reliance on foreign companies to supply cutting-edge technologies had resulted from the lack of a robust domestic capitalist class. Agustiono et al. (2020) reflected a similar phenomenon that large companies frequently benefit from the advantage of obtaining funding for their investment in digital transformation, which is different from the normative condition small Indigenous entrepreneurs in the region can access. Although studies continuously show that information technology is crucial to the success of business operations, the majority of Indigenous microenterprises still do not make full use of IT owing to a lack of IT expertise and knowledge as well as the complexity of the IT applications (Hairuddin et al., 2012). Moreover, Indigenous enterprises operate spontaneously without proper registration and operation in line with governmental regulations and policies due to the lack of knowledge from education and fear of unhandled taxation due to poverty and poor living conditions (Rahman et al., 2020). Governments in the region need to be more capable of comprehensively understanding the needs and problems of Indigenous enterprises and communicating support programmes effectively for these entrepreneurs to join, leading to a gap between government support and actual benefits for Indigenous communities (Zainol & Daud, 2011). Despite the government's extensive entrepreneurship training and development programs, a sizable proportion of Indigenous business owners have been unable to maintain their companies, which is more common in the technology-based sector (Kohar, 2013). As a result, Indigenous businesses fall behind remarkably compared to large corporates and need help maintaining business in the long run. Specifically, 13% of Indigenous business owners failed to make a profit in the first five years of operation, reflecting its weaker market viability than other businesses (Kadir & Rosli, 2011).

Nevertheless, on the positive side, several Indigenous enterprises have taken advantage of Indigenous resources and succeeded in scaling up their business and creating economic and social benefits for the community in Southeast Asian countries. Successful Indigenous business owners in the wood-based manufacturing sector applied the best techniques and approaches that cater to customer needs, such as the capacity to produce high-quality goods, offer competitive prices, provide good customer services, consider time constraints, and good networking, particularly with families, suppliers, and governmental organisations in the Kelantan region of Malaysia (Hassan et al., 2014). ICT helped define the roles that will be played in the socio-technical systems developed to support the business and research operations of Indigenous microenterprises. Thus it became one of the initiatives in improving batik-making works and the management of batik microenterprises of the Indigenous community in Malaysia (Noor & Nordin, 2012). ICT adoption can address two main concerns of batik makers: the over-reliance on tacit knowledge to make batik and the fear of batik culture eroding, which the efficiency-emphasised production systems cannot resolve (Noor & Nordin, 2011). Governments, related bodies, and organisations have spent more effort improving support programmes for Indigenous enterprises nationally (Huff, 2011). The Department of Orang Asli Development (JAKOA), as in Fig. 2.2 (Zahari, 2022) and the Ministry of Rural and Regional Development of Malaysia regularly offered a variety of financial and non-financial aid, training, courses, and encouragement to help Orang Asli entrepreneurs succeed (Mokhtar & Hanafi, 2020). For instance, contract farming is utilised as a part of an affirmative action initiative in the Malaysian state of Sarawak to teach Indigenous Bumiputra smallholders in the production of commercial poultry, support the minorities without intensifying competition between these entrepreneurs as a part of the nationwide efforts to reduce poverty, increase income in the rural regions through improve Indigenous entrepreneurship (Morrison et al., 2006). Efforts towards improving the well-being of life and empowering human capital among the Indigenous community are the main focus of a wide range of Malaysian entrepreneurship programmes and national development policies (Amiruddin et al., 2021). Indonesia is another country in the region amplifying Indigenous entrepreneurship in national objectives and development plans. The Special Autonomy (OTSUS) law for the Papua community, which states that Papuans should promote entrepreneurship through community-based economic development, states that the government's top priority is the empowerment of Indigenous Papuans (Wambrauw et al., 2019).

Scholars investigating Indigenous entrepreneurship in Southeast Asia, albeit limited in quantity and quality compared to other areas in the world, spent a notable effort identifying and conceptualising the entrepreneurial landscape of Indigenous business. A study by Amiruddin et al. (2021) qualitatively identified factors contributing to Malaysian Indigenous youth becoming successful entrepreneurs,

Fig. 2.2 *Note.* Orang Asli Entrepreneurs Carnival (KUOA) 2022 organised by The Department of Orang Asli Development (JAKOA) for Indigenous entrepreneurs. From "Galak Orang Asli ceburi keusahawanan dalam talian", by B. J. Zahari, 2022. *Source*: https://api.bharian.com.my/berita/nasional/2022/06/969894/galak-orang-asli-ceburi-keusahawanan-dalam-talian). Copyright 2020 by New Straits Times Press (M) Bhd

including demographic factors, the appropriate direction of entrepreneurship, entrepreneurial characteristics suitable for Indigenous people, transferrable skills and financial support to scale up the enterprise. Based on that, a framework categorising the factors into their source of impact, such as external determinants (financial, mentoring and business advice, networking, government policies and stakeholder objectives, research—university, entrepreneurial education and entrepreneurial skill, physical and logistical infrastructure, technology support) and internal determinants (demographics, field of entrepreneurship, characteristics of entrepreneurs) (Amiruddin et al., 2020). Another study by Wambrauw et al. (2019) researching Papuan women in Indonesia found their motivation to associate with the informal agricultural sector as Indigenous entrepreneurs such as sustaining family needs and obligations with social and cultural heritage, as well as their openness to innovation, awareness of the market, and the engagement with the cash economy. They also examined the motivation to become an Indigenous entrepreneur (Wambrauw et al., 2019). However, Cheng and Hong (2021) discovered a different set of results among Orang Asli people, which are the expansion of working opportunities, income, funding for people in the community, demand increase for tourism in the area, personal interest, cultural preservation and promotion, and enhancement of perception towards Orang Asli people. This Indigenous community was also studied by Simpong et al. (2018), particularly in the mainstream tourism industry, in which the success of these Orang Asli entrepreneurs was associated with internal determinants such as attitudes, role models, encouragement, knowledge, skill and competency, interest, patience, persistence and external determinants such as support from the government, the networking and the community itself. In another paper by Jamak et al. (2014), scholars suggested a breakout model approach that can be used as a foundation to identify crucial success factors in creating tools to support microbusiness owners, such as drivers to start a business, factors required to run a business, and disablers and enablers of forming an Indigenous enterprise.

Due to the limited knowledge and adaptation catering to each Indigenous community, Indigenous entrepreneurship studies in Southeast Asia are significantly distanced from standard research investigated more extensively in North America and Oceania, such as Canada, Australia, and New Zealand (Croce, 2017). Particularly when examining Indigenous entrepreneurship and conducting research in the Southeast Asia context, Rembulan et al. (2022) also found this gap to be similarly significant with more studies in Australia, New Zealand, the US, and Taiwan. Thus, several studies still use entrepreneurship concepts and theories to research Indigenous entrepreneurs. A significantly positive association between entrepreneurial orientation, personality characteristics, and company performance was discovered in the study by Zainol and Ayadurai (2011), which gave the empirical test in understanding Indigenous entrepreneurship in Malay family enterprises in Malaysia. In combination with the theory of planned behaviour, the study by Simpong et al. (2022) sought to determine how adaptive resilience in Indigenous entrepreneurs was related to traits of a sustainable mindset, sustainability norms, sustainability behaviours, and opportunity recognition. Consequently, most Indigenous groups assessed that, compared to sustainability standards, adaptive resilience among entrepreneurs has risen in terms of attitudes, behaviours, and opportunity perception (Simpong et al., 2022). Therefore, it is crucial to acknowledge the role of Indigenous entrepreneurship research in improving practical implications in Southeast Asia countries by conducting an extensive and comprehensive review of contemporary knowledge and literature.

Methodology and Results

A systematic review has been conducted for this study by following the PRISMA (Preferred Reporting Items for Systematic Reviews and Meta-Analyses) methodology (Maheshwari et al., 2021). The PRISMA method was initially introduced in 2009 and was created with the aim of improving the clarity, transparency, and quality of the systematic review of papers (Sohrabi et al., 2021). The scope of this study was identifying the papers published in the area of indigenous entrepreneurship in Southeast Asia and hence our selection criteria was based on that. We have followed a three-step approach method to finalise the papers for this review. As a first step, the data for this study was collected from 2006 until 2022 using the key search word "Indigenous entrepreneur*" from the Web of Science database, resulting in 201 papers. In the next screening stage, only the papers written in English and journal articles were included (excluding other conference papers and others), resulting in the final sample size of 171 articles. As a final step of article selection, we focused on identifying the studies conducted in Southeast Asia on Indigenous entrepreneurship (IE), and there were 41 such papers extracted.

Publication analysis

For the initial analysis, we considered all papers ($N = 171$) to determine the trend of papers published in IEover the years, as shown in Fig. 2.3, and it can be seen that specifically, 75% of the studies ($N = 128$) have been conducted in the last decade since 2013.

Next, the studies were analysed to see which research methods have been used by the studies conducted in IE so far, and the results show that most of the studies (81%) were qualitative studies, and the rest of the studies were quantitative or mixed study, as seen in Table 2.1.

Further, we analysed the studies conducted region-wise on IE, and results indicate that most of the studies are done in Asia (27%), although this research topic first originated in the United States and Europe (Bruton et al., 2022). The rest of them were conducted either in one region or mixed regions (as seen in Fig. 2.4).

After doing the overall analysis of 171 papers, we focused our further analysis on the studies conducted only in Southeast Asia ($N = 41$), and most of the studies were focused on Malaysia ($N = 21$), followed by

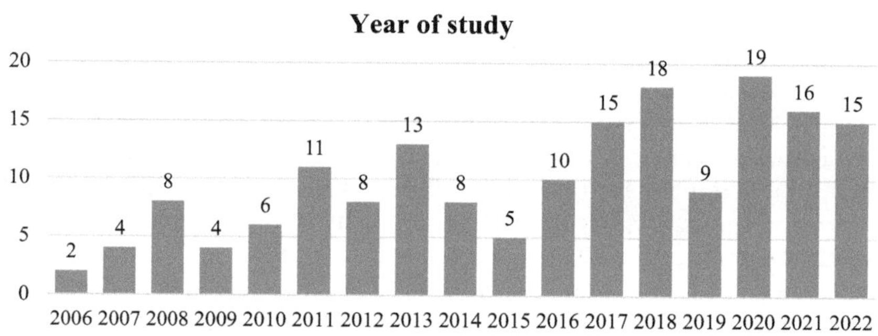

Fig. 2.3 Trend of research studies

Table 2.1 Methods used in various research studies

Research method	*Number of studies*
Qualitative	139
Quantitative	22
Mixed method	10

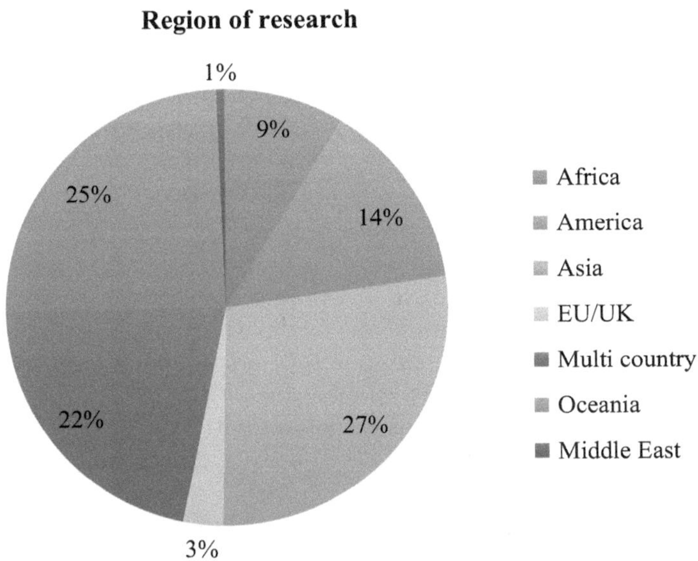

Fig. 2.4 Region of research studies

Indonesia ($N = 10$) (see Fig. 2.5). Of these total 41 studies, 30 were qualitative, nine were quantitative, and the other two were mixed.

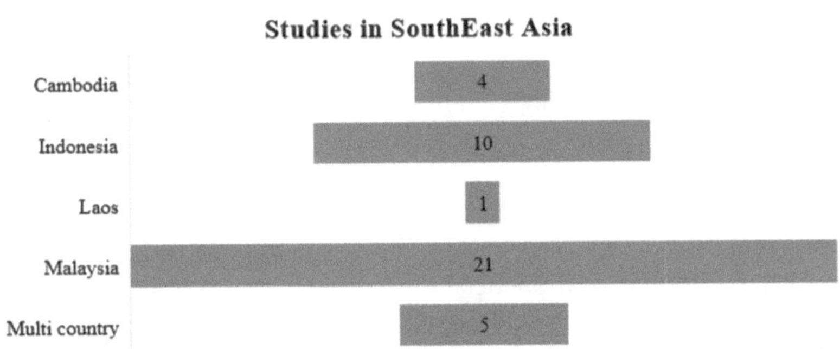

Fig. 2.5 Number of studies in Southeast Asian countries

Content Analysis

We further did the content analysis on all papers ($N = 171$), and it was found that women entrepreneurship was the most prominent research area in IE literature, and the most researched industries were tourism and traditional manufacturing/craftmanship. A few other prominent areas of research in IE identified were geared towards (as seen below):

- Finding concepts, definitions, and sub-categories of Indigenous entrepreneurship through literature review.
- Examining the establishment and development of Indigenous entrepreneurship based on political, social, and anthropological factors.
- Characteristics of successful Indigenous entrepreneurs.
- The concern about Indigenous resources such as wildlife, alienation, and environment.
- Successful case studies and portrayal of how it contributes to the Indigenous communities and society.
- Impact of Indigenous knowledge, culture, traditions, and value on Indigenous enterprises and Entrepreneurs.
- Enablers and barriers from the Indigenous entrepreneurs' perspectives.
  - o Internal factors (lack of entrepreneurial skills, families).
  - o External factors: Social network/capital, economic investment, financial institutions, governments.
- Comparison between Indigenous entrepreneurship with commercial entrepreneurship in terms of definitions, operations, and performance.

These above themes resonated with the study conducted by Croce (2019), who also determined three dimensions of IE related to sociocultural, institutional, and financial dimensions.

Next, we did a content analysis on papers from Southeast Asia ($N = 41$). We found that IE is an under-researched area in this region with relatively low impact (more than half the papers have less than ten citations). Unlike rising research efforts on this topic globally, research studies of Indigenous entrepreneurship in Southeast Asia did not show signs of an increase in quantity, with a mean of 2.93 papers/year, compared to the mean of more than 10 papers/year globally. This research area was mainly focused on Malaysia and Indonesia (as seen in Fig. 2.5) and was completely missing in countries like Laos, Vietnam, Philippines, Timor-Leste, Myanmar, Singapore, Thailand, and Brunei. Similar to most prominent themes identified globally, we also identified the prominent topics researched in Southeast Asian countries as listed below:

- Literature review & conceptual framework proposal for examining Indigenous entrepreneurship in Southeast Asian countries.
- Examination of the establishment and development of Indigenous entrepreneurship based on political, social, and anthropological factors.
- Application of commercial entrepreneurship conceptual models in testing entrepreneurial factors (performance, orientation, personality traits).
- Sustainability in Indigenous enterprises.
- Enablers and barriers from the Indigenous entrepreneurs' perspectives
    - o Internal factors (lack of entrepreneurial skills, families, IT/digital knowledge and systems)
    - o External factors (governmental support, resources)
- Case studies assessing Indigenous entrepreneurship activities separately
- Contribution of Indigenous entrepreneurship to Indigenous communities and society

Hence, the analysis of our papers globally and in Southeast Asia clearly states that there is further need for research in Southeast Asian countries on IE, and also, the topics discussed are few compared to global studies.

Discussion and Conclusion

In conclusion, the study has systematically reviewed literature from 2006 to 2022 to understand the research conducted in the Indigenous entrepreneurship (IE) area. The study first identified the articles published in IE globally and identified 171 such articles. Further, the analysis of the study was focused on the research conducted in the Southeast Asia region. The study has identified several theoretical gaps regarding the landscape of Indigenous entrepreneurship in the Southeast Asia region and the findings are discussed in the following paragraph.

Regarding the number of published studies of different Indigenous communities globally ($N = 171$), with an average of around 10 studies/year, there is a remarkable gap in global and regional (Southeast Asia) publications ($N = 41$) of around 3 articles/year, leading to a disparity in the knowledge of the phenomenon. Adding to the content gap, it is also noteworthy between the Southeast Asia region and its countries in comparison with other areas global-wide, which includes a difference in the level of extensiveness and in-depth level of understanding being reported in different themes. Further, especially in Southeast Asia, the IE has been examined in Indonesia and Malaysia compared to the remaining countries of the region, while IE is not much researched in countries such as Laos, Vietnam, Philippines, Timor-Leste, Myanmar, Singapore, Thailand, and Brunei. Another noteworthy shortcoming of Indigenous entrepreneurship studies is the investigated industries' limitations. Current publications heavily emphasised the tourism and craftmanship of Indigenous enterprises, while a few papers focused on Indigenous produce, hence a wide range of industries are still needed to be explored in future studies. Sharing similarities with global studies, a monotony in methodology and theoretical framework based on unique characteristics of the Indigenous population is acknowledged since numerous studies are primarily elaborated based on concepts of commercial entrepreneurship. This leads to a lack of systematic and quantitative comprehension of Indigenous entrepreneurship practices based on the distinctiveness of the community in the regions. Empirical studies are minimal as well, especially in cross-country examinations.

Theoretical contributions

Our study makes significant contributions to the scholarship on Indigenous entrepreneurship in Southeast Asia in several ways. Firstly, it highlights the pressing need to address a substantial theoretical gap in our understanding of Indigenous entrepreneurship in this region. By identifying this gap, we provide a catalyst for future research, drawing attention to unexplored aspects of Indigenous entrepreneurship. Our research systematically examines industries, countries, and methodologies, pinpointing areas that require additional investigation. Secondly, our study acts as a call to action for scholars. We underscore the urgency of investigating and diversifying knowledge in Southeast Asia, especially in regions where Indigenous entrepreneurship research is scarce. This call for research serves as an invitation for academics to explore Indigenous entrepreneurship in greater depth and detail, thus enriching the body of knowledge in this field. Thirdly, we aim to bridge knowledge gaps not only within the Southeast Asian region but also between this region and global studies. This broader perspective allows us to draw connections between Indigenous entrepreneurship practices in Southeast Asia and those in other parts of the world, shedding light on both commonalities and unique characteristics.

Practical implications

In terms of practical implications, Indigenous people, Indigenous entrepreneurs, and other stakeholders on the ground can draw valuable insights from our study. We emphasise the importance of multifaceted investment in technology, education, and funding from the private sector. Indigenous entrepreneurs should actively seek out opportunities to collaborate with private enterprises, which can lead to mutually beneficial partnerships. Governments, policymakers, and NGOs play a pivotal role in facilitating these collaborations, fostering an environment where Indigenous knowledge and social capital can resonate for the betterment of Indigenous entrepreneurs. Institutions and governments can also acknowledge a comprehensive landscape of the phenomenon in the region, therefore overcoming the drawbacks of contemporary approaches to support Indigenous enterprises and their communities (Jamak et al., 2014; Zainol & Daud, 2011). Furthermore, our study advocates for the expansion of Indigenous entrepreneurship into a diverse range of industries. Indigenous businesses should explore new sectors that align with their skills and resources, thereby unlocking the untapped potential for growth, creating joint profits, and addressing financial challenges within their communities. It is essential for practitioners to recognise that diversifying the industries in which Indigenous entrepreneurship thrives can have a profound impact on both economic prosperity and community development.

Limitations and Directions for Future Research

While our study offers valuable insights, we acknowledge its limitations. We aimed to capture studies from 2006 to 2022; however, there may still be overlooked research due to the wide variety of databases available. Future research should explore additional databases to ensure comprehensive coverage and gain a more holistic understanding of Indigenous entrepreneurship in Southeast Asia. Additionally, we suggest that future studies delve into comparative analyses, both within the Asian region (e.g., South Asia versus Central Asia) and on a global scale. These comparative studies can uncover specific similarities and disparities in Indigenous entrepreneurship practices, facilitating cross-regional learning and policy development. Furthermore, researchers should consider expanding their focus beyond Asia to compare Indigenous entrepreneurship across different continents. Such comparative analyses can provide a broader perspective on how Indigenous entrepreneurship varies globally and offer insights that transcend regional boundaries. Also, we might have missed out few studies due to the term "indigenous" used as a search keyword in our study, but some studies in Myanmar or any other countries might have used the word "minority ethnic groups" and hence future studies can focus on their search by using alternative keywords to expand their search. Most of the studies conducted in Southeast Asia were qualitative ($N = 30$ out of 41) and hence future studies can focus more on quantitative or mixed methodologies. Finally, the research on IE was mainly from the Indonesian and Malaysian regions and hence future studies can explore other countries in the Southeast Asian region.

References

Affizzah, A. D., Salbiah, E., Afiza, A. N., & Norimah, R. (2016). Indigenous entrepreneurs and ecotourism product: Success or collapse? *International Journal of Academic Research in Business and Social Sciences, 6*(12), 425–437.

Agbim, K. C., Ayatse, F. A., & Oriarewo, G. O. (2013a). Entrepreneurial learning: A social and experiential method of entrepreneurship development among indigenous female entrepreneurs in Anambra State, Nigeria. *International Journal of Scientific and Research Publications, 6*(3), 2250–3153.

Agbim, K. C., Oriarewo, G. O., & Owocho, M. (2013b). Indigenous female entrepreneurs' leadership styles and innovativeness in Tiv land, Benue State, Nigeria. *International Journal of Business and Management Invention, 2*(4), 45–52.

Agustiono, W., Chan, C., Kam, B., Yusron, R. M., & Yasid, A. (2020). Barriers of digital transformation: The case of small indigenous businesses in Indonesia during COVID-19.

Akpor-Robaro, M. O., & Erigbe, P. A. (2019). Globalization and indigenous entrepreneurship development in developing economies: A case study of manufacturing and commerce (Trade) in Nigeria. *Journal of Small Business and Entrepreneurship, 7*(2), 61–72.

Amiruddin, M. H., Suib, S. N., Che Ibrahim, A., & A Jalil, S. A. (2020). Determining the factors influencing indigenous youth become a successful entrepreneurs. *Gading Journal for Social Sciences, 23*(1), 5–12.

Amiruddin, M. H., Suib, S. N., Sumarwati, S., Razali, N., & Hamzah, U. (2021). A framework of entrepreneurship incubator for indigenous youth to become successful entrepreneurs. *Online Journal for TVET Practitioners, 6*(2), 1–10.

Amofah, S. (2021). Indigenous women social entrepreneurship; Poverty alleviation tool used by development NGOs in Ghana. *Athens Journal of Social Sciences, 8*(2), 151–168.

April, W. I., & Itenge, D. I. (2020). Fostering indigenous entrepreneurship amongst San people: An exploratory case of Tsumkwe. *International Journal of Business and Globalisation, 24*(4), 496–512.

Austin, B. J., & Garnett, S. T. (2018). Perspectives on success from indigenous entrepreneurs in Northern Australia. *International Journal of Entrepreneurship and Small Business, 33*(2), 176–201.

Baba, S., & Fortin-Lefebvre, E. (2020). Indigenous entrepreneurship, marginal ontologies and sustainable development goals. In W. Leal Filho, A. M. Azul, L. Brandli, A. Lange Salvia, & T. Wall (Eds.), *Industry, innovation and infrastructure* (pp. 1–12). Springer International Publishing. https://doi.org/10.1007/978-3-319-71059-4_152-1.

Banerjee, S. B. (2022). Decolonizing management theory: A critical perspective. *Journal of Management Studies, 59*(4), 1074–1087.

Bastien, F., Coraiola, D. M., & Foster, W. M. (2023). Indigenous peoples and organization studies. *Organization Studies, 44*(4), 659–675.

Brueckner, M., Spencer, R., Wise, G., & Marika, B. (2014). Indigenous entrepreneurship: Closing the gap on local terms. *Journal of Australian Indigenous Issues, 17*(2), 2–24.

De Bruin, A., & Mataira, P. (2018). Indigenous entrepreneurship. In *Entrepreneurship: New perspectives in a global age* (pp. 169–184). Routledge.

Bruton, G. D., Zahra, S. A., & Cai, L. (2018). Examining entrepreneurship through indigenous lenses. *Entrepreneurship Theory and Practice, 42*(3), 351–361. https://doi.org/10.1177/1042258717741129

Bruton, G. D., Zahra, S. A., Van de Ven, A. H., & Hitt, M. A. (2022). Indigenous theory uses, abuses, and future. *Journal of Management Studies, 59*(4), 1057–1073.

Cahn, M. (2008). Indigenous entrepreneurship, culture and micro-enterprise in the Pacific Islands: Case studies from Samoa. *Entrepreneurship and Regional Development, 20*(1), 1–18.

Cheng, M. L., & Hong, H. T. S. (2021). The motivation to become indigenous entrepreneur: A case of Orang Asli in Malaysia. *Asia Proceedings of Social Sciences, 8*(1), 60–62.

Clarke, G. (2001). From ethnocide to ethnodevelopment? Ethnic minorities and indigenous peoples in Southeast Asia. *Third World Quarterly, 22*(3), 413–436.

Croce, F. (2017). Contextualized indigenous entrepreneurial models: A systematic review of indigenous entrepreneurship literature. *Journal of Management and Organization, 23*(6), 886–906.

Croce, F. (2019). Indigenous entrepreneurship, society, and the dimensions of diversity: An overview of the Canadian national context. *Diversity within Diversity Management, 21*, 359–371.

Dana, L.-P. (2007). Toward a multidisciplinary definition of indigenous entrepreneurship. *International handbook of research on indigenous entrepreneurship*, 3–7.

Dana, L. P. (2015). Indigenous entrepreneurship: An emerging field of research. *International Journal of Business and Globalisation, 14*(2), 158–169.

Evans, M. M., & Williamson, I. O. (2017). Understanding the central tension of Indigenous entrepreneurship: Purpose, profit and leadership. Academy of Management Proceedings.

Filatotchev, I., Ireland, R. D., & Stahl, G. K. (2022). Contextualizing management research: An open systems perspective. *Journal of Management Studies, 59*(4), 1036–1056.

Foley, D. (2008). Indigenous (Australian) entrepreneurship? *International Journal of Business and Globalisation, 2*(4), 419–436.

Frederick, H., Kuratko, D. F., & Hodgetts, R. M. (2006). Entrepreneurship: Theory, process and practice (Asia-Pacific Edition). Cengage Learning Pty. Ltd.

Furneaux, C., & Brown, K. (2008). Australian Indigenous entrepreneurship: A capital-based view. *The International Journal of Entrepreneurship and Innovation, 9*(2), 133–144.

Hairuddin, H., Noor, N. L. M., & Kassim, E. S. (2012). Developing therapy-based IT adoption model for microenterprises. *Journal of Innovation Management in Small and Medium Enterprises, 2012*, 1.

Hassan, T. M. R. T., Yaacob, M. R., & Abdullatiff, N. K. (2014). Sustaining SMEs wood-based product manufacturing through best practices–The case of indigenous entrepreneurs in Kelantan. *Procedia-Social and Behavioral Sciences, 115*, 221–234.

Henderson, G. E. (2018). Indigenous entrepreneurship and social entrepreneurship in Canada. *Supreme Court Law Review, 83*(2), 241–278.

Hindle, K., & Lansdowne, M. (2005). Brave spirits on new paths: Toward a globally relevant paradigm of indigenous entrepreneurship research. *Journal of Small Business and Entrepreneurship, 18*(2), 131–141.

Hindle, K., & Moroz, P. (2010). Indigenous entrepreneurship as a research field: Developing a definitional framework from the emerging canon. *International Entrepreneurship and Management Journal, 6*, 357–385.

Huff, G. (2011). Finance and long-term development issues in Southeast Asia. *Asian-Pacific Economic Literature, 25*(1), 56–78.

Jamak, A. B. S. A., Ali, R. M. M., & Ghazali, Z. (2014). A breakout strategy model of Malay (Malaysian indigenous) micro-entrepreneurs. *Procedia-Social and Behavioral Sciences, 109*, 572–583.

Kadir, S. A., & Rosli, M. M. (2011). Managerial skills of the small indigenous entrepreneurs in Malaysia. *International Journal of Business and Social Science, 2*(10).

Khanal, B. R., & Babar, J. T. (2007). Community based ecotourism for sustainable tourism development in the Mekong region. *Policy Brief, 1*, 2007.

Kohar, U. H. A. (2013). *The factors that influence the sustainability of Malaysian Bumiputera (indigenous) new technology-based small firms* RMIT University].

Kuratko, D. F. (2011). Entrepreneurship theory, process, and practice in the 21st century. *International Journal of Entrepreneurship and Small Business, 13*(1), 8–17.

Macpherson, W. G., Tretiakov, A., Mika, J. P., & Felzensztein, C. (2021). Indigenous entrepreneurship: Insights from Chile and New Zealand. *Journal of Business Research, 127*, 77–84.

Maheshwari, G., & Maheshwari, A. (2021). Growing inequalities in the Covid-19 pandemic and their effect on women entrepreneurship: A case of Vietnam. *International Entrepreneurship Review*, *7*(4), 65–73.

Maheshwari, G., Nayak, R., & Ngyyen, T. (2021). Review of research for two decades for women leadership in higher education around the world and in Vietnam: a comparative analysis. *Gender in Management: An International Journal*, *36*(5), 640–658.

Mokhtar, M., & Hanafi, W. N. W. (2020). Indigenous Entrepreneurship Sustainability in Malaysia. *Global Business & Management Research*, *12*(4).

Molina-Ramírez, E., & Barba-Sánchez, V. (2021). Embeddedness as a differentiating element of indigenous entrepreneurship: Insights from Mexico. *Sustainability, 13*(4), 2117.

Morrison, P. S., Murray, W. E., & Ngidang, D. (2006). Promoting indigenous entrepreneurship through small-scale contract farming: The poultry sector in Sarawak, Malaysia. *Singapore Journal of Tropical Geography, 27*(2), 191–206.

Morton, M. F., & Baird, I. G. (2019). From Hill tribes to indigenous peoples: The localisation of a global movement in Thailand. *Journal of Southeast Asian Studies, 50*(1), 7–31.

Noor, N. L. M., & Nordin, A. (2011). Contextual inquiry into business requirements elicitation of indigenous enterprise: A case of the Malaysian Batik microenterprise. The European Conference on Information Systems Management.

Noor, N. L. M., & Nordin, A. (2012). Requirements elicitation for the technology conception of a community information system for the indigenous microenterprise: A contextual multi-analysis approach on business and community requirements of Batik Making. *Electronic Journal of Information Systems Evaluation, 15*(1), 102–115.

Onwuegbuzie, H. N., & Mafimisebi, O. P. (2021). Global relevance of scaling African indigenous entrepreneurship. *Technological Forecasting and Social Change, 166*, 120629.

Padilla-Meléndez, A., Plaza-Angulo, J. J., Del-Aguila-Obra, A. R., & Ciruela-Lorenzo, A. M. (2022). Indigenous entrepreneurship. Current issues and future lines. *Entrepreneurship and Regional Development*, *34*(1–2), 6–31.

Patierno, K., Kaneda, T., & Greenbaum, C. (2019). World population data sheet. *Population Reference Bureau.*

Peredo, A. M., & Anderson, R. B. (2006). Indigenous entrepreneurship research: Themes and variations. In *Developmental entrepreneurship: Adversity, risk, and isolation* (Vol. 5, pp. 253–273). Emerald Group Publishing Limited.

Peredo, A. M., Anderson, R. B., Galbraith, C. S., Honig, B., & Dana, L. P. (2004). Towards a theory of indigenous entrepreneurship. *International Journal of Entrepreneurship and Small Business, 1*(1–2), 1–20.

Persoon, G., Eindhoven, M., Modina, R., & Aquino, D. (2007). Indigenous peoples in southeast Asia, sharing knowledge, building capacity, fighting poverty, saving diversity.

Rahman, S. A., Said, H. M., & Ali, S. R. (2020). Exploring Development of Indigenous Entrepreneurship among the Semai community at Batang Padang District Perak, Malaysia. In (pp. 269–280). Sciendo.

Ratten, V., & Dana, L.-P. (2017). Gendered perspective of indigenous entrepreneurship. *Small Enterprise Research, 24*(1), 62–72.

Rembulan, C. L., Kusumowidagdo, A., & Rahadiyanti, M. (2022). Exchanged actors behind the creation of sense of place value in indigenous tourism enterprise Karangrejo Borobudur Indonesia. *Journal of Enterprising Communities: People and Places in the Global Economy*(ahead-of-print).

Salamanca, A. (2019). *Indigenous Peoples of Southeast Asia reaffirm their rights*. Stockholm Environment Institute. https://www.sei.org/perspectives/indigenous-peoples-of-southeast-asia-reaffirm-their-rights/.

Salmon, E., Chavez, R. J. F., & Murphy, M. (2023). New perspectives and critical insights from Indigenous peoples' research: A systematic review of Indigenous management and organization literature. *Academy of Management Annals*, *17*(2), 439–491.

Simpong, D., Rahim, M., & Zulkefli, N. (2022). The sustainability entrepreneurship in adaptive resilience among indigenous community in Malaysia. *GeoJournal of Tourism and Geosites*.

Simpong, D., Zahari, M., Ahmad, R., & Hanafiah, M. (2018). Indigenous entrepreneurs and the mainstream tourism industry related businesses: A case of Orang Asli in Malaysia. *Journal of Fundamental and Applied Sciences*, *10*(2S), 436–462.

Sohrabi, C., Franchi, T., Mathew, G., Kerwan, A., Nicola, M., Griffin, M., Agha, M., & Agha, R. (2021). PRISMA 2020 statement: What's new and the importance of reporting guidelines (Vol. 88, pp. 105918). Elsevier.

Statistics Division of the Department of Economic and Social Affairs - United Nations. (1999). UNSD—Methodology: Standard country or area codes for statistical use (M49). United Nations. Retrieved August 27 from https://unstats.un.org/unsd/methodology/m49/.

Tessier, J. (2015). *Indigenous Peoples and ASEAN Integration*. Asia Indigenous Peoples Pact (AIPP) Foundation.

Tipton, F. B. (2009). Southeast Asian capitalism: History, institutions, states, and firms. *Asia Pacific Journal of Management*, *26*, 401–434.

United Nations. (2021). Indigenous Peoples: Respect NOT Dehumanization. United Nations. https://www.un.org/en/fight-racism/vulnerable-groups/indigenous-peoples.

Vázquez-Maguirre, M. (2020). Sustainable development through Indigenous community-based enterprises. In *Indigenous Wellbeing and Enterprise* (pp. 263–281). Routledge.

Wambrauw, L. T., Martin, S., & Addison, R. (2019). The Nature of papuan women indigenous entrepreneurship in informal agricultural sector (A case of papuan women traders in manokwari and surrounding areas of West Papua-Indonesia). *Salasika*, *2*(1), 77–94.

Zahari, B. J. (2022, June 25). Galak Orang Asli ceburi keusahawanan dalam talian. *BH Online*. https://api.bharian.com.my/berita/nasional/2022/06/969894/galak-orang-asli-ceburi-keusahawanan-dalam-talian.

Zainol, F. A., & Ayadurai, S. (2011). Entrepreneurial orientation and firm performance: The role of personality traits in Malay family firms in Malaysia. *International Journal of Business and Social Science*, *2*(1).

Zainol, F. A., & Daud, W. N. W. (2011). Indigenous ("Bumiputera") Malay entrepreneurs in Malaysia: Government supports, entrepreneurial orientation and firms performances. *International Business and Management*, *2*(1), 86–99.

CHAPTER 3

Poverty and Indigenous Entrepreneurship: A Case Study of the Mah Meri People in Malaysia

Sharon G. M. Koh, Audrey K. L. Siah, and Andrei O. J. Kwok

Introduction

Countries worldwide experience accelerated economic development due to technological advancement. The digital age presents new opportunities for governments to foster strong linkages via flows of trade, finance, and factors of production (capital, labour, and land). As such, the new economy provides greater access to jobs, thus lowering poverty levels (Ratcheva et al., 2020). The competitive landscape benefits societies that

S. G. M. Koh (✉) · A. K. L. Siah · A. O. J. Kwok
Monash University, Subang Jaya, Malaysia
e-mail: koh.geokmay@monash.edu

A. K. L. Siah
e-mail: audrey.siah@monash.edu

A. O. J. Kwok
e-mail: andrei.kwok@monash.edu

E. L. Eijdenberg et al. (eds.), *Indigenous Entrepreneurship in Southeast Asia*, Palgrave Studies in Equity, Diversity, Inclusion, and Indigenization in Business, https://doi.org/10.1007/978-3-031-54457-6_3

adapt well to the global market. However, some communities cannot catch up and continue to be left behind in the face of economic development. A revival of literature centred around the new economy saw attempts to introduce inclusive growth into the policy agenda (Erlando et al., 2020; Hall et al., 2012; Rauniyar & Kanbur, 2010).

While the new economy has provided extensive opportunities over the past decades, it also creates barriers for minority groups that need more knowledge and skills, such as the indigenous community. The United Nations (2023a) estimates that approximately 476 million indigenous people live across 90 countries, equivalent to approximately 5% of the global population. Global estimates contained in the recent International Labour Organisation (2019) report revealed that Asia Pacific is home to the largest population of indigenous people, with approximately 335.8 million indigenous people living in the region. While the Southeast Asian countries Malaysia, Singapore, Indonesia, and Vietnam share some similarities in terms of a history of colonisation by Western powers, the impact of colonialism on their national identities differed, and the postcolonial legacy continues to influence the countries today.

The fast-changing economy is a challenge to the indigenous population, who are often handicapped by their lack of basic skills. Most indigenous communities share common problems such as discrimination, poor health, and low literacy compared to nonindigenous groups (Gracey & King, 2009; Hall & Patrinos, 2012). The underlying cause of these issues is extreme poverty. The current literature views entrepreneurship as an effective mechanism to reduce poverty (Alvarez & Barney, 2014; Sutter et al., 2019). There has been an emergent trend to create entrepreneurial ventures while embracing indigenous culture to lessen socioeconomic challenges (Colbourne, 2021). The need to expand indigenous entrepreneurship scholarship bridges Western-centric perspectives with local cultural values to preserve and contribute to the global discourse in the mainstream entrepreneurship literature.

The integration of the indigenous entrepreneurship outlook into the mainstream entrepreneurship literature is critical and timely. There has been increasing attention given to indigenous people to ensure inclusion in achieving the Sustainable Development Goals by 2030. To turn the belief of "leaving no one behind" into the practice of inclusive economic development, four Sustainable Development Goals (SDGs) are focused on indigenous status. They are (1) Goals 1.4.2 and 5.a.1 in securing tenure rights to land; (2) Goal 2.3.2, which aims to increase small-scale food producers' income; and (3) Goal 4.5.1, which emphasises equal opportunity in accessing all levels of education.

By undertaking a case study approach, this chapter provides a richer understanding of the experiences of the indigenous community in Malaysia. The question "what are the underlying factors that hinder or enhance indigenous entrepreneurship among the Mah Meri?" calls for qualitative methods. This approach deepens the understanding of conceptualisation in the indigenous entrepreneurship literature. The study provides three main findings that have salience for academics, policy-makers, and researchers in the field and contribute to the indigenous entrepreneurship literature. These findings may potentially reshape scholars' worldviews on the indigenous community.

This chapter provides a novel contribution to the literature on indigenous communities in Malaysia by providing a contextual understanding of the Mah Meri. Earlier studies by Croce (2017) highlighted a gap whereby contextual factors often influence the identification of indigenous entrepreneurship, and commonalities can enrich entrepreneurship models and assist in policy advocacy to support these communities. However, its integration is still lacking in the literature. While government support is available to improve livelihoods and empower these communities, Croce (2017) posits that the absence of specific information addressing the barriers and contextualisation of indigenous issues may have contributed to the failure of government initiatives.

The overall structure of the chapter is organised as follows. First, we present the related literature in Sect. 2 to enrich our understanding of the literature on poverty and indigenous entrepreneurship. Next, the chapter provides a background of the case study in Sect. 3, followed by an overview of the research design and data collection. The discussion of the findings of the study is covered in Sect. 4. The final section offers concluding remarks.

Insights into Poverty and Indigenous Entrepreneurship Literature

This section seeks to provide insight into indigenous entrepreneurship to establish a common understanding of the scope and literature related to the indigenous population, poverty, and entrepreneurship.

A commonly used definition of "indigenous" people is presented in the International Labour Organisation Indigenous and Tribal Convention,[1] 1989 (No. 169), which defines indigenous people objectively as those *descended from populations who inhabited the country or geographical region at the time of the conquest, colonisation or establishment of present state boundaries. They retain some or all of their own social, economic, cultural and political institutions, irrespective of their legal status.* More recent definitions in many parts of the world recognise indigenous identity as self-determined (Padilla-Meléndez et al., 2022) or produced through an upbringing and practice of indigenous lifestyles, traditions, or rituals. Regardless of the definitions, the size and population show the immense diversity of the indigenous population.

On the other hand, poverty is often understood in terms of economic opportunities and access to necessities such as education, health, water, sanitation, transportation, and housing (United Nations, 2023b; Moser, 1998). Internationally, poverty is indicated by the USD 2.15 per day threshold, which represents the minimum income to meet basic necessities (World Bank, 2022). The United Nations (2023a) estimates that approximately 15% of indigenous people live in extreme poverty. The high poverty rate among the indigenous community is alarming since it leads to a wide range of long-term problems, especially if there are no active interventions by the government. High poverty levels have also led to persistent health problems such as high morbidity and premature death. Additionally, low literacy and lack of access to primary health care have increased noncommunicable diseases among indigenous people. Due to poverty, the indigenous community is among the most disadvantaged and vulnerable groups worldwide (International Labour Organisation, 2019). They have yet to gain adequate access to the economic opportunities presented by the new economy.

Entrepreneurs play an essential role in the economic growth of a country. The concept of entrepreneur primarily originates from the works of Schumpeter (1942). Schumpeter was an Austrian economist who posited that entrepreneurs stimulate new employment and accelerate economic development by creating and innovating new products and services. Schumpeter's historical research on entrepreneurial actions, such

[1] Source: https://www.ilo.org/global/topics/indigenous-tribal/WCMS_503321/lang--en/index.htm.

as the "mechanisms of creative response", serves to advance entrepreneurship theory (Wadhwani et al., 2020, p. 10). Accordingly, entrepreneurship is often seen as an individual's innovation, and individuals have been the focus of research in this field (Welter, 2011; Yan & Yan, 2016). Such a view fails to recognise the role of a "collective or community-based orientation" or the desire to be included in the economy "on their own terms", which are characteristics of indigenous peoples (Peredo et al., 2004). Furthermore, Banerjee (2022, p. 1076) highlights the need to differentiate "indigenous as referring to local practices", which is rooted in the sociological and anthropological literature, from the characteristics of indigenous people in the management literature. He adds that this distinctive characteristic emphasises the heritage that shapes the macro environment (relationship between businesses and the indigenous community).

Indigenous entrepreneurship is often viewed as "a process of drawing value from community-based resources (people, land, capabilities, culture, etc.) and contributing value back that is responsive to a community's particular set of socioeconomic conditions" (Colbourne et al., 2023, p. 3). Indigenous entrepreneurship is a field that is often overlooked and neglected in entrepreneurship studies (Sutter et al., 2019). Departing from mainstream entrepreneurship models, contextual factors such as sociocultural, historical, and philosophical factors often affect the identification of indigenous entrepreneurship models (Bruton et al., 2022; Croce, 2019; Lindsay, 2005). Of particular concern is that theoretical foundations in this field are often Western-centric, established in North American and European contexts (Filatotchev et al., 2022). The Western theoretical underpinnings create a challenge, as many indigenous characteristics do not fit in the typical narrative these scholars have generated (Sutter et al., 2019). Increasingly, academic scholars recognise the need to develop indigenous theory to explain entrepreneurship in the context of extreme poverty (Bruton et al., 2022). The literature commonly defines indigenous entrepreneurship as "the creation, management, and development of new ventures by indigenous peoples for the benefit of indigenous peoples" (Hindle & Lansdowne, 2005: p. 132). This definition proves that entrepreneurship can be a crucial avenue for empowering indigenous people, improving their earnings, and lifting them out of poverty (Predo et al., 2004; Hindle & Moroz, 2010). The definition also shows distinctive features that differentiate them from nonindigenous entrepreneurs.

However, entrepreneurial activities among indigenous communities tend to be subsistence-based and involve day-to-day small businesses, mainly due to their deep connection to nature. These communities primarily depend on available resources accessible through hunting or fishing (Dana & Anderson, 2011; Dana et al., 2005). Subsistence entrepreneurs usually refer to poor individuals who exist at the bottom of the pyramid (Viswanathan et al., 2010, 2014). They care only about their survival; hence, their microscale businesses face tremendous challenges in expanding or developing into larger ventures (Seja, 2013). They usually face social vulnerabilities caused by their working and living conditions (Ratten, 2014).

Globally, indigenous peoples are among the poorest and most vulnerable groups, and venturing into entrepreneurial activities can improve their well-being to ensure a more sustainable future, i.e., engaging in new entrepreneurial ventures beyond those solely for survival (Giraldo et al., 2020). While existing research recognises the critical role played by entrepreneurial ventures, it can only be meaningful for indigenous peoples if mainstream ideas are transformed to enhance individual, collective, and societal well-being through entrepreneurial activities (Giraldo et al., 2020). Transformative entrepreneurship indicates that societal and economic impacts can be improved equally (Maas & Jones, 2019) while exploring opportunities to enhance economic and social well-being (Rayburn & Ochieng, 2022). Businesses can reexamine the way in which they provide opportunities for entrepreneurs to contribute equally to the economy. These actions may help reduce welfare dependency among indigenous people.

Despite the potential benefits of entrepreneurial activities, their engagement remains low. The literature highlights several barriers. For instance, Saffu (2003) indicates that entrepreneurial capital (in categories such as human, financial, physical, social, organisational, and technological) acts as a potential barrier to indigenous entrepreneurial activity. Flamsteed and Golding (2005) posit that low earnings and a lack of asset ownership are crucial factors that curtail the ability to raise capital to kick-start a business. Moreover, poor infrastructure is the critical bottleneck facing most indigenous communities in very remote areas, making the distribution of goods and services to the marketplace a significant challenge (Gouvea et al., 2022). Furthermore, the inaccessibility of electricity, telecommunications services, and roads has also significantly disrupted the operation of indigenous entrepreneurs (Gouvea et al., 2022). The authors also identify the need for more access to finance as a critical barrier that limits the promotion and expansion of indigenous entrepreneurship. Entrepreneurship in this remote community is typically characterised by self-sufficiency that leans on available techniques from heritage practices in extracting natural resources (Mason et al., 2008).

Some scholars identify the lack of education and training (Flamsteed & Golding, 2005), a lack of basic business skills (Baguley, 2007), and a limited pool of skilled labour (Flamsteed & Golding, 2005) as significant bottlenecks faced by potential indigenous entrepreneurs. A recent study by Inimiesi (2023) states that inadequate expertise or knowledge and a negative mindset are the two crucial factors that hinder indigenous communities from fostering sustainable socioeconomic development. Furthermore, Baguley (2007) implies that low human and social capital levels reduce indigenous people's incentive to be involved in entrepreneurial activity and make them more welfare dependent. In addition, in a study of 211 Kiwi indigenous entrepreneurs, Maritz (2006) demonstrates that greater independence is the primary driver of new ventures, and many entrepreneurs lack the ambition to grow personal wealth. Dana (2015) further illustrates that the perception of opportunity among indigenous communities is very different from that among nonindigenous groups, which is influenced by their culture and easily disrupted by entities outside the indigenous communities. Table 3.1 summarises some factors that influence indigenous entrepreneurship.

Background of Case Study: Mah Meri, Pulau Indah

Case selection

Recognising the need for contextualised research on specific indigenous communities, the study used a case study to explore the social and economic circumstances preventing indigenous entrepreneurship in Malaysia. The case study approach (Creswell & Creswell, 2017) allows us to draw meaningful insights from the various stakeholders' views of the community and the real-life context of indigenous peoples. Inherently, the disadvantageous environment hinders the indigenous community from embracing entrepreneurial ventures beyond subsistence economic activities.

The Mah Meri people were chosen mainly because the villagers live in extreme poverty despite efforts by nongovernmental organisations

Table 3.1 Factors that influence indigenous entrepreneurship

Author (year)	*Indigenous population*	*Potential factors that influence Indigenous entrepreneurship*
Baguley (2007)	Australia	Corporations can step in to build capabilities among indigenous entrepreneurs who mostly rely on tourism and artistic enterprises
Dana (2015)	Canada	Heterogeneity among indigenous peoples. Indigenous people rely on immediately available resources, kinship ties, a sustainable reliance on informal markets, and community and cultural influence opportunities
Flamsteed and Golding (2005)	Australia	Indigenous business differs by context, and learning must be tied to earning with customised content while putting it into practice
Gouvea et al. (2022)	Latin America	Indigenous entrepreneurship collaborations can be fostered on shared culture, religion, and traditions
Hindle and Moroz (2010)	Australia	The importance of "community" is emphasised among indigenous entrepreneurs
Mason et al. (2008)	Canada	Many indigenous entrepreneurs rely on traditional local resources
Maritz (2006)	New Zealand	Independence is valued as a primary driver of new ventures
Saffu (2003)	South Pacific Island countries	Culture impacts the characteristics of indigenous entrepreneurs

(NGOs) and the government to improve their well-being. The chosen site is an indigenous village in Pulau Indah, an island in the Klang district (Fig. 3.1). The village consists mainly of the Mah Meri tribe, internationally known for its animistic dance and culture. Mah Meri are known as "forest or sea people" because they live near the forest and sea in Selangor (Chong et al., 2018) and mainly speak an Austroasiatic language. Poverty eradication is more challenging due to their inherited way of life, and many families face intergenerational poverty. Notably, the indigenous people in Peninsular Malaysia are commonly known as Orang Asli or Orang Asal, loosely translated as original people. According to Nah (2008), the conceptualisation and social understanding of natives and indigenous people are rooted in concepts developed by the colonial administration in the eighteenth and nineteenth centuries. Prior to the 1960s, when the term Orang Asli was coined, the population was known as aborigines, a term still used today in legal documents. The Orang Asli in Peninsular Malaysia are defined by their language, customs, and way of life. This categorisation differs from that of the natives of East Malaysia, who are defined by their ancestry (Nah, 2008).

Fig. 3.1 Site location at Pulau Indah indigenous village. The village is an hour's drive from Kuala Lumpur, Malaysia's capital city. *Source* Authors' illustration with information taken from Google Maps

Jabatan Kemajuan Orang Asli (JAKOA), a department under the purview of the Ministry of Rural and Regional Department, is responsible for the development and welfare of the indigenous population. The department works to improve the indigenous people's socioeconomic status and quality of life while maintaining their rich heritage. According to Jabatan Kemajuan Orang Asli[2] (2022), there are 209,575 indigenous people in Peninsular or West Malaysia, but only 534 registered indigenous entrepreneurs. The small number of indigenous entrepreneurs in Malaysia illustrates the difficulties of starting new ventures among this minority group.

Generally, the indigenous people in Malaysia are divided into three major ethnic groups (namely, the Senoi, Melayu Proto and Negrito) and 18 subethnic groups. The latest figures from JAKOA (2022) indicate that the largest ethnic group in West Malaysia is Senoi, which constitutes slightly more than 55.21% of the population, followed by Melayu Proto (41.77%) and Negrito (3.02%). The Mah Meri tribe is a subethnic tribe of the Senoi group.

Data Collection

The chapter draws on data from two sources, namely, document analysis, such as government websites and media, combined with primary data from fieldwork conducted in an indigenous village in Malaysia. Before the face-to-face interviews, the researchers laid the groundwork through secondary data analysis of government reports, newspaper articles, and websites maintained by nongovernmental organisations (NGOs). The team reached out to an NGO that was familiar to the villagers. Volunteers from the NGO provided further understanding of the Mah Meri community. Face-to-face interviews started after the villagers were familiar and felt comfortable with the team. As the Mah Meri were cautious of outsiders, initial site visits were accompanied by a volunteer from the local nongovernmental organisation whom the villagers trusted. Through qualitative interviews and observation, the researchers were able to delve into the daily lives of the Mah Meri. Spending time with the indigenous community was crucial to building mutual trust and fostering good relationships and meaningful engagement. This stage was necessary to

[2] See https://www.jakoa.gov.my/public/vision-mission-objective/?lang=en and Jabatan Kemajuan Orang Asli (2016), Pelan Strategik 2016–2020, Kuala Lumpur, Malaysia.

understand the indigenous population's living conditions and way of life. The researchers also interviewed a JAKOA representative and four local NGO volunteers.

The interviews were conducted during field visits between April 2018 and October 2019. The purposive sampling method was employed in that adults (18 years and above) in all households in the village were included as part of the study population. However, only adults in 10 families were willing to participate in this study. Data collected from the interviews were transcribed, coded and thematically analysed to identify recurring themes using NVivo. Before starting primary data collection, consent from JAKOA and ethics approval from the Monash University Human Research Ethics Committee (MUHREC) were obtained. Based on secondary sources and interviews with the Mah Meri people and stakeholders involved with the community, we were able to identify three main inhibitors of indigenous entrepreneurship.

Indigenous Entrepreneurship Inhibitors

Lack of Formal Education

The family unit and community are influential units in developing indigenous children's knowledge. Many of the villagers struggled to assimilate into the formal education system. A volunteer from a nongovernmental organisation working with the community remarked that indigenous children prefer more freedom, as it is how they are brought up. Unlike the formal education system, which involves structured learning and examination, indigenous children traditionally learn from nature and the environment. Most learning occurs in an informal way, whereby children learn how to fish or collect sea yields as they watch their parents or others in the community. Interviews with representatives from two nongovernmental organisations reveal the following:

> The indigenous people have limited opportunities due to their low education (levels). They often skip school because they like freedom.
> (NGO representative 1)

High absenteeism and dropout rates may be due to the lack of numerical and reading skills when they enter primary school. He explained,

I think it is a mixed bag of reasons. I think different (indigenous) communities will have different reasons. In some of the communities we meet, the necessary knowledge and skillsets to start primary school are missing. Therefore, a lot of catching up... It affects the children's motivation; it affects their interest in studying. I think there are also many mindset issues... like during harvest season. Maybe not mindsets alone, but in terms of how parents do not push to make sure their kids go to school. Therefore, again, if you are not going to school regularly, you are struggling to meet good attendance [expectations].
(NGO representative 2)

The widening educational gaps between indigenous communities and other groups are alarming. Preliminary findings reveal that approximately half of the villagers interviewed reported having only completed primary school, and less than 10% had completed secondary school. At the same time, most villagers lived in poverty with less than the basic necessities, as illustrated in Fig. 3.2.

Way of Life

The Mah Meri community in Pulau Indah considers itself to be a steward of the environment. They lived nomadically in the past and depended on the jungle and sea to survive, a practice passed down through the generations. Most of the villagers in Pulau Indah are coastal fishermen and heavily rely on sampans or small boats. During the field visits to the village, the researchers noted that the surrounding areas in Pulau Indah were undergoing massive development. Despite this vast development, the Mah Meri in Pulau Indah struggled with their daily needs. Furthermore, the large-scale transformation in the Pulau Indah has somewhat disrupted the natural ecosystem, indirectly affecting their livelihood. A JAKOA representative explained that historically, the Mah Meri in Pulau Indah were nomadically scattered along riverbanks, fringes of the river and mangrove swamps on Carey Island. He explained in the following quote:

This was before the river embarkment project to develop the port. It was in 1985 that the department decided to put them together in villages. Houses were built to place them. We provided houses equipped with water and electricity facilities. We provided oil palm aid, and for fishermen, we gave (Yamaha) 15HP (horsepower) engines for boats. The aid is provided based

Fig. 3.2 Pulau Indah indigenous village and surrounding. Top left to bottom right- Fig. 3.1 Makeshift shelters- some families stay in this temporary accommodation while waiting for houses built by the local authorities. Figure 3.2 Homes built by the local government are painted in blue or white. Figure 3.3 Local fishing jetty. The indigenous population uses this modest fishing jetty. Most rely on sampan or small boats to go to the sea. Figure 3.4 School near to the village

> on our annual budget. However, there are conditions. The fishermen need an operating licence and register with the Fishing Association. However, we help them to get the licence.
> (Jabatan Kemajuan Orang Asli representative)

While the JAKOA helped the Mah Meri settle down in houses and provided aid for starting small ventures, many opportunities were left unexplored. For instance, as Pulau Indah develops into a significant industrial hub, entrepreneurial opportunities arise to develop tourism packages to introduce the indigenous culture in the village. However, a volunteer who has worked with the community remarked that it would be challenging to maintain a sustainable business model without outside help.

> They live by the day. They do not plan. Most stay in the village without venturing out.
> (NGO representative 3)

The absence of a continuous income stream significantly indicates a material disadvantage for the community. Most households in the village are involved in small-scale fishing. Due to competition from large trawlers, villagers faced depleting fishing resources, as their small boats could not go further into the sea.

Lack of Skills and Collateral for Financing

At the same time, they face problems obtaining sufficient finance or know-how to start a new business. Mah Meri are well known for their weaving skills and wooden crafts. During field visits to the village, the researchers observed beautiful handwoven mats and handicrafts produced and displayed at one of the homes. Upon further probing, the team was informed that weaving and wood crafting were necessary skills taught to them from a young age. One of the Mah Meri respondents explained that they would like to market and sell their products but cannot reach out to the broader community. He faced challenges in understanding how marketing or pricing works (Respondent 4).

In addition to the lack of knowledge to start an entrepreneurial venture, indigenous villagers lack financing. One of the main challenges in obtaining finance is the lack of collateral, as they do not own the land they are occupying. The local government provides housing assistance through various schemes, such as the Housing Assistance Programme (PBR), and these projects involve providing utilities, infrastructure and other resources for the basic needs of the communities. However, a lack of land ownership rights means they must vacate the land to give way for development. One of the villagers remarked that this was the second time she had to move because of the development in Pulau Indah. She mentioned that this was often the case when a new highway or factory needed to be built (Respondent 1).

According to Hooker (1996), the 1954 Aboriginal Peoples Act and, subsequently, the 1963 Policy Paper have inconsistencies in terms of land ownership. The acquisition of land by corporations is mainly due to the lack of formal ownership rights. In many parts of Malaysia, the indigenous community had to contest approval given by the state to corporations such as logging companies or developers. Without land ownership, obtaining financing to start entrepreneurial ventures is difficult.

What Can be Done to Overcome the Barriers to Indigenous Entrepreneurship Among the Mah Meri?

The chapter identified three main inhibitors of indigenous entrepreneurship among the Mah Meri in Pulau Indah. All three factors are interlinked. For instance, parents' low educational attainment deters their children from understanding the value of education or the know-how related to financing and land ownership. This situation leads to the intergenerational transmission of poverty. Many villagers need help with basic skills required in daily life and do not know how to seek help. Their low literacy rate limited their opportunities for starting new ventures. In the final section, we discuss the implications for policy-making and what the government can do to promote indigenous entrepreneurship.

Croce (2017) posits that government strategies identify indigenous entrepreneurship as a primary source of economic development and poverty alleviation among the indigenous population. Even with government efforts to promote entrepreneurship to improve economic standards among indigenous people, the take-up rate has been slow.[3] Studies find that contextualisation plays a crucial role in ensuring the sustainability of these entrepreneurship efforts (Croce, 2019; Mrabure, 2019; Welter et al., 2019).

Government policies must first target the three primary sources of poverty, which are the lack of access to education, health care services, and infrastructure. By addressing indigenous communities' basic needs, policies to promote indigenous entrepreneurship can then achieve a higher rate of success. Better education can improve their economic well-being and health and rights awareness. Consequently, better-educated parents can break the cycle of intergenerational poverty, as they will

[3] Source: https://www.nst.com.my/news/nation/2022/06/808145/orang-asli-urged-participate-online-entrepreneurship-highlight-products.

be more aware of the importance of education. Data from JAKOA[4] (2021) revealed that RM14 million was allocated to build new preschools, which benefitted 420 indigenous children. However, improving access to education will not be successful if prevention efforts are insufficient to curtail the high dropout rate of indigenous primary school children (Nor et al., 2011; Saifullah et al., 2021). Educating indigenous students requires teachers trained and equipped to handle a different learning culture (Renganathan, 2016), as the formal education system is not suitable for this culture (Renganathan, 2022). According to Rosnon et al. (2021), the education policy for indigenous people works best via self-determination by empowering them to take control of their education system. One model that worked was an NGO partnership with indigenous people within the community.

> We all work via the teachers and the (Orang Asli) community. Therefore, it is an empowerment project. We do not run the schools. We do not call the schools our schools. The schools are the community schools we support. Therefore, the development of the (Orang Asli) teachers would also be an important factor for us. The teachers are people from the community. (NGO representative 2)

Improving access to education is also contingent on the availability of basic infrastructure, starting from preschools and amenities such as roads, utilities, houses and hospitals. According to Kamaruddin and Jusoh's (2008) findings, schools in remote locations or that are at a distance from communities have adverse effects on school attendance.

Saifullah et al.'s (2018) study indicated that poverty incidences among indigenous people could be reduced by providing land ownership for small-scale plantations. This finding is supported by Ceddia et al.'s (2019) study on Latin America, which demonstrated that agricultural productivity could be improved significantly in tandem with indigenous land ownership and administration. Thus, government policy on indigenous people's land rights plays a crucial role in fostering indigenous subsistence and independence (Krishnan, 2020). As Subramaniam (2013) pointed out, equality for indigenous people can be extended by recognising and protecting indigenous customary land rights.

[4] Source: https://www.jakoa.gov.my/orang-asli/pendidikan-2/.

Public policies can be geared towards capability investment to enhance entrepreneurial behaviour. For instance, the Orang Asli Entrepreneurship Aid grant program (i.e., Bantuan Bimbingan Usahawan Orang Asli) is provided by JAKOA to support indigenous entrepreneurs. This aid not only supports indigenous entrepreneurs in terms of assistance and advice to accelerate the development of business ventures but also creates an opportunity for entrepreneurs to improve the quality of the products in the marketplace by providing access to finance (Jabatan Kemajuan Orang Asli, n.d.). Additionally, training is provided to enhance know-how and skills among indigenous entrepreneurs. Greater partnerships and collaborations with various public (government agencies) and private stakeholders will foster a greater chance of success.

As entrepreneurship can help improve the economic status of indigenous people, some ventures, such as cultural tourism or cultural experience, offer indigenous villages a chance to preserve their way of life while showcasing their culture to nonindigenous communities. Indigenous entrepreneurs can also offer products, food or cuisine, and performances that are unique to their community. JAKOA has showcased several successful indigenous entrepreneurs on the website, and these entrepreneurs serve as role models to other indigenous communities. Overall, the promotion of indigenous entrepreneurship ultimately becomes effective by first addressing their inhibitors, which are very context dependent.

Conclusion

In conclusion, our chapter contributes to the current scholarship on entrepreneurship by conducting a case study based on a minority indigenous group in Malaysia. The chapter provides several implications for promoting indigenous entrepreneurship research. First, indigenous entrepreneurship remains a nascent but emerging field of research that focuses on contextual factors and cultural values. Unlike mainstream entrepreneurship theoretical models, indigenous entrepreneurs rely on community-based resources, which include sea, land, people and culture, giving recognition to the unique socioeconomic context of the community. As many indigenous entrepreneurs are firmly rooted in their traditional beliefs and practices, their practices are seen as a counterbalance to mainstream entrepreneurship theoretical models. Drawing parallels with mainstream literature, the preservation of traditional knowledge vis-à-vis reliance on the resource-constrained environment is necessary to shape business practices among indigenous people. Acknowledging that indigenous entrepreneurship knowledge is applied and practised in different cultures and situations helps integrate the indigenous and nonindigenous outlook.

The chapter also highlights the factors that influence indigenous entrepreneurship, such as their way of life, a lack of formal education and a lack of the proper knowledge and financing to start a new venture. The barriers faced by the Mah Meri do not mean that they will be worse off not embracing modern values and business know-how, but we propose that practitioners (indigenous peoples, indigenous entrepreneurs) and NGOs working with the community integrate indigenous and nonindigenous perspectives when addressing the challenges faced by the indigenous people. For instance, indigenous know-how can be combined with commercial practices for sustainable business models and opportunities. One suggested area of future research with the Mah Meri community is to examine how indigenous knowledge, such as traditional carved masks, can serve as an indigenous business venture that is rooted in cultural and traditional knowledge and is environmentally sustainable. Finally, opportunities to address the plight of indigenous people arise by putting in place supportive policies to develop indigenous entrepreneurs by working closely with other stakeholders (private and nongovernmental organisations).

Acknowledgements We acknowledge that the study is supported by Seed Grants B-7-18 and GA-MA-18-S01 from Monash University Malaysia.

References

Alvarez, S. A., & Barney, J. B. (2014). Entrepreneurial opportunities and poverty alleviation. *Entrepreneurship Theory and Practice, 38*(1), 159–184. https://doi.org/10.1111/etap.1207

Baguley, D. (2007). Indigenous business. *Management Today, 3*, 22–25.

Banerjee, S. B. (2022). Decolonizing management theory: A critical perspective. *Journal of Management Studies, 59*(4), 1074–1087. https://doi.org/10.1111/joms.12756

Bruton, G. D., Zahra, S. A., & Cai, L. (2018). Examining entrepreneurship through indigenous lenses. *Entrepreneurship Theory and Practice, 42*(3), 351–361. https://doi.org/10.1177/1042258717741129

Bruton, G. D., Zahra, S. A., Van de Ven, A. H., & Hitt, M. A. (2022). Indigenous theory uses, abuses, and future. *Journal of Management Studies, 59*(4), 1057–1073. https://doi.org/10.1111/joms.12755

Ceddia, M. G., Gunter, U., & Pazienza, P. (2019). Indigenous peoples' land rights and agricultural expansion in Latin America: A dynamic panel data approach. *Forest Policy and Economics, 109*, 102001. https://doi.org/10.1016/j.forpol.2019.102001

Chong, S. P., Appannah, G., & Sulaiman, N. (2018). Household food insecurity, diet quality, and weight status among indigenous women (Mah Meri) in Peninsular Malaysia. *Nutrition Research and Practice, 12*(2), 135–142. https://doi.org/10.4162/nrp.2018.12.2.135

Colbourne, R., Peredo, A. M., & Henriques, I. (2023). Indigenous entrepreneurship? Setting the record straight. *Business History*, 1–23. https://doi.org/10.1080/00076791.2023.2166034

Colbourne, R. (2021). Indigenous entrepreneurship. In T. M. Cooney (Ed.), *The Palgrave Handbook of minority entrepreneurship* (pp. 319–348). Springer Nature.

Creswell, J. W., & Creswell, J. D. (2017). *Research design: Qualitative, quantitative, and mixed methods approaches*. Sage publications.

Croce, F. (2019). Indigenous entrepreneurship, society, and the dimensions of diversity: An overview of the Canadian national context. In *Diversity within diversity management* (Vol. 21, pp. 359–371). Emerald Publishing Limited. https://doi.org/10.1108/S1877-636120190000021017.

Croce, F. (2017). Contextualised indigenous entrepreneurial models: A systematic review of indigenous entrepreneurship literature. *Journal of Management and Organization, 23*(6), 886–906. https://doi.org/10.1017/jmo.2017.69

Dana, L. P. (2015). Indigenous entrepreneurship: An emerging field of research. *International Journal of Business and Globalisation, 14*(2), 158–169.

Dana, L. P., & Anderson, R. B. (2011). The evolution of entrepreneurship in Arviat: The southernmost community of mainland Nunavut. *International Journal of Entrepreneurship and Small Business, 14*(4), 509–532. https://doi.org/10.1504/IJESB.2011.043473

Dana, L. P., Dana, T. E., & Anderson, B. (2005). A theory-based empirical study of entrepreneurship in Iqaluit, Nunavut. *Journal of Small Business and Entrepreneurship, 18*(2), 143–151. https://doi.org/10.1080/08276331.2005.10593336

Erlando, A., Riyanto, F. D., & Masakazu, S. (2020). Financial inclusion, economic growth, and poverty alleviation: Evidence from eastern Indonesia. *Heliyon, 6*(10), e05235. https://doi.org/10.1016/j.heliyon.2020.e05235

Filatotchev, I., Ireland, R. D., & Stahl, G. K. (2022). Contextualizing management research: An open systems perspective. *Journal of Management Studies, 59*(4), 1036–1056. https://doi.org/10.1111/joms.12754

Flamsteed, K., & Golding, B. (2005). *Learning through indigenous business: The role of vocational education and training in indigenous enterprise and community development*. National Centre for Vocational Education Research Australia. https://www.ncver.edu.au/__data/assets/file/0014/4712/nr1023.pdf.

Giraldo, M., Garcia-Tello, L., & Rayburn, S. W. (2020). Street vending: Transformative entrepreneurship for individual and collective well-being. *Journal of Services Marketing, 34*(6), 757–768. https://doi.org/10.1108/JSM-08-2019-0322

Gouvea, R., Lehneman, L., & Terra, B. (2022). Tribal economic development and entrepreneurship: A Latin American perspective. *World Development Perspectives, 26*, 100403. https://doi.org/10.1016/j.wdp.2022.100403

Gracey, M., & King, M. (2009). Indigenous health part 1: Determinants and disease patterns. *The Lancet, 374*(9683), 65–75. https://doi.org/10.1016/S0140-6736(09)60827-8

Hall, G. H., & Patrinos, H. A. (2012). Indigenous peoples, poverty, and development. Cambridge University Press. https://doi.org/10.1017/CBO9781139105729.

Hall, J., Matos, S., Sheehan, L., & Silvestre, B. (2012). Entrepreneurship and innovation at the base of the pyramid: A recipe for inclusive growth or social exclusion? *Journal of Management Studies, 49*(4), 785–812. https://doi.org/10.1111/j.1467-6486.2012.01044.x

Hindle, K., & Lansdowne, M. (2005). Brave spirits on new paths: Toward a globally relevant paradigm of indigenous entrepreneurship research. *Journal of Small Business and Entrepreneurship, 18*(2), 131–141. https://doi.org/10.1080/08276331.2005.10593335

Hindle, K., & Moroz, P. (2010). Indigenous entrepreneurship as a research field: Developing a definitional framework from the emerging canon. *International Entrepreneurship and Management Journal, 6*, 357–385. https://doi.org/10.1007/s11365-009-0111-x

Inimiesi, O. P. (2023). Indigenous entrepreneurship behaviour and local economic development of otuke community. *International Journal of Entrepreneurship and Business Development*, *6*(1), 15–24. https://doi.org/10.29138/ijebd.v6i1.2104.

International Labour Organisation. (2019). Implementing the ILO indigenous and tribal peoples—convention no. 169 towards an inclusive, sustainable and just future. https://www.ilo.org/global/publications/books/WCMS_735607/lang--en/index.htm.

Jabatan Kemajuan Orang Asli. (2022). Ethnic Distribution of Orang Asli by Ethnicity/Sub Ethnicity by State. https://www.jakoa.gov.my/orang-asli/taburan-etnik-orang-asli-mengikut-etnik-sub-etnik-mengikut-negeri/.

Jabatan Kemajuan Orang Asli. (n.d.). Orang Asli Entrepreneurs' Guidance Support Grant Distribution Program. https://www.jakoa.gov.my/public/orang-asli-entrepreneurs-guidance-support-grant-distribution-program/?lang=en.

Krishnan, L. (2020). The vulnerability of the aboriginal community in relation to customary land rights. In T. Kananatu, & S. G. Koh (Eds.) *Vulnerable groups in Malaysia* (pp. 69–88) Walter de Gruyter. https://doi.org/10.1515/9783110610970

Latip, N. A., Rasoolimanesh, S. M., Jaafar, M., Marzuki, A., & Umar, M. U. (2018). Indigenous participation in conservation and tourism development: A case of native people of Sabah Malaysia. *International Journal of Tourism Research, 20*(3), 400–409. https://doi.org/10.1002/jtr.2191

Lindsay, N. J. (2005). Toward a cultural model of indigenous entrepreneurial attitude. *Academy of Marketing Science Review, 5*, 1–17.

Maas, G., & Jones, P. (2019). *Transformational Entrepreneurship Practices*. Palgrave Pivot.

Maritz, A. (2006). Indigenous enterprise in the social context: The New Zealand indigenous entrepreneur. *International Indigenous Journal of Entrepreneurship, Advancement, Strategy and Education, 2*(2), 1.

Mason, A., Dana, L. P., & Anderson, R. B. (2008). Entrepreneurship in Coral Harbour, Nunavut. *The International Journal of Entrepreneurship and Innovation, 9*(2), 111–126. https://doi.org/10.5367/000000008784489453

Moser, C. O. (1998). The asset vulnerability framework: Reassessing urban poverty reduction strategies. *World Development, 26*(1), 1–19. https://doi.org/10.1016/S0305-750X(97)10015-8

Mrabure, R. O. (2019). Indigenous business success: A hybrid perspective. *Journal of Enterprising Communities: People and Places in the Global Economy, 13*(1/2), 24–41. https://doi.org/10.1108/JEC-10-2018-0076

Nah, A. M. (2008). Recognizing indigenous identity in postcolonial Malaysian law: Rights and realities for the Orang Asli (aborigines) of Peninsular Malaysia. *Bijdragen Tot De Taal-, Land- En Volkenkunde, 164*(2), 212–237. https://doi.org/10.1163/22134379-90003657

Nor, S. M., Roslan, S., Mohamed, A., Hassan, K. H. A., Ali, M. A. M., & Manaf, J. A. (2011). Dropout prevention initiatives for Malaysian indigenous orang asli children. *International Journal on School Disaffection, 8*(1), 42–56. https://doi.org/10.18546/IJSD.08.1.07

Padilla-Meléndez, A., Plaza-Angulo, J. J., Del-Aguila-Obra, A. R., & Ciruela-Lorenzo, A. M. (2022). Indigenous entrepreneurship. Current issues and future lines. *Entrepreneurship & Regional Development, 34*(1–2), 6–31. https://doi.org/10.1080/08985626.2021.2011962

Peredo, A. M., Anderson, R. B., Galbraith, C. S., Honig, B., & Dana, L. P. (2004). Towards a theory of indigenous entrepreneurship. *International Journal of Entrepreneurship and Small Business, 1*(1–2), 1–20. https://doi.org/10.1504/IJESB.2004.005374

Ratcheva, V., Leopold, T. A., & Zahidi, S. (2020, February). Jobs of tomorrow: mapping opportunity in the new economy. *World Economic Forum*. https://www3.weforum.org/docs/WEF_Jobs_of_Tomorrow_2020.pdf.

Ratten, V. (2014). Future research directions for collective entrepreneurship in developing countries: A small and medium-sized enterprise perspective. *International Journal of Entrepreneurship and Small Business, 22*(2), 266–274. https://doi.org/10.1504/IJESB.2014.062505

Rauniyar, G., & Kanbur, R. (2010). Inclusive growth and inclusive development: A review and synthesis of Asian development bank literature. *Journal of the Asia Pacific Economy, 15*(4), 455–469. https://doi.org/10.1080/13547860.2010.517680

Rayburn, S. W., & Ochieng, G. (2022). Instigating transformative entrepreneurship in subsistence communities: Supporting leaders' transcendence and self-determination. *Africa Journal of Management, 8*(3), 271–297. https://doi.org/10.1080/23322373.2022.2071574

Renganathan, S. (2016). Educating the Orang Asli children: Exploring indigenous children's practices and experiences in schools. *The Journal of Educational Research, 109*(3), 275–285. https://doi.org/10.1080/00220671.2014.945150

Renganathan, S. (2022). Research concerning the Indigenous Orang Asli and education: A review of problem representations. *Diaspora, Indigenous, and Minority Education, 16*(3), 200–211. https://doi.org/10.1080/15595692.2021.2007073

Rosnon, M. R., Talib, M. A., & Azam, M. N. D. (2021). Symbolic self-determination: The case of Malaysia and Australia's indigenous education policy. *Kajian Malaysia, 39*(1), 25–204. https://doi.org/10.21315/km2021.39.1.2

Saffu, K. (2003). The role and impact of culture on South Pacific island entrepreneurs. *International Journal of Entrepreneurial Behavior and Research, 9*(2), 55–73. https://doi.org/10.1108/13552550310461045

Saifullah, M. K., Masud, M. M., & Kari, F. B. (2021). Vulnerability context and well-being factors of Indigenous community development: A study of Peninsular Malaysia. *AlterNative: An International Journal of Indigenous Peoples, 17*(1), 94–105. https://doi.org/10.1177/117718012199516

Saifullah, M. K., Kari, F. B., & Othman, A. (2018). Poverty among the small-scale plantation holders: Indigenous communities in Peninsular Malaysia. *International Journal of Social Economics*. https://doi.org/10.1108/IJSE-10-2016-0296

Schumpeter, J. A. (1942). *Capitalism, socialism and democracy.*

Seja, M. (2013, September). *Placing your bets: Subsistence or Transformational Entrepreneurship.* https://blogs.worldbank.org/psd/placing-your-bets-subsistence-or-transformational-entrepreneurship.

Subramaniam, Y. (2013). Affirmative action and the legal recognition of customary land rights in Peninsular Malaysia: The Orang Asli experience. *Australian Indigenous Law Review, 17*(1), 103–122.

Sutter, C., Bruton, G. D., & Chen, J. (2019). Entrepreneurship as a solution to extreme poverty: A review and future research directions. *Journal of Business Venturing, 34*(1), 197–214. https://doi.org/10.1016/j.jbusvent.2018.06.003

United Nations. (2023a). *International Day of the World's Indigenous Peoples- 9 August*. https://www.un.org/en/observances/indigenous-day.

United Nations (2023b). Ending poverty. https://www.un.org/en/global-issues/ending-poverty.

Viswanathan, M., Echambadi, R., Venugopal, S., & Sridharan, S. (2014). Subsistence entrepreneurship, value creation, and community exchange systems: A social capital explanation. *Journal of Macromarketing, 34*(2), 213–226. https://doi.org/10.1177/0276146714521635

Viswanathan, M., Sridharan, S., & Ritchie, R. (2010). Understanding consumption and entrepreneurship in subsistence marketplaces. *Journal of Business Research, 63*(6), 570–581. https://doi.org/10.1016/j.jbusres.2009.02.023

Wadhwani, R. D., Kirsch, D., Welter, F., Gartner, W. B., & Jones, G. G. (2020). Context, time, and change: Historical approaches to entrepreneurship research. *Strategic Entrepreneurship Journal, 14*(1), 3–19. https://doi.org/10.1002/sej.1346

Welter, F. (2011). Contextualizing entrepreneurship—conceptual challenges and ways forward. *Entrepreneurship Theory and Practice, 35*(1), 165–184. https://doi.org/10.1111/j.1540-6520.2010.00427.x

Welter, F., Baker, T., & Wirsching, K. (2019). Three waves and counting: The rising tide of contextualization in entrepreneurship research. *Small Business Economics, 52*, 319–330. https://doi.org/10.1007/s11187-018-0094-5

World Bank (2022, September 14). Fact sheet: An adjustment to global poverty lines. https://www.worldbank.org/en/news/factsheet/2022/05/02/fact-sheet-an-adjustment-to-global-poverty-lines.

Yan, J., & Yan, L. (2016). Individual entrepreneurship, collective entrepreneurship and innovation in small business: An empirical study. *International Entrepreneurship and Management Journal, 12*, 1053–1077. https://doi.org/10.1007/s11365-015-0380-5

CHAPTER 4

Malay-Bumiputera Halal Herbs Industry in the Post-pandemic Context: Developing SME Performance Through Economic Stimulus Packages, Supply Chain Management, and Internationalisation

Aida Idris, Siti Nur Husna Tukiran, Nazzatush Shimar Jamaludin, Nurhidayah Bahar, and Shaiful Azlan Abdul

Introduction

Indigenous people, also known as native people, refer to the original inhabitants of a particular region or country who have historically been occupied or colonised and continue to have a strong cultural, social, and often political connection to that land (Padilla-Meléndez et al., 2022). They can be found in regions all over the world, from the Arctic to tropical rainforests, deserts, and urban areas. These populations are

A. Idris (✉) · S. N. H. Tukiran · N. S. Jamaludin
Universiti Malaya, Kuala Lumpur, Malaysia
e-mail: aida_idris@um.edu.my

E. L. Eijdenberg et al. (eds.), *Indigenous Entrepreneurship in Southeast Asia*, Palgrave Studies in Equity, Diversity, Inclusion, and Indigenization in Business, https://doi.org/10.1007/978-3-031-54457-6_4

often distinct from the dominant or settler populations that arrived later through colonisation or migration (Bastien et al., 2023; Padilla-Meléndez et al., 2022).

In Malaysia, the term "indigenous community" generally refers to Malay and other native ethnic groups broadly known as Bumiputera or "Sons of the Soil" (Idrus, 2022; Ali, 2022). Many Bumiputera communities possess extensive knowledge and practices related to the use of traditional products for medicinal, culinary, and cultural purposes. Previous studies show that Malay-Bumiputeras and other indigenous communities in Malaysia have relied on traditional herbal remedies for centuries to treat various ailments and maintain good health (Abdulrahman et al., 2018; Ong et al., 2012; Samuel et al., 2010). Kardooni et al. (2014) reported that indigenous communities in Malaysia had documented a minimum of 500 local plants possessing economic or medicinal properties as early as the 1960s. These traditional discoveries have yielded significant economic returns, estimated at approximately US$32 billion worldwide according to the Rural Advancement Foundation International (RAFI). Research suggests that the global herbal products market is currently valued at around US$62 billion (Ghosh, 2013) and is projected to grow at a rate of 7% annually, reaching between US$5–7 trillion by the year 2050.

The anticipated growth presents significant economic opportunities for countries with established herbal industries, such as Malaysia, to further expand their market share and contribute to the global herbal products market's growth. The industry has been included as one of the National Key Economic Area (NKEA) agricultural initiatives in the Economic Transformation (ETP) Programme because of its significant

S. N. H. Tukiran
e-mail: 22064446@siswa.um.edu.my

N. S. Jamaludin
e-mail: shimar@um.edu.my

N. Bahar
Universiti Kebangsaan Malaysia, Bangi, Malaysia
e-mail: nbahar@ukm.edu.my

S. A. Abdul
Universiti Teknologi MARA, Shah Alam, Malaysia
e-mail: shaiful71@uitm.edu.my

potential to contribute to Malaysia's economic growth. As stipulated in the Twelfth Malaysia Plan 2021–2025 (12MP), the local herbal industry aligns closely with the government's initiatives and plans to position Malaysia as a leading nation in the production and export of halal products. This has led to the emergence of a burgeoning halal herbs industry in Malaysia, which holds significant potential for economic growth and development potential for Malay-Bumiputera SMEs because of their religious connection with Islamic values and practices. The increasing global demand for herbal and natural products (Rajendran & Kamarulzaman, 2023) presents a significant opportunity for the Malay-Bumiputera halal herbs industry to expand its reach beyond national borders. Engaging in the production, processing, and trade of halal herbs will enable this community to generate income, foster job opportunities, and enhance their overall livelihoods. Additionally, it can alleviate poverty and reduce socio-economic disparities, while also fostering economic empowerment within this indigenous community.

However, despite Malaysia's potential to become a leader in the halal herbs market (Othman et al., 2009), the country remains a net importer of herbal products, posing a significant challenge for the Malay-Bumiputera herbs industry (Zakaria et al., 2019). This over-dependence on imports not only affects the industry's profitability but also undermines its potential to contribute to the country's economic growth and development. Addressing this challenge requires effective measures to increase the availability of local raw materials (Tan et al., 2020), such as promoting sustainable cultivation and harvesting practices, research and development efforts to identify suitable plant varieties for cultivation and support for small-scale producers to enhance their productivity and competitiveness. The ability of the Malay-Bumiputera community to penetrate international markets relies on every aspect of the halal herbs supply chain, emphasising the necessity of a comprehensive approach to foster the industry's growth and development.

The recent COVID-19 pandemic has further exacerbated problems regarding the supply chain. The disruption to the global supply chain caused by the pandemic, coupled with the Russia–Ukraine war that began in February 2022, has led to shortages of critical raw materials and introduced new challenges for producers (Cui et al., 2023; Xu et al., 2020). The conflict has introduced geopolitical tensions, disrupted transportation routes, and raised concerns about the stability of key commodity supplies, thereby intensifying the strain on an already fragile supply chain ecosystem. On the plus side, the pandemic has influenced consumer behaviour, leading to an increasing demand for natural and herbal products to boost immunity and promote overall health. While this presents a tremendous growth opportunity for the industry, disruptions to the global supply chain have made it challenging for producers to meet this demand.

Realising the full potential of the Malay-Bumiputera halal herbs industry and addressing the obstacles it faces will require a concerted effort from multiple stakeholders. This includes the Malaysian government, which must enact supportive policies and provide resources to foster the growth of the industry. Given adequate support and resources, the industry possesses the potential to emerge as a global frontrunner in the halal herbs market, making substantial contributions to Malaysia's economy. Hence, sustaining and increasing the demand is crucial. Small and medium-sized enterprises in the industry must have access to financing and other resources to improve their productivity and competitiveness. By addressing these shortcomings, the industry can contribute to the country's economic growth and development while preserving its indigenous cultural and natural heritage.

In response to the challenges faced by the Malay-Bumiputera halal herbs industry prior to the COVID-19 pandemic, the government had initiated numerous programmes to accelerate the industry's internationalisation process. These programmes aimed to support halal herbs SMEs by providing access to financing and other resources to improve their productivity and competitiveness (Ahmad et al., 2020; Mustapa & Mohamad, 2021). The government had also sought to create new market opportunities for halal herbs and related products by promoting their exports to new markets and encouraging foreign direct investment in the industry.

When the COVID-19 crisis hit in 2020, many businesses were affected. At the height of the pandemic, followed by the early stages of the economic recovery from mid-2021 to late 2022, the government introduced a series of economic stimulus packages (ESP) intended to help SMEs to withstand the effects of the outbreak. Some of the actions taken were also designed to overcome supply chain disruptions that were affecting import-based businesses, such as the halal herbs SMEs. Among the elements of the ESP were wage subsidies, moratoria, digital transformations, tax incentives, utility bill discounts, and financing facilities. However, these programmes have been severely derailed by the pandemic and subsequent changes in political leadership as well as economic policies, following the results of the 15th general election.

As a result, there now exists a research gap concerning the effectiveness of government assistance in bolstering the Malay-Bumiputera halal herbs industry. While prior studies have acknowledged the industry's potential and the obstacles it confronts, further exploration is necessary to assess the actual impact of government policies and support in fostering its growth and development. Undertaking such exploration can significantly contribute to evidence-based decision-making, pinpoint areas for improvement, and offer valuable insights into the most effective strategies for facilitating the internationalisation of the industry, particularly in a specific socio-economic context (Filatotcheva et al., 2022; Welter et al., 2019).

Therefore, the aim of this chapter is to develop a comprehensive theoretical framework that can facilitate further research on the effects of various forms of government assistance on the internationalisation of the halal herbs industry. By providing a theoretical foundation for such research, this chapter can help identify key factors that contribute to the industry's success and inform the development of effective policies and interventions to support its growth and development. This will ultimately support the economic prosperity and social well-being of the indigenous community and the nation as a whole.

Literature Review

Indigenous Communities in Malaysia

Malaysia is home to a diverse range of indigenous groups, each with its own unique cultural practices, languages, and historical significance. These groups include the Malays and Orang Asli in Peninsular Malaysia, as well as various indigenous ethnic groups in Sabah and Sarawak such as the Rungus, Iranun, Tatana, Iban, Bidayuh, Kenyah, and Kedayan. These communities contribute to the cultural richness and heritage of Malaysia, preserving traditional knowledge and sustainable practices that are deeply rooted in their respective environments.

The indigenous population in Malaysia, also known as the Bumiputera community, is primarily composed of Malays and Orang Asli in Peninsular Malaysia. However, this definition differs from that of Sabah and

Table 4.1 Malaysia's population by ethnicity (2019–2022)

Characteristic	*Bumiputera*	*Chinese*	*Indians*	*Others*
2019	69.3	22.8	6.9	1
2020	69.6	22.2	6.7	0.7
2021	69.6	23	6.7	0.7
2022	69.9	22.8	6.6	0.7

Source Statista Research Department (6 April 2023)

Sarawak, where the term Bumiputera can be applied to a variety of indigenous ethnic groups such as Kadazan-Dusun, Bajau, Dayak, and Murut (Siddique & Suryadinata, 1981). Bumiputera literally means "son of the soil" in Malay, and it refers to the ethnic groups in Malaysia that are considered to be the original inhabitants of the land (Idrus, 2022; Ali, 2022). The Bumiputera community is a significant part of Malaysia's population, comprising about 69.9% of the total population, as shown in Table 4.1.

Indigenous communities in Malaysia have a deep connection with nature, viewing it as an integral part of their way of life. Their traditional knowledge systems are deeply embedded in the understanding and sustainable management of natural resources. They have developed intricate systems of ecological knowledge, passed down through generations, which allow them to navigate and utilise the diverse ecosystems they inhabit (Ong et al., 2012; Samuel et al., 2010). These communities often practise sustainable resource management, relying on traditional agricultural practices, fishing, hunting, and gathering techniques that have minimal impact on the environment. They possess an intricate understanding of the local flora and fauna, including the medicinal properties of various plants and herbs.

Traditional healers, known as "bomohs" or "dukuns," play a vital role in providing healthcare within indigenous communities. The use of herbal medicine among indigenous communities is often deeply connected to cultural and spiritual practices. Traditional healers combine their knowledge of plants and spirituality to diagnose and treat illnesses, considering the mind, body, and spirit as interconnected. The healing practices of these communities have gained recognition for their efficacy in treating

Table 4.2 Examples of Malaysian indigenous herbs and their uses

No.	*Local name*	*Medicinal uses*	*Plant part*	*Preparation method*	*Preparation category*
1	Limau purut	Dandruff	Fruit	Squeeze	Extraction
2	Mengkudu	High blood pressure	Leaf	Eaten fresh	Direct usage
		Diarrhoea	Leaf	Smearing, seared	Direct usage
		Increase white blood cells	Root	Boiled	Decoction
		Cancer	Fruit	Eaten fresh	Direct usage
		Diabetes	Fruit	Eaten fresh	Direct usage
		Skin disease	Fruit	Smearing	Direct usage
		Cough	Fruit	Blended	Extraction
		Hypertension	Fruit	Eaten fresh	Direct usage
3	Tongkat Ali	Reproductive	Root	Boiled	Decoction
		Tonic	Root	Boiled	Decoction
		Antiviral	Root	Boiled	Decoction
4	Tea tree	Wound	Leaf	Crushed	Extraction

Source Malaysia indigenous herbs knowledge representation (2012)

various ailments, leading to increased interest from modern medical practitioners and researchers. Table 4.2 provides a representation of the knowledge regarding some of the indigenous herbs in Malaysia.

Role of Government Policies in Malay-Bumiputera Entrepreneurship Development

Indigenous entrepreneurship refers to the practice of creating and operating businesses by indigenous peoples (April & Itenge, 2020). This can play a significant role in promoting economic self-sufficiency and cultural preservation within indigenous communities. It also contributes to the broader economy by fostering innovation, job creation, and economic development. Indigenous entrepreneurship differs from other forms of entrepreneurship in terms of its context, goals, outcomes, and the organisation of the enterprise. From an indigenous perspective, indigenous entrepreneurship is not primarily driven by economic gain but is more oriented towards benefiting the indigenous community (April & Itenge, 2020). Scholars agree that indigenous entrepreneurs often have a strong connection to the land and natural resources (Ulluwishewa et al., 2008). As a result, they may prioritise sustainable and environmentally friendly business practices that align with their cultural values.

The recognition of indigenous peoples as Bumiputera is an important policy in Malaysia (Siddique & Suryadinata, 1981). In the context of affirmative action and socio-economic development programmes, Bumiputera refers to the ethnic groups in Malaysia that are considered the original inhabitants of the land. The Bumiputera status is considered an important criterion for various socio-economic policies and affirmative action programmes aimed at promoting the economic advancement and social well-being of Malays and other indigenous groups. These policies and programmes seek to address historical inequalities as a result of colonisation, and empower Malays and other indigenous groups by providing them with opportunities for economic advancement and social well-being.

The role of government policies and support in promoting Bumiputera SMEs is significant. Being the majority population, Bumiputera businesses are essential to the country's economy, and supporting their growth and development can have a positive impact on Malaysia's overall economic performance and social well-being. The government typically provides financial assistance, business development services, market access support, and support for innovation and technology adoption to help Bumiputera SMEs gain access to capital, knowledge, and skills that are needed to grow their businesses. Such policies provide Bumiputera SMEs with affirmative action treatment in government procurement, access to financing, and other forms of support to promote their growth and development.

Since the late 1960s, the Malaysian government has established specific policies, starting with the New Economic Policy (NEP), to promote Bumiputera economic participation. The NEP, launched in 1971, was Malaysia's first affirmative action programme aimed at reducing the economic disparities between Bumiputera and non-Bumiputera communities (primarily ethnic Chinese and Indians). It allocated a certain percentage of opportunities, such as business licences, government contracts, and procurement, to Bumiputera-owned businesses, and provided various forms of assistance and incentives to Bumiputera entrepreneurs. Since the introduction of the NEP, numerous other affirmative action programmes have been implemented to further promote the economic advancement and social well-being of the Bumiputera community. These programmes have included the National Development Policy (NDP), the Ninth Malaysia Plan, and the New Economic Model (NEM).

Malay-Bumiputera Halal Herbs Industry

The Malay-Bumiputera halal herbs industry plays a crucial role in the Malaysian economy and serves as a significant contributor to the global halal market (Rajendran & Kamarulzaman, 2017). This industry capitalises on Malaysia's abundant biodiversity, which offers a wide range of indigenous herbs renowned for their healing properties and cultural significance. It encompasses the cultivation, processing, and marketing of halal-certified herbs. According to the Department of Statistics Malaysia, the halal food sector contributed significantly to the country's economy, accounting for 7.6% of the total Gross Domestic Product (GDP) in 2020. The industry caters to both domestic and international markets, with a primary focus on meeting the dietary and medicinal needs of Muslim consumers. Leveraging Malaysia's diverse flora, which includes over 12,500 species of flowering plants, including numerous indigenous herbs, further adds to its value.

Halal, which means "permissible" in Arabic (Hanzaee & Ramezani, 2011), refers to products and practices that are lawful and allowed according to Islamic law, as defined in the Quran and the Hadith (teachings and practices of Prophet Muhammad). The concept of halal, deeply rooted in Islamic principles, holds significant importance in the international trade of halal herbs and related products. Halal certification ensures that products meet the stringent requirements and standards set by Islamic law throughout the entire supply chain, from sourcing raw materials to processing, packaging, and distribution.

The halal herbs industry is a significant segment within the global herbal and natural products market. The industry encompasses the production, processing, and distribution of herbal and natural products that comply with Islamic dietary laws and regulations. This sector has witnessed remarkable growth in recent years, driven by various factors, including rising awareness about health and wellness, increased consumer spending power, and a growing Muslim population worldwide. While precise figures may vary, studies suggest that the global halal market is rapidly expanding and is estimated to reach trillions of dollars by 2050

(Ghosh, 2013). The halal herbs industry is expected to contribute significantly to this growth (Ahmad et al., 2015), driven by the increasing popularity of halal-certified products among Muslim consumers and the broader market.

In general, the herbal industry is seen as offering several important advantages to support the financial performance of the country. According to Rajendran and Kamarulzaman (2017), more than RM5.4 billion in gross profits were produced by herbal-related products in a single year. The combination of Malaysia's multiracial nation expands the country's opportunities for the herbal industry. Numerous past studies have discovered that there is a wide range of options that can be produced from a single herbal plant, which is not only limited to food items but also healthcare products, cosmetics, fragrances, and medicinal products. Some typical herbal plants found in Malaysia include *nenas kerang* (moses-in-the-cradle) and *bunga telang* (butterfly pea), as shown in Fig. 4.1.

In line with the increasing demand for halal products around the world, it is important to emphasise the development of the halal herbs industry in Malaysia as a feasible investment and trade option. To achieve this, the role of each halal herbs supply chain player, which consists of suppliers, manufacturers, transporters, retailers, and consumers is extremely important to strengthen the market for the halal herbal industry. It has been a great challenge for these businesses to recover from the recent pandemic, and the government holds a huge responsibility to take progressive and interventionist actions to lessen the burden on industry players.

The supply chain of the Malay-Bumiputera halal herbs industry plays a crucial role in facilitating its entry into the global market. Previous studies have proposed logistics as a mediator within the broader framework for halal pharmaceutical supply chain resilience (Aigbogun et al., 2014). These studies recognised the importance of considering specific requirements and considerations related to halal practices in the pharmaceutical industry. The industry's halal supply chain encompasses various stages, starting from cultivation and harvesting to processing, packaging, distribution, and retailing (Hasan, 2021; Rajendran & Kamarulzaman, 2017). Each stage is essential in ensuring the integrity, quality, and compliance with halal standards of the products. In the context of the global market, the supply chain becomes even more significant. Here's an overview of

Moses-in-the-Cradle

Butterfly Pea

Fig. 4.1 Common herbal plants in Malaysia

how the Malay-Bumiputera halal herbs supply chain intersects with the global market:

1. Cultivation and Harvesting: The cultivation and harvesting of halal herbs in accordance with halal requirements provide the foundation

for producing authentic and compliant products. Cultivating high-quality herbs with specific characteristics and cultural significance can contribute to the industry's competitiveness in the global market.

2. Processing and Packaging: The processing stage, which includes drying, grinding, and extracting essential oils, enhances the shelf life and usability of the herbs. Adhering to halal standards during processing ensures that the products meet the dietary requirements of Muslim consumers worldwide. Proper packaging, labelling, and certification verification are also essential for product identification, traceability, and market acceptance.
3. Quality Control and Halal Certification: Stringent quality control measures throughout the supply chain are crucial to ensure product safety, purity, and compliance with halal standards. This includes testing for contaminants, verifying the absence of non-halal ingredients, and conducting microbial analysis. Halal certification by recognised bodies adds credibility and enhances consumer trust, particularly in Muslim-majority countries and regions with a significant Muslim population.
4. Distribution and Global Market Access: Efficient distribution networks and logistics are vital for entering the global market. Collaborating with distributors, wholesalers, and retailers with established international networks helps expand market reach and ensure timely delivery. International trade regulations, including import/export requirements, customs procedures, and documentation, must be complied with to facilitate the smooth flow of products across borders.

By integrating these aspects into the supply chain, the Malay-Bumiputera halal herbs industry can access the global market more effectively, tap into larger consumer bases, diversify revenue streams, and establish a global presence. This will create economic growth opportunities, generate export revenues, attract foreign investments, and enhance the industry's reputation and recognition worldwide.

Challenges and Barriers in the Halal Herbs Industry

The Malay-Bumiputera halal herbs industry often encounters considerable hardship that impedes its growth and competitiveness. The first challenge faced by the Malay-Bumiputera halal herbs industry is its dependence on imports (Zakaria et al., 2019). Statistics reveal that the industry heavily relies on imported raw materials and finished products. According to trade data, over 60% of halal herbs and related products in the market are imported. This reliance increases production costs, compromises quality control, and exposes the industry to international market fluctuations. To address this weakness, promoting local cultivation is crucial. It is estimated that by expanding local herb cultivation by 20%, the industry could reduce imports by approximately 30%, leading to substantial cost savings.

Limitations in the availability of local raw materials pose another significant barrier. Despite the country's rich biodiversity, the industry faces obstacles in cultivation practices, infrastructure, and funding. To overcome these limitations, investing in research and development is vital. Allocating resources to research and development activities can foster the identification and cultivation of new halal herbs, improve processing techniques, and develop value-added products. This will not only enhance the availability of local raw materials but also stimulate innovation and economic growth within the industry.

As mentioned earlier, the COVID-19 pandemic had severely disrupted global supply chains, adversely affecting the halal herbs industry. According to industry reports, the pandemic caused a significant decline in exports and disrupted the procurement of raw materials (Xu et al., 2020; Cai, 2020). A survey conducted among industry stakeholders revealed that 80% of businesses experienced delays in shipments, while 60% faced scarcity of raw materials due to lockdown measures and logistical challenges. These disruptions had a direct financial impact, with the industry suffering an estimated 25% decrease in revenue in 2020 compared to the previous year.

One of the key impacts of the pandemic on the global supply chain was the disruption of logistics and transportation networks. Lockdowns and travel restrictions imposed by governments worldwide have led to delays and cancellations in shipments, hindering the timely delivery of raw materials and finished goods. The Malay-Bumiputera halal herbs SMEs, which relied on imports for a large portion of their raw materials, then faced considerable difficulties in securing timely and consistent supply. A number of herb plantations in Malaysia, such as Nasuha Herbs and Spice Farm, which is the largest halal herbs and spice plantation in Asia, reported that one of the greatest hardships caused by COVID-19 was the loss of foreign labourers who left the country at the outset of the pandemic. Until now, the costs and risks of operating such a farm are so huge that most SMEs prefer to source their raw materials from abroad.

The change in consumer behaviour during the pandemic has also affected the supply and demand dynamics of the halal herbs industry. During the pandemic, the export segment of the industry had difficulty accessing international markets. With restrictions on international travel and logistics, the industry encountered obstacles in reaching overseas customers and fulfilling export orders. This led to decreased revenue and limited market expansion opportunities for SMEs. Furthermore, the shift towards online shopping has altered consumption patterns and created challenges in meeting evolving customer preferences. The industry has had to adapt to the surge in e-commerce, invest in online platforms, and establish efficient last-mile delivery networks to cater to the changing needs of consumers.

Future Direction

The COVID-19 pandemic has significantly impacted economies globally, including the Malay-Bumiputera halal herbs industry. One of the most significant impacts of the pandemic was disruptions of its global supply chains (Cai & Luo, 2020; Xu et al., 2020). To mitigate this problem, the industry needs to develop new and more robust supply chain networks. Collaborative efforts among growers, processors, distributors, and retailers can improve reliability and streamline the flow of raw materials and finished products. Smallholders of commodities such as rubber and palm oil should be encouraged to take up herb planting as a supplementary source of income. For housewives and single mothers, herb planting (see Fig. 4.2) can become an avenue to improve their economic productivity and family livelihood.

Additionally, exploring partnerships with other countries for sourcing raw materials and diversifying markets can enhance supply chain resilience and reduce dependency on a single source. However, the above task is extremely challenging for Malay-Bumiputera SMEs due to their limited international networking (Zain et al., 2012). Hence, government intervention is crucial to help them gain access to international market information, investment and joint-venture opportunities, human capital, et cetera.

From the government's point of view, various programmes had been introduced in the past to boost the growth of the halal industry, whereby

Fig. 4.2 Malay women as herb growers

one of the primary benefits was the provision of financial assistance to SMEs. These programmes were expected to have positive effects on the internationalisation of Malay-Bumiputera halal herbs industry, since they would have had the potential to expand their operations, invest in research and development (R&D), and enhance their international competitiveness. With improved financial stability, industry players could allocate resources towards developing and executing internationalisation strategies, such as market research, product customisation, and establishing distribution networks in target markets.

During the COVID-19 pandemic, special economic stimulus packages were established by the government. Through grants, loans, moratoriums, and subsidies, these packages offered a lifeline to Malay-Bumiputera halal herbs industry players, helping them overcome the severe financial depression caused by the pandemic (Ahmad et al., 2020). However, changes in leadership and economic policies following the 15th general election have stalled the recovery path chartered by the former administration. There is also no present attempt to measure the effectiveness of the various stimulus packages introduced earlier. For the Malay-Bumiputera halal herbs sector to achieve the goals set out in MP12, these stimulus packages need to be reviewed, revised, and revived, especially to address supply chain challenges in the post-pandemic environment.

Economic stimulus packages often include measures to promote exports and facilitate market access. By organising trade missions, providing export incentives, and establishing trade promotion agencies, the government can assist the Malay-Bumiputera halal herbs industry in expanding its international reach. These initiatives play a vital role in helping industry players connect with potential buyers, explore new international markets, and increase their export volumes. Additionally, trade agreements and preferential trade arrangements facilitated through these packages can create favourable conditions for the international trade of halal herbs, further boosting the industry's globalisation efforts.

Stimulus packages often prioritise investments in innovation, research, and development. By allocating resources to these areas, the government will be able to encourage the creation of new products, improve production processes, and enhance the overall competitiveness of the Malay-Bumiputera halal herbs industry. The development of innovative products, such as value-added herbal extracts or novel formulations, can attract international buyers seeking unique offerings. Additionally, investments in research and development help ensure compliance with international standards and regulations, positioning the industry as a leader in the global halal herbs market. These efforts will contribute to the industry's internationalisation by increasing its market share and differentiating its offerings from competitors.

Economic stimulus packages often include provisions for skills training and capacity building. By investing in human capital, these packages equip industry players with the necessary knowledge and skills to compete effectively in international markets. Training programmes can focus on various areas, such as product quality improvement, market research, branding, and export management. By enhancing the skills and capabilities of industry professionals, stimulus packages contribute to improved product quality, adherence to international standards, and a better understanding of target markets. This, in turn, facilitates the internationalisation process by enabling industry players to develop tailored marketing strategies, establish strong business relationships with international partners, and effectively navigate cultural and regulatory barriers in foreign markets.

While economic stimulus packages provide significant support to the Malay-Bumiputera halal herbs industry, it is essential to consider the challenges and limitations that may persist. Cultural and regulatory barriers in foreign markets, such as varying halal certification requirements or preferences for certain herbal products, can pose challenges to internationalisation efforts. Limited access to market information and networks may also hinder industry players' ability to identify and tap into potential international markets. Furthermore, the need for customised marketing strategies and localised product adaptations to meet the preferences and regulations of different countries can require additional resources and expertise. Addressing these challenges requires close collaboration between industry players, government agencies, and relevant stakeholders to ensure that stimulus packages effectively address specific industry needs and provide comprehensive support for internationalisation.

Applying the Resource-Based View

Resource-Based View (RBV) theory has its roots in the field of strategic management (Donnellan & Rutledge, 2019; Freeman et al., 2021; Hoskisson et al., 1999). It offers a framework for understanding how organisations can achieve a competitive advantage by leveraging their unique resources and capabilities. According to RBV, organisations possess both tangible and intangible resources (Wernerfelt, 1995). These resources can include human capital (skills and knowledge of employees), physical capital (such as infrastructure and technology), and organisational capital (structures, routines, and culture). The idea that organisations can be viewed as a collection of resources was initially proposed by Penrose (Rugman & Verbeke, 2002). Her work laid the foundation for the RBV theory by emphasising the role of resources within organisations. The development of RBV theory was further advanced by scholars like Wernerfelt and Barney. Wernerfelt's work contributed to the understanding of how resource heterogeneity and immobility influence competitive advantage. Barney's contributions are notable for his focus on strategic resources as sources of competitive advantage for organisations. His work emphasised the rareness, value, inimitability, and non-substitutability (VRIN) of resources as key determinants of competitive advantage.

RBV can be applied to strategically map the relationships between the resources and capabilities of indigenous entrepreneurship within the context of the COVID-19 pandemic and economic stimulus packages. This mapping helps in identifying and understanding the unique assets and competencies that indigenous entrepreneurs possess. RBV theory offers valuable insights into the Malay-Bumiputera halal herbs industry's competitive advantage and internationalisation strategies. This industry possesses a unique set of tangible and intangible resources, ranging from its access to rare herbal varieties and skilled labour force to its deep knowledge of halal production processes and established distribution networks. These resources exhibit the VRIN characteristics highlighted by RBV, which collectively contribute to its competitive edge. Therefore, these are assets that are essential to understanding how the industry can maintain a strong position in the global market.

Malaysia's economic stimulus packages will enable Malay-Bumiputera halal herbs businesses to channel their supply chain activities towards internationalisation. Targeted financial support, export promotion, infrastructure development, and community-based upskilling collectively maximise the impact of supply chain management on the industry's competitiveness and capacity to penetrate international markets. In turn, internationalisation is expected to improve firm performance. In other words, it can be proposed that economic stimulus packages moderate the relationship between supply chain management and internationalisation, while internationalisation mediates the relationship between supply chain management and firm financial performance.

Based on the discussion above, this chapter proposes a conceptual framework as shown in Fig. 4.3.

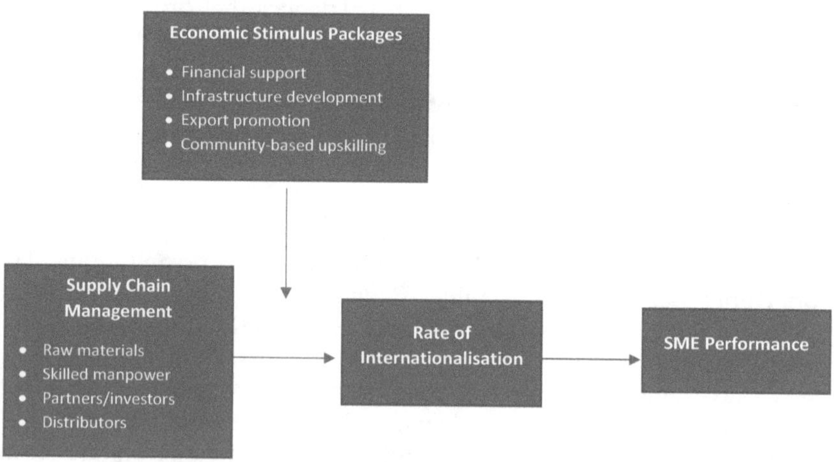

Fig. 4.3 Proposed conceptual framework

The above framework is expected to make a significant contribution to research on Malay-Bumiputera halal herbs SMEs because it provides a platform for testing the effects of government assistance on their supply chain management, internationalisation, and firm performance. The framework posits that for the halal herbs industry to achieve financial sustainability, its growth in international markets must be facilitated through effective supply chain management. However, the effects of supply chain management on internationalisation are dependent on post-pandemic economic stimulus packages, which should include financial support, export promotion, infrastructure development, and community-based upskilling. The development of this framework will enable future researchers to quantify the impacts of different forms of government assistance on the internationalisation and the performance of the Malay-Bumiputera halal herbs industry, particularly in the context of its recovery from COVID-19.

Conclusion

This chapter highlights the rich traditional knowledge and practices of indigenous communities in Malaysia regarding herbal medicine and the use of herbs for medicinal, culinary, and cultural purposes. Malay-Bumiputeras, in particular, have inherited and preserved valuable knowledge about the medicinal properties of local plants and their applications in healing practices. In line with Padilla-Meléndez et al. (2022), the importance of acknowledging indigenous experience and incorporating it with modern practices is emphasised to create a more sustainable and culturally sensitive approach to business. The integration between indigenous and modern knowledge is presented above through the connection between Malay-Bumiputeras—and their mastery of Islamic healing practices—and contemporary business concepts such as supply chain management and internationalisation. It is further argued that the application of indigenous knowledge can also contribute to the economic empowerment of Malay-Bumiputeras, whose socio-economic status has been deeply troubled by the COVID-19 pandemic.

On an international level, the halal herbs industry has gained significant attention due to growing consumer preference for natural and organic products, coupled with an increasing demand for halal-certified goods. Involvement in the production, processing, and trade of halal herbs can help generate considerable income and create job opportunities among Malay-Bumiputeras, thus reducing socio-economic disparities between them and other ethnic groups in the country. However, for Malay-Bumiputera entrepreneurs, competing globally is a daunting challenge due to their limited international networks which hamper their supply chain capacity (Zain et al., 2012). Although the Malaysian government has implemented various measures to empower and encourage the development of Malay-Bumiputera businesses, they have continued to underperform mainly because of the difficulty they face in gaining access to international market information, partnerships, raw materials, distribution channels, et cetera. It is therefore vital that in the current post-pandemic environment, fresh economic stimulus packages are introduced to address these specific weaknesses related to supply chain management and internationalisation among Malay-Bumiputera SMEs.

Government initiatives for SMEs typically aim to provide them with access to financing, infrastructure, and training. According to the Resource-Based View theory (Donnellan & Rutledge, 2019; Freeman et al., 2021; Hoskisson et al., 1999), economic stimulus packages are expected to play a crucial role in supporting the growth and internationalisation of halal herbs businesses, particularly in light of their financial constraints and networking limitations. Consistent with Boussebaa (2023), this chapter argues that the internationalisation processes and needs of SMEs in developing countries greatly differ from large western multinational corporations. For indigenous entrepreneurs, community-focused initiatives such as youth financial literacy training and business mentoring are especially important because of their limited business backgrounds. Strategic collaborations and a comprehensive approach to internationalisation can also help the industry to successfully navigate the global market landscape through coordinated efforts and standardised halal certification systems. Thus, by leveraging these packages, Malay-Bumiputera SMEs can overcome the economic lethargy left by the COVID-19 pandemic, enhance their productivity and competitiveness, and expand their reach beyond Malaysia's borders.

The arguments forwarded in this chapter connect economic stimulus packages, supply chain management, internationalisation and firm performance of halal herbs Malay-Bumiputera SMEs in a single theoretical framework. This framework highlights the urgency of introducing fresh interventionist measures to help Malay-Bumiputera halal SMEs to recover from the COVID-19 pandemic. It can be applied in future research to quantify the impact of different forms of government assistance on the internationalisation and performance of the Malay-Bumiputera halal herbs SMEs, post-pandemic.

Acknowledgements The authors would like to thank the Ministry of Higher Education, Malaysia, for its financial support towards the completion of this chapter (Fundamental Research Grant Scheme Project No. FP037-2022).

References

Abdulrahman, M. D., Ali, A., Fatihah, H. N. N., Khandaker, M. M., & Mat, N. (2018). Traditional medicinal knowledge of Malays in Terengganu, Peninsular Malaysia. *Malayan Nature Journal, 70*(3).

Ahmad, F., Zaidi, M. A. S., Sulaiman, N., & Majid, F. A. A. (2015). Issues and challenges in the development of the herbal industry in Malaysia. *Prosiding Perkem, 10*(1), 227–238.

Ahmad, N. N., Hanafi, W. N. W., Abdullah, W. M. T. W., Daud, S., & Toolib, S. N. (2020). The effectiveness of additional PRIHATIN SME economic stimulus package (PRIHATIN SME+) in Malaysia post-COVID-19 outbreak: A conceptual paper. *Global Business and Management Research, 12*(4), 754–763.

Aigbogun, O., Ghazali, Z., & Razali, R. (2014). A framework to enhance supply chain resilience in the case of the Malaysian pharmaceutical industry. *Global Business and Management Research, 6*(3), 219–228.

April, W. I., & Itenge, D. I. (2020). Fostering indigenous entrepreneurship amongst San people: An exploratory case of Tsumkwe. *International Journal of Business and Globalisation, 24*(4), 496–512. https://doi.org/10.1504/IJBG.2020.106955

Bastien, F., Coraiola, D. M., & Foster, W. M. (2023). Indigenous peoples and organisation studies. *Organisation Studies, 44*(4), 659–675. https://doi.org/10.1177/01708406221141545

Boussebaa, M. (2023). Decolonizing international business. *Critical Perspectives on International Business*. https://doi.org/10.1108/cpoib-12-2022-0121.

Cai, M., & Luo, J. (2020). Influence of COVID-19 on manufacturing industry and corresponding countermeasures from supply chain perspective. *Journal of Shanghai Jiaotong University (science), 25*(4), 409–416. https://doi.org/10.1007/s12204-020-2206-z

Cui, L., Yue, S., Nghiem, X.-H., & Duan, M. (2023). Exploring the risk and economic vulnerability of global energy supply chain interruption in the context of Russo-Ukrainian war. *Resources Policy, 81*, 103373.

Donnellan, J., & Rutledge, W. L. (2019). A case for resource-based view and competitive advantage in banking. *Managerial and Decision Economics, 40*(6), 728–737.

Filatotcheva, I., Ireland, R. D., & Stahl, G. K. (2022). Contextualising management research: An open systems perspective. *Journal of Management Studies, 59*(4), 1036–1056. https://doi.org/10.1111/joms.12754

Freeman, R. E., Dmytriyev, S. D., & Phillips, R. A. (2021). Stakeholder theory and the resource-based view of the firm. *Journal of Management, 47*(7), 1757–1770. https://doi.org/10.1177/0149206321993576

Ghosh, S. P. (2013). Promotion of medicinal and aromatic plants in the Asia-Pacific region. *Expert Consultation on Promotion of Medicinal and Aromatic Plants in the Asia-Pacific Region: Proceedings*, 33.

Hanzaee, K. H., & Ramezani, M. R. (2011). Intention to halal products in the world markets. *Interdisciplinary Journal of Research in Business, 1*(5), 1–7.

Hasan, Z. (2021). Making Indonesia as integrated halal zone and world halal sector hub through the implementation of Halal supply chain. *Journal of Islamic Economic and Business Research, 1*(1), 1–14.

Hoskisson, R. E., Hitt, M. A., Wan, W. P., & Yiu, D. (1999). Theory and research in strategic management: Swings of a pendulum. *Journal of Management, 25*(3), 417–456. https://doi.org/10.1177/014920639902500307

Idrus, R. (2022). Competing for the 'indigenous' slot: Layered histories and positionings in Peninsular Malaysia. *Sojourn: Journal of Social Issues in Southeast Asia*, 37(1), 58–84.

Kardooni, R., Kari, F. B., Yahaya, S. R. B., & Yusup, S. H. (2014). Traditional knowledge of Orang Asli on forests in peninsular Malaysia. *Indian Journal of Traditional Knowledge, 13*(2), 283–291.

Mustapa, A. N., & Mohamad, A. (2021). Malaysian government business support and assistance for small and medium enterprises: A case of COVID-19 pandemic crisis. In *Modeling economic growth in contemporary Malaysia* (pp. 291–305). Emerald Publishing Limited. https://doi.org/10.1108/978-1-80043-806-420211022.

Ong, H. C., Lina, E., & Milow, P. (2012). Traditional knowledge and usage of medicinal plants among the Semai Orang Asli at Kampung Batu 16, Tapah, Perak Malaysia. *Studies on Ethno-Medicine, 6*(3), 207–211. https://doi.org/10.1080/09735070.2012.11886440

Othman, P., Sungkar, I., & Hussin, W. S. W. (2009). Malaysia as an international halal food hub: competitiveness and potential of meat-based industries. *ASEAN Economic Bulletin*, 306–320.

Padilla-Meléndez, A., Plaza-Angulo, J. J., Del-Aguila-Obra, A. R., & Ciruela-Lorenzo, A. M. (2022). Indigenous entrepreneurship. Current issues and future lines. *Entrepreneurship and Regional Development, 34*(1–2), 6–31. https://doi.org/10.1080/08985626.2021.2011962.

Rajendran, S. D., & Kamarulzaman, N. H. (2023). Review of issues and challenges in the growing use of herbal-based products. *Science Letters*(1), 16–31%V 17. https://doi.org/10.24191/sl.v17i1.18516.

Rajendran, S. D., & Kamarulzaman, N. H. (2017). Preserving halal Integrity in herbs and herbal industry supply chain. *Journal of Contempory Islamic Studies, 3*(2), 93–104.

Rugman, A. M., & Verbeke, A. (2002). Edith Penrose's contribution to the resource-based view of strategic management. *Strategic Management Journal, 23*(8), 769–780. https://doi.org/10.1002/smj.240

Samuel, A. J. S. J., Kalusalingam, A., Chellappan, D. K., Gopinath, R., Radhamani, S., Husain, H. A., Muruganandham, V., & Promwichit, P. (2010). Ethnomedical survey of plants used by the Orang Asli in Kampung Bawong, Perak, West Malaysia. *Journal of Ethnobiology and Ethnomedicine, 6*, 1–6. https://doi.org/10.1186/1746-4269-6-5

Siddique, S., & Suryadinata, L. (1981). Bumiputra and pribumi: Economic nationalism (Indiginism) in Malaysia and Indonesia. *Pacific Affairs, 54*(4), 662–687. https://doi.org/10.2307/2757890

Tan, T. Y. C., Lee, J. C., Yusof, N. A. M., Teh, B. P., & Mohamed, A. F. S. (2020). Malaysian herbal monograph development and challenges. *Journal of Herbal Medicine, 23*, 100380.

Ulluwishewa, R., Roskruge, N., Harmsworth, G., & Antaran, B. (2008). Indigenous knowledge for natural resource management: A comparative study of Māori in New Zealand and Dusun in Brunei Darussalam. *GeoJournal, 73*(4), 271–284. https://doi.org/10.1007/s10708-008-9198-9

Welter, F., Baker, T., & Wirsching, K. (2019). Three waves and counting: The rising tide of contextualization in entrepreneurship research. *Small Business Economics, 52*, 319–330. https://doi.org/10.1007/s11187-018-0094-5

Wernerfelt, B. (1995). The resource-based view of the firm: Ten years after. *Strategic Management Journal, 16*(3), 171–174.

Xu, Z., Elomri, A., Kerbache, L., & El Omri, A. (2020). Impacts of COVID-19 on global supply chains: Facts and perspectives. *IEEE Engineering Management Review, 48*(3), 153–166. https://doi.org/10.1109/EMR.2020.3018420

Zain, Z. M., Anas, Y., Hassan, F. H., Lehar, H., & Shamsuddin, S. (2012). Challenges, opportunities and performance of Bumiputera SMEs in the food industry: A Malaysian perspective. In *2012. International Conference on Innovation Management and Technology Research.*

Zakaria, M. H., Abdullah, A. M., Kamarulzaman, N. H., & Abdul Latif, I. (2019).Transformation of herbal industry in Malaysia. *Macro Outlook of Herbal Industry in Malaysia, Agribusiness. Food and Fertiliser Technology for the Asian and Pacific Region (FFTC-AP), Malaysia.*

CHAPTER 5

Between Assimilation and Cultural Pluralism for Indigenous Livelihood and Entrepreneurship: Case of Lumad in the Philippines

Emmanuel Mushimiyimana

Introduction

Indigenous theory highlights that there is a distinctiveness of local context when determining who is indigenous and who is not, and the global context of indigenous often refers to non-Western persons (Bruton et al, 2021). The focus is on the uniqueness of the local people in terms of culture, traditions, beliefs, and economic production. Indigenous people are often presented as marginalized and left-behind communities in terms of politics, socio-economic development, and cultural values. This is a vast difference from managerial theory originating from the West that assumes indigenous people are those who are not in the dominant modes of

E. Mushimiyimana (✉)
University of Rwanda, Kigali, Rwanda
e-mail: mushimiyimana.emmy@gmail.com

E. L. Eijdenberg et al. (eds.), *Indigenous Entrepreneurship in Southeast Asia*, Palgrave Studies in Equity, Diversity, Inclusion, and Indigenization in Business, https://doi.org/10.1007/978-3-031-54457-6_5

production (i.e., the industrial realm), those who did not embrace liberal or socio-democratic progress (i.e., the political realm), and generally those who did not attain civilization (i.e., the cultural realm) (Filatochev et al., 2022). This was due to the rapid advancement from the industrial revolution to liberal social and political thoughts since the sixteenth century. The rest of the world has been considered as the left-behind groups and are therefore assimilated or included for the purpose of achieving global civilization.

The indigenous people are considered as native and conservative in their own way of life—mostly traditional and stagnant in their mode of production, entrepreneurial activities, and development. Moreover, they are considered as people who do not embrace tangible changes over time or have resisted changes to embrace local and international ideologies and beliefs including dominant religions such as Christianity and Islam. This hinders their development as their values become distant from the progressing beliefs, and their economic practices are still very traditional in not using financial institutions (Croce, 2019).

The indigenous theory is pertinent to understanding entrepreneurship as it highlights "the diversity not just between indigenous groups and indigenous cultures, but also at the national context in which they are situated" (Croce, 2019, p. 360). For many who share a common experience of discrimination, colonization, and abuse, the historical and political aspects affect how they practice entrepreneurship as these groups of people face financial and moral marginalization and a sense of inferiority complex (Croce, 2019).

This research focuses on the Lumad indigenous people of Mindanao, an island in the Southern part of the Philippines. It seeks to observe how historically, the adoption of neo-liberal, assimilation practices impact on the livelihood and entrepreneurial practices of this group of indigenous people facing marginalization and impoverishment. The next section highlights the theoretical underpinnings of concepts like assimilation and cultural pluralism followed by the methodology adopted to analyze the treatment of the Lumad people by the government and other stakeholders. The findings and discussion uncover some of the nuances of the government–Lumad people relationship and the extent of marginalization faced by the Lumad people as a result of different focus exercised by the NGOs and the MNCs. It concludes with some recommendations, limitations, and gaps in research.

Assimilation Versus Cultural Pluralism: Theories and Practices

Assimilation happens when people who have power over indigenous people want them to look, live, and act like them without due consideration for indigenous culture, values and practices. This process goes hand in hand with political, economic, and cultural sanctions to stimulate changes in the society. Assimilation also promotes both socio-political and economic aims, inclusion and exclusion of individuals, and at times with the price of losing indigenous values and culture. This causes conflict between indigenous people, various stakeholders including government, NGOs, and the multinational companies (MNCs).

Research has shown that continuous discrimination and marginalization against indigenous peoples are counter-productive to human rights, freedom, and economic progress (Banerjee, 2022; Bastien et al, 2023). For example, government assimilation (i.e., into mainstream Western society) impacted on many aspects of Canadian Aboriginal people resulting in health inequities, loss of tradition and traditional practices, and breakdown of the family unit (MacDonald & Steenback, 2015). Boussebaa (2023) highlights that MNCs are playing an increasing significant role in international business in the neo-liberal world order, aspects of which negatively affect the livelihood and entrepreneurship of indigenous people.

On the other hand, cultural pluralism accommodates societal differences and tolerance of multiple cultures where smaller groups within a larger society maintain their unique cultural identities and their values and practices are accepted by the dominant culture (William & Madelon, 1973). This modern way of treating humans by recognizing the values of inclusion and differences of cultures serves to resist malpractices of colonialism. It accepts differences in religious beliefs and political organizations. It allows the creation of different civil society organizations (CSOs) and provides a form of state mechanism to guarantee the rights of the majority as well as minority groups. For example, cultural pluralism has been demonstrated in the local response to having Aboriginal advisory boards in some municipalities that include urban indigenous input (Heritz, 2018) enabling the inclusion of indigenous culture in the society and consideration of their ways of life and production. Cultural pluralism enhances the recognition of formally marginalized people and changes the discourses of cultural imperialism of the last century (Banerjee, 2022).

Most developed societies embraced cultural pluralism after experiencing atrocities from practices of cultural imperialism, segregation, Nazism, and apartheid practices. In current practices, Western countries and other nations adopted cultural pluralism for the sake of inclusive governance and development.

In the neo-liberal world order where freedom in movement of companies from one country to another and the facility of communication, exchange, and ease of doing regional and international business exist, multiculturalism is seen as the sole practice that helps to overcome stigma of cultural inequalities and imperialism. Bastien et al. (2023) emphasize that there is a need to decolonize the management and organization of the society by stopping discrimination against indigenous production and livelihood. This is crucial as traditionally colonialism always downplays the relevance of indigenous rights over property, production, and earnings. The discrimination and impoverishment of many indigenous people worldwide at the hands of a few dominant groups have resulted in global inequality, terrorism, and resentment. For society to get rid of the past colonial legacy, most of the developed and developing nations are decolonizing the structure and values of their society to embrace respect of diversity and differences through their constitution and culture.

As indigenous knowledge is pivotal to decolonization, we need to revisit the kind of governance practiced worldwide and in the Philippines in particular to trace the threats to indigenous livelihood and culture. The purpose is to have a better society which is inclusive and to get rid of traditions of governing citizens in a coercive manner, especially the minority groups.

The different forms of governance or political ideologies used worldwide such as liberalism, republicanism, assimilationism, multiculturalism, and cosmopolitanism have effects on the livelihood and entrepreneurship practices of indigenous people in their societies.

Liberalism is equated with equality of citizens where dominant groups in the society treat others with respect and tolerance and guarantee individual rights and freedom to all, including minority groups. In this realm, there is market economy and minimal or limited government interference. The government fosters the interests of people including minorities and indigenous groups and in this system of governance, political, cultural, and economic spaces are open to all, and people's participation is guaranteed. Besides, liberalism paces with neo-liberalism in assuming free movement of goods and services, and investment of MNCs in a borderless world. This form of governance also has aspects of free market economy, freedom of movement, and freedom to do business as enshrined in the political ideology.

The Republicanism form of governance emphasizes public and general interests, but not necessarily individual rights and interest since these are subjugated to the state interest. Only a few can lead and look after the interests of many and participation in governance is restricted and indirect. Assimilationism requires that minority groups and specifically indigenous people adopt the customs, values, and practices of the majority population. Thus, the rights are limited especially when customs are not appreciated by the majority. There is a feeling that indigenous practices contradict or jeopardize their interests if they are not changed and adjusted to the culture of the majority. Therefore, minority groups have to be assimilated whether they want or not.

Cosmopolitanism assumes no differences in human beings and that everyone is entitled to the same conditions of life. People are treated equally and equitably. It hinges on inclusion and consequently creates an environment conducive to generalization or commonness.

Cosmopolitanism is very close to multiculturalism—or cultural pluralism because it relies on the assumption that diverse groups, no matter ethnic, cultural and linguistic differences, receive equal treatment, right to self-determination, and/or representation. This is crucial for the interests of the whole society in general and each group in particular. People understand their differences and the government establishes conditions and sets up regulations that promote the peaceful co-existence of different groups especially in the example given of Canada (Croce, 2019).

In the Philippines, the country's indigenous population makes up 10% to 20% of the national population, which currently stands at around 102.9 million (IWGIA, 2023). Geographically, they are predominantly located in Mindanao (61%) and Northern Luzon (33%) (Angara, 2023). They are clustered into groups such as the Negrito, Cordillera, Cagayan, Mangyan Mindaro, Palawan, Visayan, Lumadnon (Lumads), and Bangsamoro (ADB, 2002). Overall, while indigenous people represent a sizeable chunk of the population, they continue to be among the most disadvantaged groups in the country as many still retained much of their traditional, pre-colonial culture, social institutions, and living practices. They live in geographically isolated areas with lack of access to basic social services, few opportunities for major economic activities, education, or political participation. While commercially valuable natural resources such as minerals, forests, and rivers are found mainly in their areas, they are continuously subjected to aggression against development and land grabbing (IWGIA, 2023).

The Lumads are regarded as the original inhabitants of Mindanao and include the Bagobo, Blaan, Bukidnon People, Higaonon, Kalagan, Kamigin, Mamanwa, Mandaya, Manobo, Magsaka, Matigsalug, Sangil, Subanon, Tagabawa, Tagakaulo, Talaandig, Tasaday, Teduray, Tigwahonon, and Umayamnon (Limos, 2021). They are the non-Muslim and non-Christian indigenous peoples of Mindanao (ADB, 2002). Based on the 2010 National Census, they comprised about 14.38% of the population in the upland and lowland areas of the Agusan, Cotabato, Davao, Misamis, Surigao, and Zamboanga Provinces, Bukidnon, Compostela Valley, Maguindanao, Sultan Kudarat, and Sarangani (National Museum Philippines, 2023). Some of them are now Christians and others are Muslims. Their productive culture focuses mainly on T'nalak weaves (textile), T'boli brassware (belt), and agriculture. They have developed such a range of specific production culture for many centuries.

Generally, the indigenous groups in the Philippines have their own traditional way of production in farming, hunting, and tattooing. As in any other indigenous groups and societies, diversification of activities in the lens of economic liberalism is very limited. They have established their own education system to cater to local needs with integration into the global education system. Therefore, they teach literacy, mathematics, social sciences, technology, and livelihood education in addition to locally sustainable agriculture and indigenous arts and culture. In partnership with the government, they operate under the Department of Education—the DepEd's K-12 curriculum, and their schools are called the Lumad schools (La Vina & Vergara, 2021).

The relevance of this research hinges on the following facts: (1) Indigenous people worldwide face impoverishment as a result of being subjugated by strong or dominant groups (Croce, 2019), (2) There exists the exercise of violence or aggression against them in the process of integration and development—quite like the former colonial period, and (3) There is low transformation of indigenous livelihood and entrepreneurship in these societies.

This study focuses on the theories of assimilation and cultural pluralism as they have been used by dominant groups worldwide in different places and regions to control the production and entrepreneurship of indigenous people through colonialism. The study seeks to examine the adoption of neo-liberal, assimilation practices by the government of the Philippines and the impact these have on the Lumad indigenous people. As MNCs play an increasingly significant role in international business in the neo-liberal world order, it is paramount to consider the neo-colonial aspects that negatively affect the livelihood and entrepreneurship of indigenous people. It also analyzes what can be done to redress some of the challenges faced by indigenous entrepreneurs and how to move forward with their progress.

Methodology

This study uses qualitative research through document and discourse analysis to examine the impact of adopting neo-liberal, assimilation practices by the Philippines government and its stakeholders such as the multinational companies (MNCs) on the Lumad indigenous people. The Lumad people are selected for the case study due to their distinctiveness as indigenous local people who fall into the category of marginalized groups in the Philippines. They were chosen also based on their level of cultural entrepreneurship including the establishment of the Lumad schools, and traditional weaving and the recent structural violence faced by this group of people.

The research draws from the multi-culturalism lens embedded in inclusive governance as articulated by the United Nations Development Programme (UNDP) and the World Bank (WB). Multiculturalism and inclusive practices give rise to representation, equal treatment and fair access to national economic resources, property ownership, and freedom to economic opportunities and production.

The research examines online data, scholarly journals, and official documents to analyze the impact of treatment by the government, NGOs, and MNCs on the livelihood and entrepreneurial experiences of the Lumad indigenous people. It sheds light on the impact of treatment resulting in poverty, socio-cultural hardship, and political marginalization and the extent to which indigenous people are integrated into the society. Besides, the research assesses the level of tolerance for differences, and the ways to improve productivity of the indigenous people through increasing the rights, values, profitability, and access to the market of their products.

Findings

This section highlights the findings of different approaches and policies implemented by the government and other stakeholders that impact on the Lumad indigenous people's livelihood and entrepreneurial practices.

There exists different understanding of ideology that has created conflict between the government of the Philippines and the Lumad people. The ideology of the government is centered on capitalism and globalization while the Lumad elites focused on communism and communal use of their property, including the use of land. Hence, the Lumads have resisted change including refusal to accept the idea of attracting and bringing foreign and domestic companies to the native land. This resentment was associated with their ideological understanding of protecting their land, common ownership of the means of production, and general mistrust of liberal capitalism.

The lack of understanding of capitalist entrepreneurship among the Lumad leaders in embracing new culture of working with bigger global companies to advance the Lumad economy enabled the rebel groups to exploit the situation by directing them to the common control of land and property which has resulted in the direct conflict with government and foreign companies. The concern of the government in applying liberal entrepreneurial endeavors was to end poverty in the Lumad society while the Lumad leaders wanted to continue with their communist and traditional ways.

This has resulted in resistance by the Lumad people and the use of force by government to compel them to follow. Consequently, the Lumad people were influenced by communist ideology of the CPP (Communist Party of The Philippines) that hinges on Marxism–Leninism political thought—fighting against liberal capitalism and more specifically foreign investments that were often linked with exploitation of rich nations at the detriment of the poor. Liberal capitalism on the contrary as subscribed by the government could bring jobs, money, and wealth not only to the Philippines but also to the Lumad land in particular (Nawal & Salaverria, 2018).

The Lumad people only saw the contrary and viewed the pro-government plans as self-benefiting for the government and the international companies, and an opportunity for the military to plunder their resources. While President Duterte promised to provide lots of funding for agriculture as compensation in the Lumad areas and to increase the local content and their corporate social responsibility, this was not sufficient to satisfy and convince the local indigenous people. The opposing ideological views and approaches of the government and the Lumad people have significantly affected the political, economic, social, and entrepreneurial development of the Lumad areas in Mindanao.

In terms of education, the Lumad people have established their own schools and advocated the right of education for the benefit of their community. Therefore, the Lumad communities are eager to learn and be educated for the betterment of their livelihood and be connected with the rest of the world. Since 2007, many schools were established and came under the purview of the Department of Education. The Government initially supported and included their local curriculum such as farming and weaving into the national teaching agenda. However, the Lumad schools were invaded by the military forces of the same government (Rey, 2017) who accused the Lumad people for providing a safe haven to the NPA (New People's Army) rebels. Despite the success stories of the Lumad schools, some were closed, and others destroyed. In 2019, majority of students in those schools that were attached could not finish their academic year. An estimate indicated that only 30 out of 55 Salugpongan schools managed to finish the academic year of 2019–2020 (La Vina & Vergara, 2021).

The Lumad people have an autonomous region in the Muslim Mindanao as defined by the Republic Act No.6734 where they are provided with the basic structure of government within the framework of the Constitution and national sovereignty and the territorial integrity of the Republic of the Philippines (Official Gazette, 1989). Politically, these could help them set up affirmative and empowerment actions to bring about self-determination, a cultural pluralistic society, and a democratic governance—but this was not to be the case!

On political inclusion, the Lumad people of Mindanao have a political voice, organizations, and traditional leaders to advocate for them (Cagoco-Guian, 1999). The problem lies in the ideological differences between them and the government as discussed earlier on. One of the signs of their capacity to organize themselves was the formation of the Lumad Mindanao Peoples Federation (LMPF) in June 1986. It had staged different demonstrations against the abuses from state agents and their leaders had engaged with the government and its stakeholders. However, their positive bargaining power was too weak as the government used force to impose its policies. There has been development of conflict over time since the globalization era in 2000 until now with increasing killing of the Lumad leaders and displacement of people—around 30,000 people were displaced in the last 8 years (Go, 2015; Nawal & Salaverria, 2018).

The government and the paramilitary forces were responsible for the Lumads' displacement with killings and bombing in their territories. Some of the atrocities included the invasion of the Lumads and the Manabo people by the paramilitary group, the Magahat-Bagani as well as the massacre of the traditional leaders, Dionel Campos and Jovillo Sinzo after beating them up in public (Go, 2015). The same fate also befell the headmaster of a local school which used to give technical education services to children (Go, 2015). The government deployed about 65 battalions in defense of international investment groups or corporations especially those investing in mining (Nawal & Salaverria, 2018; Rey, 2017).

In terms of religion, justice, and morality, the Lumads are non-Muslims with an orientation of Islamic culture according to the Republic Act 6734. However, there are no cases of compelling the Lumads to adopt any religion in the current Philippines, where previously some were compelled to adopt Christianism (Filipinas Heritage Library, n.d). The morality and justice system in Mindanao is based on respecting others' property and their personality, making peace and harmony in the society largely due to the work of *Kefeduwans* who are like mediators or judges who ensure all conflicting parties reach an agreement (Rodil, 2020). This works hand in hand with the Western justice system being established by the government.For social inclusion, the Lumads are generally poor and hence stigmatized and marginalized compared to others. They have been deprived of their fertile swampy lands before and were compelled to abandon their lands to go to the highlands—a threat that they seemingly faced again in new era of globalization. Investors and government are likely grabbing their land by force and without compensation.

The economy of the Lumad people is very much based on traditional ways of production in agriculture and weaving although some traces of modernization are seen in the access of weaving machines. Their products range from chocolate cacao, turmeric granules, herbal tea, carrot cakes, etc. Below is a photo (Fig. 5.1) of a hand-made carpet made by the Lumads.

It is clear from the picture that they produce nice hand-made goods. Modernization of these entrepreneurial activities can obviously trigger

Fig. 5.1 Carpet made by the Lumads. Photo anonymous, 2023

the opportunity to increase production and trade. Agricultural production and weaving can be lucrative if the Lumad people are empowered to increase their production and have access to good market regionally and globally.

In addition to the lack of modernization of these products, there is also insecurity arising from displacement of the Lumad people into the highlands, the killing of the resilient Lumad leaders, the transformation by force, and the violent acts exercised by the government. Over the years, the government allowed destructive mining and projects by foreign corporations to happen in the Lumads' ancestral lands thereby causing them to flee their very own properties. They did not have easy access to money through financial institutions nor private property rights (Filipinas Heritage Library, n.d). This hindered them from embarking on innovation and entrepreneurial activities. Most of the Lumad innovative schools and human capital have been destabilized. There were very few engaged in government or military service of the incumbent government and the voices of people were silenced and subjugated to the interests of government, and the business investors including the mining companies in Mindanao. Without security, it is difficult to embark on innovative and entrepreneurial activities.

From the records of non-governmental organizations (NGOs) in this region, the emphasis was placed on the transformation and developmental awareness of the Lumads rather than direct financial support needed by them. The Initiative PH (TIPH) helped and advocated for the Lumad youth in overcoming issues of poverty, marginalization, and insecurity that prevented their success in entrepreneurship (TIPH Blog

News, 2017). However, much effort is required to initiate modern activities for the Lumad people who require financial access, technological knowhow, and capacity to use machines for development. The Lumad people have no health care, education, and do not enjoy economic, social, and civic rights like others in the Philippines. Despite the wealth of the island, there is too much greed in the power of the government and that has not helped the Lumads to have access to wealth and wealth creation. Table 5.1 summarizes the findings on how the government and various stakeholders treated the Lumad people and their effects on their livelihood and entrepreneurship.

Table 5.1 The treatment of Lumad and its effect on their livelihood and entrepreneurship

What should be done for Lumad integration and inclusion	*What is done*	*Effect on Lumad livelihood and Entrepreneurship*
Good government–Lumad Relationship	Bad government–Lumad relationship	Conflict and more exclusion of the Lumads
Ideological harmony	Government – liberal, and Lumad, generally communist	Military incursion, rebellion, and violence. Lack of effective and productive investments in Lumad territory, enclave economy
Activities of innovation and entrepreneurship for indigenous interests	Lack of innovation, modernization, and empowerment for Lumad	Conflict with government, destruction of local schools, and activities of what the Lumad people and government have jointly initiated
Autonomy and representation	Lack of self-determination, killing of the Lumad elites and leaders	More conflict and subjugation, more internal colonization, and threats to the Lumad people's interests and land property
Social inclusion, delivery of public service to indigenous people, and socio-economic integration in entire Philippino society and empowerment	More exclusion, less political and military elites, no social and health security service, limited access to financial institutions and public services delivery	Impoverishment of Lumad

Source Author (2023)

As shown above, the findings of this research indicated the state of the government and Lumad relationship—which is not harmonious and often violent. This conflict ranges from ideological disharmony between the Lumads and the government, the creation of rebellion and resistance from government and foreign investment, destruction of infrastructure including schools, and killing and violence against the Lumad elites and leaders. The situation needs to improve for the betterment of the Lumad people's livelihood and entrepreneurship.

Moreover, there is limited social and economic inclusion of the Lumad people in terms of access to infrastructure, social-economic empowerment, political representation, health care services, and financial and public services. All these affect the working environment of the Lumad people in terms of innovation and entrepreneurship. In short, the study affirms that impoverishment of the Lumad people and aspects of marginalization still exist in the Lumad area due to forceful governance imposed on the Lumad people to accept the government's agenda. This is a hindrance to further innovation and entrepreneurship of the Lumad people.

Discussion

This research confirms that there is the colonial aspect in the treatment of indigenous people evident in existing literature (Banerjee, 2022; Boussebaa, 2023; Bastien et al., 2023; Salmon et al., 2022; Medby, 2019). Assimilation practices were being used to compel the Lumad people to adopt neo-liberal economic system by force and at the cost of their blood and property. Even though the government looks like it is aiming at reaching cultural pluralism, it is rather using assimilative violence against the Lumad people.

The treatment and mode of governance applied to the Lumad people are linked with other issues related to the aspect of neo-colonialism in developing the nation generally and applied to the indigenous community specifically. There are some aspects of using MNCs' interests in the exploitation and impoverishment of local people—who also form the resistance mechanism (Bastien, 2023). As MNCs play an increasingly significant role in international business in the neo-liberal world order, it is paramount to consider the neo-colonial aspects that negatively affect the livelihood and entrepreneurship of indigenous people. Using MNCs' interests at the detriment of the poor and marginalized indigenous is a hindrance to multiculturalism—considered as a modern form of governance that triggers inclusive society. It is also awakening the traditional form where companies were used in colonizing developing nations in the South.

The findings are also similar to the case of state–citizen relationship found in extractive industry and globalization in Southeast Asia and in African states such as Tanzania, Angola, Nigeria, Mozambique, Zambia, etc., where foreign companies had conflicts with native people while the governments were leaning to the side of MNCs (Ferguson, 2006; Mushimiyimana, 2019). The study brings to fore that in the neo-liberal world order, we can still find traces of colonialism that are detrimental to the indigenous interests, freedom, production, innovation, and entrepreneurship (Banerjee, 2022; Boussebaa, 2023).

Conclusion

This paper focuses on the governance of the Lumad indigenous people of Mindanao that impacts on their livelihood and entrepreneurship. The introduction discusses the conceptualization of indigenous people and the historical and political context faced by indigenous people facing marginalization and impoverishment (Bruton et al, 2021; Filatochev et al., 2021; Croce, 2019). The traditional way of treating indigenous people during colonial era has been assimilation—a way of peacefully or forcefully using mechanism to transform indigenous culture and beliefs while subjecting them to their interests and gradually or totally erasing their means and modes of production. Assimilation happens when people who have power over indigenous people want them to look, live and act like them without due consideration for indigenous culture, values, and practices. This process goes hand in hand with political, economic, and cultural sanctions to stimulate changes or new indoctrination in the society. It also highlights the subjugation of indigenous people to the interests of multinational companies especially during colonial period (Bastien et al, 2023; Boussebaa, 2023; Padilla-Melendez et al., 2022). These theories show that the indigenous people were treated quite badly by powerful groups in society where the government and MNCs have been using coercion against the interest of indigenous peoples.

This research examines the adoption of neo-liberal, assimilation practices and the impact these have on the Lumad indigenous people facing marginalization and impoverishment. In neo-liberalism, values such as respect, reciprocity, and tolerance should frame cultural encounters in multicultural societies, yet power differences and political domination also influence the cultural sphere and the relations between cultural groups as evident in the case of the Lumad people in the Philippines (Collste, 2019).

Using qualitative research, especially documents and discourses, the research revealed that the government of the Philippines and its stakeholders including NGOs had implemented violent assimilative policies against the Lumad people. The government initially wanted the Lumad people to change their livelihood and to bring in foreign investors in their territory without consent. In many cases, the Lumad people have been displaced without any form of compensation. The government has been using force to attack Lumad schools and kill their elites and leaders—mostly as a response to the Lumad's support of communist rebels who resisted government neo-liberal policies and found a safe haven in the Lumad territory.

Besides, there was limited social-economic integration and political representation for the Lumad people. This hampered the integration of the Lumad indigenous people to the society and the workforce. The lack of social, health, and financial services provided to the Lumad people also hindered their innovation and entrepreneurship practices. This was further compounded by the Lumad people not well represented in government organizations further increasing their marginalization. The lack of cultural pluralism in the Philippines hampers the effectiveness of government initiatives to integrate the Lumad people. Cultural pluralism is linked with inclusive governance, empowerment, and service delivery to both dominant and minority groups of the society who are mostly indigenous.

There is a serious ideological divide between the government and the indigenous Lumad people. The former is liberal in their economic pursuit of investment and creation of wealth, while the latter are communist in their ideology. The government has the responsibility of using persuasion and development projects to help the Lumad people move on with their livelihood without facing any resistance. There is a need to embrace a multicultural thinking from the leadership of the country. The method of governing requires a gradual and peaceful process of change to embrace the indigenous Lumad people. Further research should look at how this can be achieved. There is a need to use both NGOs and government agents in transformative policies and education practices that reduce politicization of identity to fight communist ideas and stop the use of violence to help the Lumad people despite the tenacity of communist rebels in Mindanao.

This research contributes to the existing knowledge on the treatment of indigenous people in the neo-liberal world order. It highlights that there are still aspects of colonialism and sometimes violent assimilation, which is considered as traditional governance method and outdated. The research affirms that there are still traces of assimilation and neo-colonialism despite their counter-productive nature, practiced in the lives of indigenous peoples. The use of modern ways of governing indigenous people such as the adoption of multiculturalism and inclusive governance will help encourage innovation, development, and change of lives among the indigenous people in general and the Lumad people in particular.

In understanding how the livelihood of the Lumad people has been affected by the governance of the country and the MNCs, the research has identified the following gaps where more work needs to be done: (1) The extent of the use of power by government military force to the Lumad territory in the course of fighting communism; (2) Whether the civilians and the Lumad infrastructures were scapegoats or victims of the conflict between government and the rebels; (3) The role of the MNCs and civil society in this issue; and (4) Whether there were other peaceful mechanisms, apart from violence that the government could have used to bring about peaceful integration of the Lumad people. One of the limitations of this study has been the methodological aspect as the researcher did not manage to make field visits to trace observable facts in the Lumad territory. Deeper observation and field visits are recommended for future research.

References

Angara, S. (2023, Aug 6). Keeping track of our indigenous people and communities. Manila Bulletin. https://mb.com.ph/2023/08/06/keeping-track-of-our-indigenous-people-and-communities.

Official Gazette (1989, Aug 1). *Republic Act No. 6734*. Government of the Philippines. https://www.officialgazette.gov.ph/1989/08/01/republic-act-no-6734/.

Banerjee, S. B. (2022). Decolonizing management theory: A critical perspective. *Journal of Management Studies, 59*(4), 1074–1087. https://doi.org/10.1111/joms.12756

Asian Development Bank [ADB] (2002). Indigenous peoples/ethnic minorities and poverty reduction Philippines. https://www.adb.org/sites/default/files/publication/28025/indigenous-peoples-philippines.pdf.

Bastien, F., Coraiola, D. M., & Foster, W. M. (2023). Indigenous peoples and organization studies. *Organization Studies, 44*(4), 659–675. https://doi.org/10.1177/01708406221141

Boussebaa, M. (2023). Decolonizing international business. *Critical Perspectives on International Business*. https://doi.org/10.1108/cpoib-12-2022-0121.

Bruton, G. D., Zahra, S. A., Van de Ven, A., H., Hitt, M. (2021). Indi*genous Theory Uses, Abuses, and Future*. John Wiley and Sons Ltd.

Bruton, G. D., Zahra, S. A., Van de Ven, A. H., & Hitt, M. A. (2022). Indigenous theory uses, abuses, and future. *Journal of Management Studies, 59*(4), 1057–1073.

Cagoco-Guiam, et al. (1999). Philippines-Mindanao. *Conciliation Resources*. Accord, Issue 6. https://www.c-r.org/accord/philippines%E2%80%93mindanao/mindanao-land-promise-1999.

Collste, G. (2019). Cultural pluralism and epistemic injustice. *Journal of Nationalism, Memory and Language Politics, 13*(2), 152–163. https://sciendo.com/downloadpdf/journals/jnmlp/13/2/article-p152.pdf.

Croce, F. (2019). Indigenous entrepreneurship, society, and the dimensions of diversity: An overview of the Canadian national context. *Diversity within Diversity Management, 21*, 359–371. https://doi.org/10.1108/S1877-636120190000021017

Ferguson, J. (2006). *Africa in the neoliberal world order*. Duke University Press.

Filatotchev, I., Ireland, R. D., & Stahl, G. K. (2022). Contextualizing management research: An open systems perspective. *Journal of Management Studies, 59*(4), 1036–1056. https://doi.org/10.1111/joms.12754

Filipinas Heritage Library (n.d). *The Lumad of Mindanao. On Philippine history and culture*. https://www.filipinaslibrary.org.ph/articles/the-lumad-of-mindanao/.

Go, V. (2015, 9 Oct). Displaced Lumads of Mindanao. *Aljazira*. https://www.aljazeera.com/gallery/2015/10/9/displaced-lumads-of-mindanao.

Heritz, J. (2018). From self-determination to service delivery: Assessing Indigenous inclusion in municipal governance in Canada. *Canadian Public Administration, 61*(4), 596–615. https://doi.org/10.1111/capa.12277

IWGIA. (2023). Indigenous peoples in the Philippines. https://www.iwgia.org/en/philippines.html.

Limos, M. (2021, Feb 18). Who are the Lumads and why are they the most vulnerable ethnic group in the Philippines? *Esquire*. https://www.esquiremag.ph/long-reads/features/who-are-the-lumads-a00293-20210218.

MacDonald, C., & Steenbeek, A. (2015). The impact of colonization and western assimilation on health and wellbeing of Canadian aboriginal people.

International Journal of Regional and Local History, 10(1), 32–46. https://doi.org/10.1179/2051453015Z.00000000023

Medby, I. A. (2019). State discourses of indigenous "inclusion": Identity and representation in the Arctic. *Antipode, 51*(4), 1276–1295. https://doi.org/10.1111/anti.12542

Mushimiyimana, E. (2019). *Regulation of mining in the East African community in the context of globalisation.* PhD Thesis, University of Leipzig. https://ul.qucosa.de/landing-page/?tx_dlf%5bid%5d=https%3A%2F%2Ful.qucosa.de%2Fapi%2Fqucosa%253A34780%2Fmets.

National Museum of the Philippines. (2023). Lumad Mindanao. https://www.nationalmuseum.gov.ph/ethnology-lumad-mindanao/.

Nawal, A., & Salaverria, L. B. (2018, Feb 4). Palace defends investors' entry into Lumad land: The President's Pan is designed to protect indigenous people in the highlands from being exploited by communist rebels. *Philippine Daily Inquirer*. https://newsinfo.inquirer.net/965932/palace-defends-investors-entry-into-lumad-land.

Padilla-Meléndez, A., Plaza-Angulo, J. J., Del-Aguila-Obra, A. R., & Ciruela-Lorenzo, A. M. (2022). Indigenous entrepreneurship. Current issues and future lines. *Entrepreneurship and Regional Development, 34*(1–2), 6–31. https://doi.org/10.1080/08985626.2021.2011962.

Rey, C. (2017, Jul 15). Increased militarization under martial law threatens Lumad teachers in the Philippines. https://intercontinentalcry.org/increased-militarization-martial-law-threatens-lumad-teachers-philippines/.

Rodil, R.B. (2020, Aug 1). Angay-Angay Lang: Harmony and conflict among the Lumad community of Mindanao: Focus on the Teduray Adat. Minda News. https://www.mindanews.com/mindaviews/2020/08/angay-angay-lang-harmony-and-conflict-among-the-lumad-communities-of-mindanao-focus-on-the-teduray-adat/.

Salmon, E., Chavez, R, J. F., & Murphy, M. (2023). New perspectives and critical insights from Indigenous peoples' research: A systematic review of Indigenous management and organization literature. *Academy of Management Annals, 17*(2), 439-491. https://doi.org/10.5465/annals.2021.0132.

The Initiative PH (TIPH) Blog News. (2017, Dec 14). Raising Awareness: Lumads of Mindanao. https://theinitiativephblog.wordpress.com/2017/12/14/raising-awareness-lumads-of-mindanao/.

La Vina, T., & Vergara, V. (2021, May 27). In defense of the Lumad schools. *Rappler*. https://www.rappler.com/voices/thought-leaders/opinion-in-defense-of-lumad-schools/.

William, H. R., and Madelon, S. (1973). Cultural pluralism and schooling: Some preliminary observations. *Cultural Pluralism in Education: A Mandate for Change* (p. 13). Appleton-Century-Crofts.

CHAPTER 6

Beyond Entrepreneurship: The Iu Mien's Silver Craft Activism in Thailand

Urai Yangcheepsutjarit

Introduction

The integration of Indigenous populations into the market has been an emerging research interest in the Management and Organisation Studies field for a time now (Dana, 2015). Instead of reproducing Western knowledge and theories to analyse non-Western peoples' approaches and practices of making a living, postcolonial and decolonial scholars in management schools encourage us to instead pay attention to the particular contexts that their entrepreneurship is conducted in. They further argue that the existing economic interest-based theoretical framework developed in the mainstream entrepreneurship and even ethnic entrepreneurship fields can no longer fully explain a particular form

U. Yangcheepsutjarit (✉)
Chiang Mai University, Chiang Mai, Thailand
e-mail: pangyayang73@gmail.com

E. L. Eijdenberg et al. (eds.), *Indigenous Entrepreneurship in Southeast Asia*, Palgrave Studies in Equity, Diversity, Inclusion, and Indigenization in Business, https://doi.org/10.1007/978-3-031-54457-6_6

of entrepreneurship undertaken by Indigenous populations (Banerjee, 2022; Bastien et al., 2023, Boussebaa, 2022; Salmon et al., 2022). This resonates with an abundance of studies which have proposed that Indigenous entrepreneurship is both socially and economically oriented. For instance, Degen (2007) revealed how the Bedouin profession of sheepherding is correspondent with the maintenance of their cultural identity and claims to their land even though it may result in economic losses. Similarly, despite being restricted by the governments of Sweden and Norway to allow their reindeer to graze, the Saami have still found reindeer herding an essential part of their livelihood as it provides them with a sense of belonging (Nilssen, 2019). Other studies have further suggested that Indigenous entrepreneurship can also strengthen the relationships among Indigenous members (Curry, 2005), maintain a particular cultural essence (Amato & Amato, 2019), and preserve Indigenous knowledge and practices while also making it marketable (Comaroff & Comaroff, 2009). A balanced examination of these two forms of value is indeed usually absent in mainstream entrepreneurship studies and it is this specific feature that sets Indigenous entrepreneurship apart from other forms of entrepreneurship. Much research has demonstrated the significance of Indigenous entrepreneurship beyond the economic realm.

Based on these multiple dimensions of Indigenous entrepreneurship, scholars have proposed that each phenomenon must be contextualised within its own distinctiveness (Bruton et al., 2022; Croce, 2017; Filatotchev et al., 2022). Following this context-based approach, this chapter will elaborate on the entrepreneurship of an Indigenous community in the field of silver craftsmanship in Thailand that extends beyond economic motivations alone. In particular, it will focus on the unequal power relations between the Iu Mien Indigenous people and the ethnic Thai majority and state officials. It will also bring attention to the significance of silver as a cultural substance within Iu Mien society. Guided by the above theoretical framework, it is argued that Iu Mien entrepreneurship in silver craftsmanship is a form of activism employed to decolonise the Thai state's internal colonial discourse which continues to devalue and deny Indigenous peoples' dignity and legitimacy while living within the Thai nation. In this regard, Indigenous entrepreneurship is inseparable from the Indigenous peoples' struggle, which seeks to alter the power relations that exist between themselves and those dominant groups that continue to marginalise them.

The chapter is organised into five sections. The first introduces the Iu Mien as members of an Indigenous population living in Southeast Asia, particularly in Thailand, since the early nineteenth century. The second reviews the theoretical perspectives on craft commodification as a form of gentle activism performed by subaltern actors. An elaboration of the research methodology will make up the third section, while the fourth will reveal the research results related to Iu Mien entrepreneurship in silver craftsmanship with an emphasis on craft activism, or "craftivism". The last section concludes that Indigenous entrepreneurship is an emerging form of social activism led by Indigenous members themselves in order to deconstruct the dominant discourse and practices that continue to marginalise them today.

Who Are the Iu Mien?

The Iu Mien is an Asian Indigenous group that mostly resides throughout various regions in China and Mainland Southeast Asia. Linguistically, they are classified as a subgroup of the Mien, who are in turn considered a subgroup of the Yao[1] (Pourret, 2002). Drawing from Andrew Gray's conception of indigeneity in the Asian context (Baird, 2016), the Iu Mien, regardless of their current place of residence, are all considered Indigenous people as they are recognised as a "colonised people", or a group that has been oppressed over long periods of time by one or various dominant groups. In Thailand, the Iu Mien's experience of internal colonisation and marginalisation is indifferent from other Indigenous groups living in the highlands of Northern Thailand. However, Thailand has never officially recognised that there are Indigenous peoples living in Thailand despite its ratification of the United Nations Declaration on the Rights of Indigenous Peoples in 2007. Similarly, members of the Iu Mien residing in other countries such as China (Litzinger, 2000), Vietnam, Laos, and the West (MacDonald, 1993) have all experienced some form of marginalisation. One way to overcome this state of inferiority is prosperity.

1 "Yao" is an exonym used in the Chinese language when referring to the four groups of the Yao people, who call themselves "Mien", "Kim Mun", "Byau Min", and "Yau Min" (Pourret, 2002). Therefore, the Iu Mien will also sometimes refer to themselves as Yao. However, this study uses the term "Iu Mien" instead as it is the autonym preferred by them.

Having descended from China—the world's silver market provoked the birth of global trade since history (Flynn & Giráldez, 2019), to Northern Thailand, the Iu Mien religious practices and belief is underpinned by silver holdings. According to Kandre (1991), the Iu Mien associate silver to every aspect of their lives as it is believed that it guarantees their prosperity and well-being in both this life and the afterlife. He further proposed that due to this aspect, the Iu Mien's choice of trade is more significant than other neighbouring groups. Despite not knowing the exact time when they began to form connections with this metal, their cultural practices tell us that they have long known, used, and traded the metal (Chanbamrung, 1991; Pourret, 2002). Although silver has a lesser economic value than gold, to the Iu Mien, silver is much more culturally valuable and meaningful. To them, silver is not simply a monetary medium, but possesses a life or spirit that brings forth prosperity and status to the possessors. Owning or engaging with silver is therefore essential for keeping the spirit of wealth within oneself for fortune and prosperity (L. Seatern, personal communication, December 5, 2022). It is possible that these particular beliefs and practices resulted in an increase in wealth accumulation, allowing them to expand beyond China and into Southeast Asia in the early nineteenth century, a period prior to the formation of new modern nation-states in the region. Tsan et al. (2016) observed that Iu Mien chiefs have long engaged in the interethnic hill-valley trade system in Mainland Southeast Asia, and according to Siamese archival records studied by Mallikamarl (2022), they were well recognised by various neighbouring principalities, in particular the Siamese Kingdom who claimed sovereignty over this Upper Mekong region. Several of these archival records prove interesting. Firstly, the Iu Mien's presence in Mainland Southeast Asia was well recognised by the tributary principalities in this region, especially the Siamese kingdom perceived them as its "citizens with a distinctive language" (พลเมืองต่างภาษา), meaning that they were recognised for their cultural distinctiveness rather than minority status. Secondly, the Iu Mien were perceived as economically well-established, resulting in the Siamese kingdom taxing them at higher rates compared to other neighbouring groups. This marks them a different class from other highlander groups. Thirdly, the archival records reveal a close relationship between Iu Mien communities and the Siamese military during the time when quasi-military Chinese refugee gangs invaded parts of the Upper Mekong region during the Haw War from 1885 to 1890. Acquainting themselves closely with these Chinese gangs, members of the Iu Mien served as spies for the Siamese military, volunteered as soldiers to fight against the gangs and supplied Siamese soldiers with rice and other basic necessities. Within this context, strong relationships between the Iu Mien and the Siamese kingdom were established and strengthened. Based on such historical accounts, the presence of the Iu Mien was not perceived as an alien threat to Siamese sovereignty, but rather as a mechanism that facilitated Siamese domination over the region.

However, later on, such perceptions and the relationships that were built upon them gradually changed, especially after the formation of the modern Thai nation-state in the late nineteenth century. The modern nation-state began labelling them with negative identifications as found in official reports written by local authorities (Rangsiyanan & Naowakarn, 1925). Although the Iu Mien were described as descending from China, their racial/ethnic characteristics were not considered to be of Chinese origin due to their perceived primitive ways of life. Similarly, official records during the creation of the Siamese nation-state also identified them as the "Other within" (Winichakul, 2000); a people that were inferior to the ethnic majority and thus deemed insignificant in relation to the process of modern nation-state building and security. It remained like this until the Cold War era, when conflicts broke out between the Thai government and the Communist Party of Thailand (CPT), who began to use the remote areas in the jungles as bases to fight against the government. Indeed, this situation placed the livelihoods of the Iu Mien in between these two competing powers. The Iu Mien would eventually strategically take sides with the dominant actor, and later be forcefully relocated from their mountain homes to the lowlands for a new episode of their lives fully under the state's control. Since then, the Iu Mien and other Indigenous populations in the uplands of Northern Thailand have become the subjects of the state's hegemonic discourse relating to the "Chao Khao" or "hill tribe problem" (Burutpat, 1975). According to this discourse, particular problems of the nation were referred to as "Hill tribe problems", encompassing issues relating to opium, primitivity, poverty, and national security (Bhruksasri, 1989; Krajaejun, 2007; United Nations, 1967). This hegemonic discourse was created by the state apparatus in order to legitimise its power over them. Often through development programmes, they were "domesticated" (McCaskill & Kampe, 1997) to the state's nationalist ideology, which emphasised the three pillars of the Thai nation, Buddhism, and Monarchy. Citizenship was granted and basic infrastructure constructed as negotiation techniques to lure them away from the influence of the CPT. Those Iu Mien and other Indigenous members who moved down to the lowland areas were classified as "good hill tribes" according to the government's plan, while "bad hill tribes" were those residing in the jungles with the CPT (Hearn, 1974 in Leepreecha et al., 2018). The Iu Mien living at Ban Huay Sanoa in the district of Pua, Nan Province was one of the communities displaced from the mountains to live under the government's control (Leepreecha et al., 2018). Many of them fought in order to confirm their loyalty to the state (Baird, personal communication, September 11, 2023). Nearby Iu Mien communities also demonstrated their loyalty to the state by presenting and gifting a Thai flag made of their traditional embroidery to King Rama IX during his visit to Phayao Province in the late 1960s. "*We had no choice. If we didn't do so, we would have been easily attacked by the authorities*" (K. Srisombat, personal communication, December 15, 2022).

It is worth noting here that without the CPT's uprising, the Thai state and monarchy would not have valued this classification of Indigenous populations in Thailand and would never have allowed them Thai citizenship. However, as Vaddhanaphuti (2005) has argued, the state's policy towards them is still a "selective integration", in which not all aspects of theirs are fully embraced, rather, many critical aspects that are relevant to their rights,[2] legitimacy, and dignity are often purposively ignored and/or excluded. The point is that the hegemonic discourse of "hill tribe" and "hill tribe problems" did not end with the conclusion of the Cold War era. It continues to freeze them in such Cold War narratives and images via daily life interactions, textbooks, development discourse, social media, and even in the tourism industry (Cohen, 1986). This demonstrates that the Thai state continues to marginalise this group of Thai people in the country. As a result, some of them, especially the younger generations, have sought to instead uphold their Thai identity in order to improve their position within the unequal power relations the embed mainstream Thai society. On the other hand, Indigenous leaders seem to have maintained resiliency in protecting their distinctive indigeneity in order to decolonise such mainstream knowledge and practices about themselves and achieve equal power or rights in relation to the Thai majority.[3] This

[2] Especially the right to land and other national resources (Witthayapak & Baird, 2018).

[3] It is of the opinion of the author that the Indigenous people's struggle in Thailand does not aim for self-determination nor self-governance such as what is found in the

can be seen in the 1991 occasion when representatives of each Indigenous group came together to establish the Inter Mountain Peoples Education and Culture in Thailand Association (IMPECT) and later the Indigenous Peoples Network in Thailand in 2007, who would later collaborate with the Asian Indigenous Peoples Pact (AIPP) (Leepreecha, 2019; Morton & Baird, 2019) in order to pressure the Thai government to issue a legal framework that would promote and protect their Indigenous knowledge, culture, and rights to cultivate and live on their ancestral lands. However, our focus here is not the movement conducted by these networks but rather the emerging phenomenon of Indigenous entrepreneurs.

Over the last decade, I have observed that there has been an increase in social activism via the economic sphere, which is led by Indigenous entrepreneurs in Thailand. Many scholars in fact have accounted for the high level of agency of Indigenous entrepreneurs in competing with others in different economic fields, however, their analyses focused solely on economic motivations and outcomes (Cohen, 2000; Saeju, 2014; Sasitranon, 2017; Takaeng, 2017; Trupp, 2020; Yun, 2010). To move beyond this scholarship, this chapter therefore seeks to demonstrate that the participation of Iu Mien in the Ban Huay Sanoa's silver craft entrepreneurship programme can be considered as a gentle form of social activism. Based on this account, I find it useful to review a few perspectives on craft commodification undertaken by subaltern populations as a means of decolonising dominant forms knowledge and practices that have until now marginalised them.

Perspectives on Craft Commodification as a Gentle Form of Decolonial Activism

Besides its use and exchange value, crafts are a site of self-expression (Campbell, 2005) and can even be considered as a gentle form of social activism (Corbett, 2017; Fitzpatrick, 2018). Historically, crafts have been considered a form of activism since the industrial revolution in the nineteenth century, when human creativity and labour were replaced by machines. As a result, producers and consumers of craft commodities during those times can no longer be explained merely by conventional

European colonial context, but rather for equal rights and dignity alongside the Thai ethnic majority.

economic perspectives. Originally, the idea of utilising crafts as a form of activism was strictly anti-capitalist in nature until it began to be applied by subaltern actors and activists in the field of politics, feminism, and environmentalism (ibid.). Besides this historical importance of craftsmanship, Bourdieu's theory of cultural production describes a distinctive mode of production which seeks to explain why cultural products such as crafts are more powerful than non-cultural products. He asserts that the field of cultural production gains its power due to the required high level of cultural capital (knowledge, creativity, intelligence), which is absent in the field of non-cultural production, where power is monopolised by those who hold the most economic capital (Bourdieu, 1993 in Hesmondhalgh, 2006). Thus, due to this powerful aspect of craftsmanship, subaltern actors widely use it as a gentle form of social activism referred to as "craft activism" or "craftivism",[4] which has commonly been mobilised by social activists across the globe to combat capitalism and dictatorships, as well as to address inequality in gender relations and promote environmental justice. Betsy Greer (2017 in Fitzpatrick, 2018) defined craftivism as a way of voicing opinions through creativity which makes one's voice stronger and compassion deeper. Furthermore, she views craftivism as a social process of collective empowerment, action, expression, and negotiation as it invites people to ask questions, reflect, and change (Greer, 2006 in Bratich & Brush, 2011). Similarly, Corbett defined the objectives of craftivists that if one wants to tackle injustice and help create long-lasting positive change, he or she must not make simply crafts but craftivist object (Corbett, 2017, p. 3). She further distinguished it from conventional forms of social activism in three ways: (i) craftivism is not aggressive and loud but focuses on a gentle form of protesting, (ii) it pursues a slow and mindful form of activism, and (iii) it is a powerful tool for change. In her same work, she provided many historical examples of craftivism; one of which illuminates the actions of female political prisoners in Chile who utilised craft commodities to help bring down Augusto Pinochet's military dictatorship from 1973–1990 and another regarding the Suffragettes who crafted and commoditised outfits and fashion accessories in three significant colours: purple, white, and green, which represented women's loyalty (white), purity (purple), and hope (green) in politics.

[4] This specific term is coined by Betsy Greer in 2003 (Fitzpatrick, 2018, p. 3).

In this respect, craftivism reflects the agency of the subaltern in taking their own struggles to the public through two significant means: crafts (culture) and the market (economy). It is through the workings of the market that facilitate the movement greater than craft alone. This proves that the commodification of things is not merely an economic practice but rather the beginning of other activities as well (Miller, 1995), as suggested by the above examples.

Through this lens, craftivism takes on a decolonial perspective in which subaltern populations, including Indigenous peoples attempt to struggle against colonial hegemony. Bastien et al. (2023) define decolonisation as the process of suspending the marginalisation of Indigenous peoples. Maori scholar, Tuhiwai Smith (1999) has argued that decolonisation concerns the recovering of Indigenous histories, acknowledging their place in the world, and moving beyond the legacy of colonialism. Similarly, Indigenous scholar and activist Simpson (2017) insisted that decolonisation is a means of reclaiming our territories, revitalising our languages, and rematriating our cultures. Furthermore, the works of scholars in management and organisation studies have suggested that decolonisation also includes changing the Western worldview towards Indigenous peoples, valuing their knowledge, and drawing to a close the continued favouring of Western epistemology as the ultimate source of knowledge (Banerjee, 2022; Boussebaa, 2022; Bastien et al., 2023; Filatotchev et al., 2022). Based on these perspectives, at its core, decolonisation centres on the reclaiming of agency, identity, and power of subaltern populations from dominant forces. This combination of decolonial theory with the concept of craftivist commodification is therefore used as a guide in the exploration of the silver crafts entrepreneurship of the Iu Mien in Ban Huay Sanao, and which reaches beyond conventional economic interest approaches.

Research Methodology

The research was conducted from 2020 to 2023 in the northern province of Nan at two fieldwork sites. The first is Ban Huay Sanao, located on the outskirts of Pua District, Nan Province. The second consists of the silver craft shops and factories owned by Iu Mien individuals which are located both within the community as well as in the towns of Pua and Muang Nan, the capital city of Nan Province. Moreover, within the city of Muang Nan, participant observation was conducted at the public fairs relating to silver and the Iu Mien. These include the Silver and Textile Festival 2021, the Iu Mien Cultural Festival and Conference 2022, and the World's Iu Mien Cultural Festival and Conference 2023 (Fig. 6.1).

As this study follows the qualitative research approach, the data was mainly collected using two methods: (i) the archival research method and (ii) ethnographic methods, particularly semi-structured interviews and participant observation.

Archival Research Method

This method involves the study of documents and texts relevant to the topic. These are not only limited to those in paper-form, but also consist of digital texts that originate from electronic databases, emails, and webpages. This approach also includes extracting data and evidence from these original archives. This method is usually carried out by historians; however, it has now become more widely employed by scholars in other fields as a tool to complement other research methods. The data extracted from these original texts are meaningful in the sense that they provide primary data for scholars to better understand existing phenomena (Ventresca & Mohr, 2002). This method is used to collect data from historical documents and texts stored at the Siam Society which are available online at their website. The chapter is also shaped by former literature both in Thai and English that is related to Indigenous entrepreneurship, the Iu Mien people, and silver.

Ethnographic Method

Following the anthropological method, I conducted extensive ethnographic fieldwork several times from 2020 to 2023. According to this method, the researcher's presence of "being there at the research site" over a period of time in order to understand the relationships people have among each other and their surroundings is described in the Geertzian sense as "think description". It involves the researcher's participation, observation, and interpretation of the data collected (Naidoo, 2015). Practically, it includes various strategies starting from the most formal and engaging form of participation such as formal interviews to less formal methods such as semi-structured interviews, participant observation, and observation from the sidelines (Adams, 2015). However,

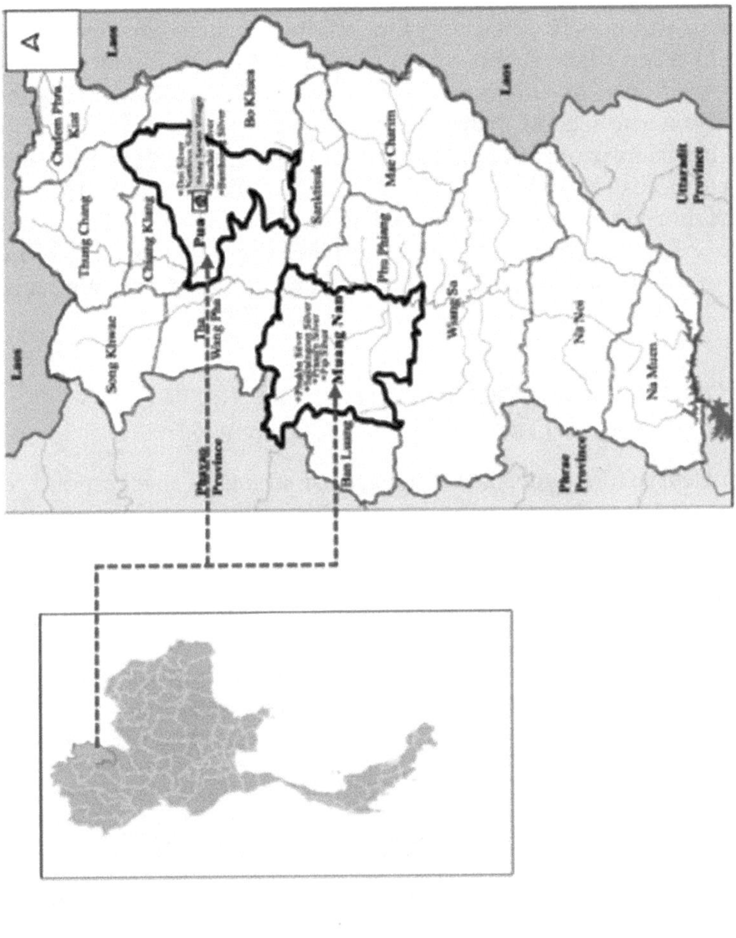

Fig. 6.1 The map of Thailand (left) shows Nan Province (right) and the two districts of Pua and Muang Nan where research was conducted

for this study, only semi-structured interviews and participant observation were crucial for data collection. Semi-structure interviews allowed me to shape my interactions with the interviewees in a more relaxed and engaging manner. Respondents consisted of five main groups: (i) twelve Iu Mien silver crafts entrepreneurs, (ii) two specialists (non-Iu Mien) assisting the entrepreneurs' craft business, (iii) ten craft producers, both Iu Mien and non-Iu Mien, (iv) four spiritual leaders knowledgeable about the Iu Mien's beliefs and rituals related to silver, and (v) six local government officials. All interviews were conducted in Thai. Participant observation was the second main source of information, which involved active looking, improving memory, informal interviewing, [and] writing detailed field notes (Kawulich, 2005, p. 2). This method allowed me to rely on the five senses to perceive and describe important events and people, especially when observing and attending the activities held at the Iu Mien entrepreneurs' factories and shopping centres, trade fairs, and exhibitions.

Results: Indigenous Entrepreneurship as a Decolonial Practice

Iu Mien entrepreneurs undertake three activist strategies that respond to and seek to reshape the power relations with mainstream Thai people and state officials, as well as deconstruct the state's hegemonic discourse. The first strategy is their entrepreneurial activity of crafting and marketing their silver crafts that effectively increases their visibility and reputation in Nan Province as the leading entrepreneurs in the Nan silver crafts industry. The second consists of the entrepreneurs' practice of gifting silver crafts to the Thai royal monarchy. The last concerns their practice of naming their silver crafts companies and museums. Each of which is elaborated upon below.

Taking Silver Crafts to Market

Ban Huay Sanoa was founded in 1968 by two displaced Iu Mien communities; those relocated by the Thai government from various districts in Nan Province as described earlier, and those who escaped from political conflict in Laos.[5] The village is part of the Paklang community, a former refugee camp reserved for the "hill tribes" during the CPT conflict. Finding limited job opportunities in the lowlands, a few entrepreneurial silversmiths in the village adapted their traditional silver craftsmanship to produce small silver items that responded to a small group of customers who visited and worked in the community. They would soon later expand their business beyond the village. After decades of crafting and trading, this village has gradually transformed itself economically from a refugee village to a silver crafts village. Moreover, with the development of their expertise and entrepreneurship, Nan Province has now become a 92.5 silver crafts[6]

Besides the increasing demand for silver crafts in the Thai market in the 1970s, the accumulated knowledge and skills of silver craftsmanship was crucial in the transformation of the village. Instead of supplying their own traditional silverware products to fellow Iu Mien, a few silversmiths led by Laopha and his family began to use their accumulated silver coins and ingots to craft modern products. This shift in focus allowed them to not only connect with the mass market but with the monarchy as well. Continuing their relationship with the Siamese monarchy that past Iu Mien entrepreneurial leaders began in the nineteenth century (National Archives of Thailand in Mallikamarl, 2022), Kamol Seatern presented a silver gift to King Rama IX in 1976 (Leepreecha et al., 2018) (Fig. 6.2).

It was this unique gift that resulted in Queen Sirikit calling to meet five Iu Mien silversmiths[7] in person several times during the late 1970s at the Phuping Palace in the nearby province of Chiang Mai. In 1978, the Queen recruited them to work at Suan Chitlada, part of the Dusit Palace in Bangkok, under her organisation, the Foundation for the Promotion of Supplementary Occupations and Related Techniques of Her Majesty Queen Sirikit of Thailand, for a few years before three of them, including Kamol, resigned in order to pursue their own work based in their

[5] Having experienced similar conditions during the Cold War, a few Iu Mien families from Xayaburi, Laos escaped to Thailand in 1972 (three years before the victory of the Pathed Lao in 1975) and sought refuge in Huay Sanoa Village.

[6] The figure "92.5" indicates the purity of sterling silver used in making a product, meaning that a product is constituted of 92.5% silver and 7.5% alloy, the global standard of any silver commodity.

[7] The five Iu Mien silversmiths were all men and close relatives; namely Kamol Seatern, Chantong Seatern, Banthoeng Seatern, and Laopa Seatern (Doi Silver, 2016).

Fig. 6.2 Kamol Seatern in conversation with King Rama IX (right) after offering his silver gift to him during the King's visit to their community on February 12, 1976 (Photo by Royal Palace Office [Leepreecha et al., 2018, p. 194])

community in Nan Province (Doi Silver, 2016). Since their return, silver craftsmanship, originally a male-dominated activity in Iu Mien society, transformed into a livelihood that all genders and ages could pursue. The other two, Laopha and Pichai, being disabled[8] remained working at the palace until they reached an advanced age; Laopha having served the longest in the palace. Meeting him in 2022, he proudly shared his memories as a "royal goldsmith" via photographs, books, and a uniform with Queen Sirikit's insignia. For the Iu Mien and other Indigenous peoples, the Queen is the patron of their craft products. Without her interest and attention, state officials would not have supported them so wholeheartedly. In this context, many Indigenous populations in Thailand associate the patronage of the monarchy, the sovereign of Thailand, to a means of shifting the balance of power in their favour in relation to state officials and most mainstream Thais who often perceive and treat them as of lower status. Thus, both gifting and serving are therefore not primarily intended for economic opportunities alone but more importantly for accumulating power and a state of exception that frees them from government harassment. Silver crafts, as one of the monarchy's items used to

[8] Laopha is deaf while Pichai was handicapped and passed away a few years ago (W. Seatern, personal communication, November 10, 2022).

denote civilisation, wealth, and power, has therefore become an effective medium for the Iu Mien to establish and maintain their relationship with the monarchy.

After leaving the Queen's foundation, the entrepreneurs began to buy old crafted silverware and ingots[9] at cheap prices from the Laotian Hmong and Iu Mien refugees at nearby refugee camps as well as started to recruit fellow villagers to work with them (K. Seatern, personal communication February 4, 2022) and sent their descendants to gain craft skills by working for the Queen's craft project in Bangkok (S. Kittipanitnan, personal communication, November 6, 2022). Later on, both groups of these recruited silversmiths became the second wave of entrepreneurs whose businesses grew both in terms of production and distribution (Uttaradit Rajabhat University, 2003). According to Charatsangpetch (1992), by the early 1990s, silver craftsmanship had become already the primary source of income for the Iu Mien in Ban Huay Sanao. To commoditise their crafts, some entrepreneurs continued to offer their silver craft products to members of the royal family, especially Her Majesty Queen Sirikit during the 1980s and Her Royal Highness Princess Sirindhorn since the 1990s. Meanwhile, according to a silver craft entrepreneur, at this time the production of silver crafts in Huay Sanao began to expand to the nearby villages of Huay Li and Baan Klang Pattana. Furthermore, a Hmong entrepreneur married to an Iu Mien woman, recollected that it was this initiative of the Iu Mien at Huay Sanao that led to a total of fifty-two entrepreneurs of mainly Iu Mien descent to form the first silver shopping centre in Nan Province called the "Chompoo Phukha Silver and Handicrafts Cooperative" in 1993 and later bought, taken over and renamed Phukha Silver by him and his wife in 1998 for 40 million bath (approximately USD 1,157,571) (T. Wannawiphusit, personal communication, March 25, 2021).

At this point, many silver entrepreneurs started to establish their own family-owned businesses by constructing showrooms and formal factories that would later attract many clients and visitors from within the country and later abroad. This economic growth led Princess Sirindhorn to visit Phukha Silver in 2004 and the silver village of Baan Klang Pattana the following year. Many of them offered silver crafts to her. Soon later

[9] These silverware and ingots were of very high quality, thus refugees carried them while escaping from Laos to Thailand.

the Princess sponsored a local school to launch an extra silver craftsmanship class. Having seen the princess's interest in such craft field, an Iu Mien couple seek collaboration from the Golden Jubilee Royal Goldsmith College[10] which founded under her patronage, to launch a free[11] dual vocational education programme at their Doi Silver factory since 2014, as a business strategy to resolve labour shortage (S. Rungrajatawanich, December 25, 2020).

Alongside this rise of Iu Mien entrepreneurs, Nan Province also began to be recognised as a popular tourist destination recently with its popularisation of the concepts of the "slow life" and "creative city". This would also prove favourable to Iu Mien entrepreneurs as it became easier for them to seek out business opportunities, especially after their silver crafts began to be promoted as a type of cultural heritage of Nan Province. Following this trend, Huay Sanao is now promoted as a silver crafts village, recognised for its exceptional expertise and entrepreneurship in silver craftsmanship (Fig. 6.3).

In 2014, the annual "Nan Silver and Textile Festival" was founded by four sectors (the Nan Provincial Industry Office, the Nan Provincial Commercial Office, the Nan Textile Cluster and the Nan Silver Cluster). Data from my participation in the 7th Silver and Textile Fair in 2021 certainly confirmed that the leading Nan Silver Cluster is Iu Mien. At the festival, I met both the former and current presidents of the Nan Silver Cluster, both of who are of Iu Mien descent. Tantikorn Wannawiphusit, the current president told me that there are about fifteen to sixteen Iu Mien family-owned enterprises; a few of these enterprises now beginning to expand their businesses into the gold jewellery industry with the Chinese in Bangkok. During my last visit to the field, there were shops and factories strategically located both within and outside of

[10] The Golden Jubilee Royal Goldsmith college is located in Bangkok and was set up by Princess Maha Chakri Sirindhorn in the 1980s for the preservation of crafts, especially gold and silver crafts, as well as to enhance their commodification.

[11] This programme becomes free for students because all expenses are covered by Doi Silver, this includes students' fees, teachers' salaries, and extracurricular activities that normally students need to pay for themselves. This is with the hope that after graduation these students will work for the company.

Fig. 6.3 A wooden sign written in English at the entrance of Huay Sanao Village serves as a marker claiming the village's specialisation in silver craftsmanship (Photo by Author)

the villages.[12] The most well-known firms include Doi Silver, Phukha Silver, Sakul Ngoen, Nan Pradup Ngoen, Pip Silver, Huern Ngoen, Prasarn Silver, and Lai Ngoen Nyam. Apart from these registered Iu Mien enterprises, it was also found that there are various small-scale household enterprises that produce and supply their products independently to the market. There are also two non-Iu Mien silver crafts firms, Sala Ngoen and Boonchuey Silver, which have also built up their reputation around ancient Nan silver craftsmanship. Perhaps due to the high level of competition, these entrepreneurs have contributed to the high ranking of Nan Province as an emerging source of high-quality silver craft commodities in Thailand, alongside Chiang Mai, Sukhothai, and Surin (Gem & Jewelry Institute of Thailand, 2018). However, only Doi Silver

[12] Those firms located nearby and within Hauy Sanao community are Banthoeng Silver, Ekkapat Silver, and Namchai Silver, while Doi Silver and Nanthiya Silver are located in Pua District. Those others that are located within the heart of Nan Province are Phukha Silver, Sakul Ngoen (formally known as Surachai Silver), Prasarn Silver, Pip Silver, Huern Ngoen, and Lai Ngoen Ngam.

has become recognised for its quality products sufficiently to become an exporter of its products to the international market, in particular the US and Canada[13] (Department of International Trade Promotion, Ministry of Thai Commerce, 2016). Most importantly, it has not only been their entrepreneurship that has been recognised, but also their expertise in the field of silver craftsmanship, which has become widely recognised both within the market and by the general public (Arts and Crafts International Centre of Thailand, 2012; Khaosod, 2016). Furthermore, the owners of these firms are frequently bestowed with higher economic titles when people refer to them; for instance, the term "hia" (เฮีย) or "sia" (เสี่ย), which are commonly used to denote a wealthy businessman, and "je" (เจ๊), a term referring to businesswomen. All of this is a result of their long engagement with the silver crafts market for almost six decades and covering three generations of entrepreneurs. Nobody could have possibly known that through the small initiative of only a few Iu Mien entrepreneurs in the past, a substantial transformation of several communities' livelihoods and overall group identity would occur. Due to this significant historical and cultural connection with the silver and gold industries, the Iu Mien in Nan Province have generally been perceived as millionaires.

With this in mind, I propose that the well-established silver crafts entrepreneurs in Nan Province make up a new fraction of the Thai middle class whose lifestyles and worldview are cosmopolitan in nature but which are beyond typical mainstream understandings. They have sufficient wealth for abroad vacations, support their children's higher education overseas, and have the capacity to extend their family businesses to other industries. Some of their children have also sought marriages with people from the upper and middle classes. Additionally, most of them, regardless of generation, have also strategically joined the Nan Provincial Chamber of Commerce in order to sharpen their business knowledge and increase their influence in local politics to benefit their own interests. Some are even involved with the Rotary Foundation in order to reshape themselves as caregivers as opposed to the previously held notion of them as donation recipients. Moreover, these Iu Mien silver crafts entrepreneurs are also the leading agents of the Iu Mien Foundation in Thailand, an organisation founded with the purpose to more effectively interact with state authorities as well as other Iu Mien organisations in Thailand and

[13] There are three firms that Doi Silver consistently trades their silver crafts with: Scott Kay, Royal Chain, and Keith & Jack.

beyond. However, the point here is that these economic transformations should not conclude our analysis due to the significance of silver and how it is culturally related to their identity. Furthermore, it is obvious from the above accounts that silver has also been used by the Iu Mien as both commodities and gifts in order to strengthen their relationship with members of the royal family, the main source of power in Thai society, and whom Indigenous peoples often associate with in order to deal with state authorities (Yangcheepsutjarit, 2021). Therefore, undoubtedly within the silver crafts industry, Iu Mien entrepreneurs tend to place representatives of the monarchy as patrons of the Iu Mien community, and proudly showcase their photographs with these royal figures in their shops and factories. The Iu Mien therefore recognise silver craftsmanship and their enterprises in a way that transcends simple material interests.

The Naming of Companies

This section tackles how company names reflect the activism of Iu Mien entrepreneurs, in particular as it relates to the upgrading of the Iu Mien's social status. Among the various names adopted by Iu Mien entrepreneurs, three of them in particular showcase their efforts to redefine their group identity: "Phukha Silver", "Doi Pradup Ngoen" (later Doi Silver), and "Sakul Ngoen".

The term Phukha refers to a mountain range in Pua District where most of the Iu Mien in Huay Sanao Village previously resided prior to their relocation into the lowlands in the 1960s. As mentioned previously, this firm originated from the Chompoo Phukha Silver and Handicraft Cooperative, and was initiated by a group of Iu Mien in Huay Sanao. The name is therefore truly significant in commemorating the history of the people of Huay Sanao. However, although the cooperative was taken over by a couple that did not come from Huay Sanao, the term "Phukha" is still retained, as it has already gained an excellent reputation in the market. "*We didn't name the company, but we bought it from the cooperative. It cost us 10 million baht* [approximately USD 280,000]" (T. Wannawiphusit, personal communication, March 25, 2021). Although the reason for keeping the name has occasionally shifted, whoever asks about the term "Phukha Silver" will certainly be referred to the history of Huay Sanao and the connection the name has to their former homeland.

In addition to the significance of the name is the logo of the company; the traditional Iu Mien earring that is used to represent Iu Mien women.

Furthermore, the owners of Phukha Silver also showcase their own silver craftsmanship heritage by providing descriptions about their crafts at a designated area within the factory. When asked the reasons for showcasing certain objects, the owner of Phukha Silver strongly stated that "*there is no need for us to hide our identity, either Mien or Hmong. How can others accept us if we don't accept ourselves first?*" (T. Wannawiphusit, personal communication, March 25, 2021).

In a similar vein, Somchai, the founder of Doi Silver strategically chose meaningful words for his company's name.

> At first, I named my company in Thai as Doi Pradub Ngeon and later renamed it to the shorter Doi Silver. Both carry the same meaning and intention that I want to express to others, that is, despite being regarded as inferior 'Khon Doi' [mountain people], we can engage with silver, a world's valuable commodity. So, it's our turn, we want others who look down on us, to know who we truly are. (S. Rungrajatawanich, personal communication, December 25, 2020)

This certainly challenges the mainstream perception of the Iu Mien as a "hill tribe", or those who are primitive, underdeveloped, inferior, ignorant, and troublemakers as discussed in the former section (Fig. 6.4).

Similarly, the name "Go High 'O", Doi Silver's eco-guesthouse and food service, also conveys a meaning in English as if someone is ascending to a summit. Although the owner claimed that this phrase literally means "the remaining distance to the chosen destination", I rather find this phrase alluding to the rise of Doi Silver and the Iu Mien's economic success in contemporary Nan Province. Corresponding to this account, the owner had once used this term to praise the Nan Governor who has always attended and supported the company; "As you [the governor] always respond to my invitation for opening each silver crafts fair, I thank and wish you to *kao naa, kao klai, and go high* 'o*'!*" (move forward, move further, and go high 'o'" (Rungrajatawanich, 2023).

Likewise, the company Sakul Ngoen literally translates as "The Clan of Silver". This signifies the entrepreneurs' attempt to incorporate family members and relatives into the silver clan, giving them a new identity in contrast to their previous one as people associated with opium and drugs. The silver business holds great importance to them as it serves as proof of their group's identity transformation; from being an uninformed "hill

Fig. 6.4 Doi Silver Museum (left) and Doi Silver Factory (right). The entrepreneurs were demonstrating a student's craft project to a distinguished guest, Kasem Wattanachai, a member of the Privy Council of Thailand, and his colleagues (Photos by Doi Silver)

tribe" to becoming more cosmopolitan lowland villagers. This assertion was further made by the owner of a family firm when he stated;

> Through our silver business, the Thai people have gradually come to realise that we are not *sue bue* (stupid/ignorant) but *sue sat* (honest/truthful/sincere). That's why now I no longer find our group's identity as a threat to our business, as it once was. (S. Khositpaphada, March 26, 2021)

The negative experiences faced by the Iu Mien undoubtedly provides an explanation for why these Indigenous entrepreneurs have chosen to incorporate terms relating to their own identity in regard to naming their companies. These names therefore are not just labels; they carry a specific image and status of the Iu Mien as an experienced group of people involved in the production and trade of this highly valuable commodity.

Turning the Factory into a Tourist Attraction

Similar to gold jewellery production sites, silver crafts factories in general are not easily accessible to outsiders. However, this has started to change after many firms decided to operate their silver crafts workshops as sites for learning and tourism. Both the small-scale household enterprises within the villages as well as the well-established formal factories proudly open their working environments to visitors free of charge. Two significant elements are usually emphasised: the Iu Mien's indigeneity, and their relationship with the monarchy. However, instead of providing details about the activism of all firms concerning this issue, only Doi Silver's practices will be elaborated upon here.

The photographs placed prominently on the showroom walls reveal to us that Doi Silver was visited by many elite groups before gradually being turned into a tourist attraction in 2014. There are two primary reasons that have attracted people to visit it. The first is the launch of the dual vocational education programme in collaboration with the Golden Jubilee Royal Goldsmith College for marginalised students. This garnered vast public attention and attracted high-profile visits to the factory, including former Thai prime ministers, government ministers, and members of the royal family. The programme was formed upon the slogan "Preservation, Promotion, and Invention" of Nan's silver craftsmanship heritage. Secondly, the construction of a silver museum in 2020 further attracted waves of visitors, including university and secondary school students, interested in exploring the craftsmanship heritage associated with silver. These two factors have led the Doi Silver factory along with the "Go High 'O" guesthouse and food service to become one of the main tourist attractions in Nan Province.

The Doi Silver Museum is attached to both the factory and a showroom. Visitors are typically guided to explore the museum first, followed by the factory, and then conclude their visit at the showroom. The factory premises are adorned with plants, flowers, a tall red bridge extending over a pond, and luxury eco-guesthouses that provide accommodation for guests.

During my first visit in late December 2020, Pimporn and Somchai, the owners of Doi Silver, treated me like any other visitor. They introduced me to the Doi Silver Museum, where Pimporn explained the significance of silver to the Iu Mien people throughout various stages of their history. She presented the history of the Iu Mien through their embroideries and the "Gia Seng Pong", believed to be an ancient Chinese emperor-issued "passport" for the Iu Mien to travel across various regions without having to pay any fees. She also reiterated the story of how Doi Silver came into existence as a family-owned company with connections to the Thai royal family through gifting practices since the late 1980s. Numerous photographs of these gifting practices in the past decades are showcased on the wall, not only to show their loyalty to the monarch but to also claim their state of exception due to being under the monarchy's patronage. In particular, Queen Sirikit and Princess Sirindhorn have become the two most significant patrons of the Iu Mein silver crafts economy. This practice of showcasing their connections to the monarchy is a common feature among other Iu Mien enterprises as well (Fig. 6.5).

Before exiting, there is a guestbook with a silver pen available for visitors to write down their thoughts and comments. On one occasion, I read through all of the comments in a total of eight guestbooks and found that most comments stated their appreciation of both the Iu Mien's preservation of this craftsmanship heritage, as well as their high level of entrepreneurship and expertise in the field.

Moving on to the factory, there is a small corner dedicated to showcasing craft pieces designed by students of the vocational programme. Inside the factory, Pimporn explained the presence of two groups of people: those wearing grey T-shirts are the "teachers", while the students usually wear purple T-shirts which represent Princess Sirindhorn, the founder of the Golden Jubilee Royal Goldsmith College. While walking

Fig. 6.5 Pimporn was explaining how her family members met and gifted silver products to members of the Thai royal family (left). Photo taken at Doi Silver by author. A painting illustrating the Iu Mien's positionality in relation to Queen Sirikit, the patron of their silver crafts (right) (Photo taken at Phukha Silver by Author)

through the factory, she introduced me to her students and provided details about their creative and innovative crafts projects. We then proceeded to the showroom, where various silver crafts are displayed, and accompanied by a team of young saleswomen ready to assist customers. Surprisingly, I later learned from these saleswomen that although they wore the traditional Iu Mien female attire, they were not in fact Iu Mien. The company encourages a specific dress code in order to maintain and showcase all aspects of Iu Mien identity. Nevertheless, they did express that they did not feel alienated due to the elegance of the dress as well as it now being accepted by mainstream Thai society.

My subsequent visits from October to November 2022 further led me to observe Pimporn and Somchai take turns leading visitors through the three sections mentioned earlier. This seemed to be their daily routine besides looking after all other parts of the business. Their narratives on their craft products and company remained largely unchanged from what I first learned from them. It was only the collections of silver crafts created by students and groups of visitors who paid to visit the site that ever changed. Some of the products can be regarded as craftivist as they are made with unique patterns and designs just for the sake of showcasing the company's high level of cultural capital and economic power. Some examples include a collection of silver craft warriors, a Suphannahong barge associated with the Thai monarchy, a dragon barge, and a water bowl crafted in unique motifs (Fig. 6.6).

In addition to these daily tours, since 2019 Doi Silver has also organised an annual event called the "Night of Silver Crafts" during their students' graduation ceremony in March. Professional models are hired to showcase the students' innovative silver crafts, and distinguished guests, such as the principal governor, district governor, and potential customers, are invited to celebrate and participate in the event. They are usually encouraged to dress in Iu Mien attire and wear the silver crafts promoted by Doi Silver to surprise the audience on stage. This event goes beyond a mere fashion show; it is a deliberate effort to captivate, inspire appreciation, and gain recognition for their distinct cultural identity and progressive economy. The intention is to create an allure that entices the audience and general public to embrace Iu Mien culture. The impact of their endeavours is exemplified by a statement of a Thai female elder who remarked;

Fig. 6.6 A collection of warrior pieces presented to Prayuth Chan-o-cha, former Thai Prime Minister, and his foreign visitors (left). Photo by Doi Silver. A dragon barge displayed at the Doi Silver showroom (right) (Photo by Author)

> They have been so successful to the extent that we now want to be Mien. In fact, we seem to be more Iu Mien than the Iu Mien themselves as we now like dressing up in their traditional attire and using their silver products more often than they do now. As we have embraced their culture, we have become representatives of their people. So, we need to behave ourselves with care and responsibility, otherwise, they might complain about us. (K. Jaroenkan, personal communication, November 17, 2022)

Overall, this section highlights two important practices undertaken by Iu Mien entrepreneurs as they strive to redefine their image from one being associated with the opium industry, to being recognised as individuals deeply involved in the silver industry and trade. This newly acquired image has gradually gained widespread recognition to the extent that entrepreneurs no longer need to hire others to create documentary videos about them. Mass media and social influencers now automatically take on this role, circulating their newly created image to a larger audience. For instance, a song composed by a Thai famous songwriter, Pongsit Kamphee, inspired by his experiences in Nan, serves as a testament to the achievements of the Iu Mien entrepreneurs in establishing themselves as the people of silver. The translated lyrics convey the significance of silver in their lives and the craftsmanship passed down through generations, as well as the beauty and precision involved in its production. The song portrays silver as an integral part of the Iu Mein's livelihoods, as well as to the province of Nan in general (Doisilver Premium, 2022). The song is now played daily at the Doi Silver shop for guests to learn more about the connection between the Iu Mien and silver while shopping. Another notable example of the Iu Mien entrepreneurs' success in reshaping their image as the people of silver is the portrayal of this identity in the plot of a Thai novel written by the renowned dramatic novelist, Ponsakorn Jindawatana.[14] This novel has certainly motivated numerous readers to visit Nan and seek out the silver villages of the Iu Mien. The impact of this plot in the novel has even extended further when a documentary team from the Thai Public Broadcasting Service (Thai PBS), a channel known for its inclusivity and fairness, visited Doi Silver in late November and chose it as the silver village to film a documentary entitled "Led by the Novel", based off of the plot of the aforementioned novel (C.

[14] The novel is titled "Reudu Dao" (ฤดูดาว), literally meaning "Season of Star" in English.

Boonkan, personal communication, 2022). This recognition and interest from both literary and media platforms have contributed to the growing awareness and appreciation of the Iu Mien people's association with the silver industry, amplifying their image as experts in the field.

Besides actively utilising this "craftivist capitalism" to reshape power relations and their Indigenous identity, under the leadership of Somchai, Iu Mien crafts entrepreneurs have also played a vital role in bringing Iu Mien people from around the globe to assemble at the heart of Nan Province during the last two years. These gatherings took place in order to celebrate the New Year via the forum known as the World's Iu Mien Festival and Conference 2022 and 2023. At the festivals, silver maintained its status as one of the main highlight features of Iu Mien identity. An exhibition of five well-known master silversmiths in Nan Province was organised, along with the providing of space for numerous silver crafts shops to display their own work. Moreover, many festival attendees including government authorities dressed up in traditional Iu Mien attire, adorned with silverware and jewellery. This was especially the case with women. These two occasions marked the entrepreneurs' attempt to increase the visibility of the Iu Mien in the urban space of Nan Province, which, as mentioned previously, is not considered an area where "hill tribes" like the Iu Mien should reside. They also challenged the mainstream perception of the Iu Mien by organising the festival around the theme, "Civilised Iu Mien". In addition to challenging perceptions, they also succeeded in fostering understanding, acceptance, and appreciation of their traditions among non-Iu Mien, especially among the elite. This was emphasised by the governor of Nan, Wiboon Weawbandit, during his opening speech at the 2022 World's Iu Mien Festival;

> I have noticed that you [Iu Mien] are spiritually tied up and don't conform to outsiders' preferences. Instead, you can influence others to embrace your culture and understand you. Look at these government leaders who have joined you today, dressed in your Iu Mien attire and adorned with your shiny silver crafts produced by you. Their presence today makes it hard for me to even recognise them. (February 5, 2022)

Even among the Iu Mien themselves, many have asserted a noticeable shift in how they are perceived, and now take pride in their achievements as they believe that mainstream Thai society can no longer criticise them due to their thorough integration into the capitalist market and their upward social mobility within Thai society. Undeniably, this significant change in Iu Mien society can be attributed, at least in part, to the social activism of the Iu Mien silver crafts entrepreneurs in Nan Province.

To summarise, through the silver crafts economy, Iu Mien entrepreneurs have been able to weave their network among various political and economic fields and actors that concerns both the individual economic growth of these entrepreneurs as well as their collective struggle for the recognition of difference, dignity, and their contribution to Thai society.

Conclusion

In the contemporary era, the geographic distancing or migration to periphery zones in order to escape from dominant powers is no longer applicable to Indigenous peoples in Southeast Asia (Scott, 2009). Likewise, integration into mainstream society by leaving behind one's difference and indigeneity is also not the fully preferred option among most Indigenous peoples. Armed struggle is also undesirable. Thus, the Iu Mien and other Indigenous groups have preferred the strategy of the deconstruction of dominant knowledge and discourse as a potential means for Indigenous peoples to achieve upward social mobility and increase their economic capital within Thai society.

This chapter has argued that Indigenous entrepreneurship has become an increasingly popular form of decolonial practice undertaken by today's Indigenous peoples in the capitalist era; one that transcends the basic measure of self-interested economic pursuit. It has demonstrated how the Iu Mien Indigenous people have struggled to become "someone" in the chosen silver crafts commodity field in order to contest the state's hegemonic discourse imposed upon them. Moreover, it has asserted that Indigenous craft entrepreneurship is a unique form of social activism that allows entrepreneurs to non-aggressively reach out to, connect and communicate with, and influence diverse groups of people in mainstream Thai society, with the objective of encouraging recognition, respect, and even the adoption of certain Indigenous ideas and practices by the general public. With this feature, Iu Mien entrepreneurship in the silver crafts market is both socially and economically oriented, and not socially oriented than economically oriented like in other contexts (Lindsay, 2005 in Croce, 2019, p. 367) since both dimensions in this context are correspondent to one another as discussed throughout the results section concerning the gifting of silver crafts, the naming of companies, and the transformation of factories into tourist destinations. They all imply both material and non-material interests and outcomes.

The chapter has further argued that Iu Mien entrepreneurship in silver be recognised as a form of activist entrepreneurship due to several factors. Firstly, their entrepreneurship is based on their Indigenous background and identity. The cultural meaning embedded within the practice of crafting and trading this specific metal is therefore a means of maintaining their difference. Secondly, upon being treated as inferior, Iu Mien entrepreneurs continue to relate themselves to members of the monarchy since the Cold War, either by the act of gifting, recruitment, or educational collaboration. These practices certainly cannot be considered for their economic motivations alone, but also for showcasing their relationship with the monarchy in order to change the power relations with state officials and mainstream Thai society. Lastly, although seemingly exotic and politically insignificant to crafts consumers, certain features of the Iu Mien silver crafts economy, such as the names, logos, attire, and tourism activities act as spaces that allow for the possibility for the Iu Mien to reconfigure the public's perception of the Iu Mien; from that of inferiority, primitivity, poverty, drugs, and troublemakers, to that of a distinguished cosmopolitan Indigenous group that has been particularly successful in engaging with this high value commodity both in terms of expertise and economic growth.

Certainly, it is totally understood that these entrepreneurial practices are in fact business strategies with the objective of accumulating wealth which has resulted in their ability to enter the Thai middle class, however, it cannot be denied as well that as the "Other within", these practices also facilitate the maintenance of their cultural identity, the redefining of their Indigenous self, and the rebalancing of power relations in their favour within Thai society.

In this regard, this research finds that these Indigenous entrepreneurs are in fact performing a type of activism, in which their products, either as gifts, cultural art showcased in museums, or as commodities, are craftivist products that can be considered as having a use value, exchange value, and sign/symbolic value. In other words, Iu Mien silver entrepreneurship does not solely constitute the objective of seeking out personal economic interest, but rather also contains a symbolic value relating to the Iu Mien's distinctive indigeneity as well as their relationship with the Thai monarchy, the sovereign of Thailand.

To an extent, this economic strategy may be regarded as one of the best practices among Indigenous communities where individual Indigenous entrepreneurs do not necessarily work only in groups to change their community's destiny. Sometimes, competition among themselves within a specific economic field can also lead to improved livelihood conditions, stronger relationships with dominant groups, and more effective maintenance of group identity as seen in the Iu Mien's case. Iu Mien entrepreneurship in silver crafts is therefore an interesting and challenging economic case study for other subdominant entrepreneurs or communities who seek to gently challenge the colonial discourse about themselves and creatively "craft" themselves into a new desirable subject based on their self-definition via the economy.

However, the analysis presented in this chapter does contain some limitations. By limiting analysis to mainly successful Iu Mien entrepreneurs, this chapter has understudied those who have not been able to obtain sufficient economic capital in order to enter the silver crafts market. This includes those such as the petty and start-up entrepreneurial classes. Therefore, it would be interesting if future research could focus on this area and see what silver crafts entrepreneurship means to those specific populations.

Acknowledgements This chapter is a part of the author's PhD dissertation, Silver Craft Entrepreneurship of the Iu Mien People in Nan Province, under supervision of Assoc. Prof. Dr. Prasit Leepreecha, Asst. Prof. Dr. Mukdawan Sakboon, and Asst. Prof. Dr. Arratee Ayuttacorn. The author would like to express gratitude to the two anonymous reveiwers for their constructive feedback on this chapter. Sincere thanks also go to Alejandro Alfredo Hute for editing and proofreading this study prior its submission to the editorial team for inclusion in this book. Urai Yangcheepsutjarit is pursuing a PhD degree programme in Social Sciences (International Programme), Faculty of Social Sciences, Chiang Mai Univeristy, under the CMU Presidential Scholarship and LX Scholarship.

References

Adams, W. C. (2015). Conducting semi-structured interviews. In K. E. Newcomer, H. P. Hatry, & J. S. Wholey (Eds.), *Handbook of practical program evaluation* (pp. 492–505). Wiley.

Amato, L. H., & Amato, C. H. (2019). Cultural entrepreneurship: An emerging field of study. *Journal of Small Business Management, 57*(2), 407–423.

Baird, I. G. (2016). Indigeneity in Asia: An emerging but contested concept. *Ethnicity, 17*(4), 501–505. https://doi.org/10.1080/14631369.2016.1193804

Banerjee, S. B. (2022). Decolonising management theory: A critical perspective. *Journal of Management Studies, 59*(4), 1074–1087.

Bastien, F., Coraiola, D. M., & Foster, W. M. (2023). Indigenous peoples and organisation studies. *Organisation Studies, 44*(4), 659–675. https://doi.org/10.1177/01708406221141545

Bhruksasri, W. (1989). Government policy: Highland ethnic minorities. In J. McKinnon & B. Vienne (Eds.), *Hill tribe today: Problems in change* (pp. 5–32). White Lotus Co.

Boussebaa, M. (2022). Unsettling west-centrism in the study of professional service firms. *Human Relations*. https://doi.org/10.1177/00187267221128262

Bratich, J. Z., & Brush, H. M. (2011). Fabricating activism: Craft-work, popular culture, gender. *Utopian Studies, 22*(2), 233–260. https://doi.org/10.5325/UTOPIANSTUDIES.22.2.0233

Bruton, G. D., Zahra, S. A., Van de Ven, A. H., & Hitt, M. A. (2022). Indigenous theory uses, abuses, and future. *Journal of Management Studies, 59*(4), 1057–1073.

Burutpat, K. (1975). *Chao Khao*. (In Thai) [Hilltribes]. Preapittaya.

Campbell, C. (2005). The craft consumer: Culture, craft and consumption in a postmodern society. *Journal of Consumer Culture*, 5(1), 23–42. https://doi.org/10.1177/1469540505049843

Chanbamrung, S. (1991). *Yao-Thai Yao Kwang Si sueapha lae khrueang-pradap*. (In Thai) [Thailand Yao-Guangxi Yao costumes and ornaments]. Chulalongkorn University.

Charatsangpetch, S. (1992). *Sara thang kansueksa nai phithikam khong chao Thai phukhao phao Mien (Yao) Baan Paklang amphoe Pua changwat Nan.* [The essence of rituals of the Mien (Yao) at Baan Palkang, Pua District, Nan Province. (In Thai) (Master thesis, Chiang Mai University).

Cohen, E. (1986). Hill tribe tourism. In J. McKinnon & W. Bhruksasri (Eds.), *Highland of Thailand* (pp. 307–325). Oxford University Press.

Cohen, E. (2000). *The commercialised crafts of Thailand: Hill tribes and lowland villages*. Cuzon Press.

Comaroff, J., & Comaroff, J. (2009). *Ethnicity Inc.* University of Chicago press.

Corbett, S. (2017). *How to be a craftivist: The art of gentle protest.* Unbound.

Croce, F. (2017). Contextualised indigenous entrepreneurial models: A systematic review of indigenous entrepreneurship literature. *Journal of Management and Organisation, 23*(6), 886–906. https://doi.org/10.1017/jmo.2017.69

Croce, F. (2019). Indigenous entrepreneurship, society, and the dimensions of diversity: An overview of the Canadian national context. *Diversity Within*

Diversity Management: Country-Based Perspectives Advanced Series in Management, 21, 359–371.

Curry, G. N. (2005). Doing 'business' in Papua New Guinea: The social embeddedness of small business enterprises. *Journal of Small Business and Entrepreneurship, 18*(2), 231–246.

Dana, L. (2015). Indigenous entrepreneurship: An emerging field of research. *International Journal of Business and Globalisation, 14*(2), 158–169.

Degen, A. (2007). Traditional livestock production among Bedouin in the Negev desert. In L. Dana & R. B. Anderson (Eds.), *International handbook of research on indigenous entrepreneurship* (pp. 115–136). MPG Books.

Department of International Trade Promotion, Ministry of Commerce. (2016). *25th prime export minister's awards: Beyond the success*.

Doi Silver. (2016). *Khrongkan sueksawichai khrueangngoen chuttaengngan Iu Mien*. (In Thai) [Research project on the Iu Mien's wedding silverware]. n.p.

Doisilver Premium. (2022, April 21). *Doi Silver* [Video]. YouTube. https://www.youtube.com/watch?app=desktop&v=X7DBnpGc2tU&feature=youtu.be&fbclid=IwAR0z6gOC_LYKwFYnJav-G-GBXfWqLOrGUa4gx374ZRFbb2zmUbUwfeNAM3M#dialog

Filatotchev, I., Ireland, R. D., & Stahl, G. K. (2022). Contextualising management research: An open systems perspective. *Journal of Management Studies, 59*(4), 1036–1056.

Fitzpatrick, T. (2018). *Craftivism: A manifesto/methodology*. Blurb Books.

Flynn, D. O., & Giráldez, A. (2019). Cycles of silver: Globalization as historical process. *The New World History, 3*(2), 503–514. https://doi.org/10.1525/9780520964297-057

Gem and Jewelry Institute of Thailand. (2018). *ASEAN gem and jewelry review*. The Gem and Jewelry Institute of Thailand.

Hesmondhalgh, D. (2006). Bourdieu, the media and cultural production. *Media, Culture, and Society, 28*(2), 211–231. https://doi.org/10.1177/0163443706061682

Kandre, P. (1991). Autonomy and integration of social system: The Iu-Mien ("Yao" or "Man") Mountain population and their neighbors. In J. Lemoine & C. Chien (Eds.), *The Yao of South China: Recent international studies* (pp. 583–638). Pangu.

Kawulich, B. B. (2005). Participant observation as a data collection method. *Forum Qualitative Sozialforschung Forum: Qualitative Social Research, 6*(2). https://doi.org/10.17169/fqs-6.2.466

Khaosod. (2016, October 21). Laopha Seatern, changtham khrueangngoen phu rai siang kap 40 pi thi fao thawai ngan mai khoei luem namprathai "nai luang". (In Thai) [Laopha Seatern, the silversmith who has no voice and his 40 years of serving the monarch]. *Khaosod*. https://www.khaosod.co.th/around-thailand/news_64314

Krajaejun, P. (2007). *Kan sang phaplak khong klum chattiphan "Chaokhao" nai sangkhom Thai.* (In Thai) [The construction of "hill tribe" ethnic images in Thai society during 1880s-1980s] (Master thesis, Chulalongkorn University).

Leepreecha, P. (2019). Becoming Indigenous peoples in Thailand. *Journal of Southeast Asian Studies, 50*(1), 32–50. https://doi.org/10.1017/S0022463419000183

Leepreecha, P. et al. (2018). *50 pii Paklang: Chak yot doi su phuen rap.* (In Thai) [50 years of Paklang: From the mountain to the lowland]. Wanida.

Litzinger, R. A. (2000). *Other Chinas: The Yao and the politics of national belonging*. Duke University Press.

MacDonald, J. L. (1993). *Reunited the white ox horn: Transnational aspects of Iu-Mien refugee identity* (Doctoral dissertation, The New School for Social Research).

Mallikamarl, S. (2022, February 12). *Iu-Mien in Muang Nan politics: A contribution from Siamese sources* [Video live]. Facebook. https://www.facebook.com/TheSiamSocietyUnderRoyalPatronage/videos/895670107774411/

McCaskill, D., & Kampe, K. (Eds.). (1997). *Development or domestication? Indigenous peoples of Southeast Asia*. Chiang Mai.

Miller, D. (1995). Consumption and commodities. *Annual Review of Anthropology, 24*, 141–161. https://doi.org/10.1146/annurev.an.24.100195.001041

Morton, M., & Baird, I. G. (2019). From hill tribe to Indigenous peoples: The localization of a global movement in Thailand. *Journal of Southeast Asian Studies, 50*(1), 7–31.

Naidoo, L. (2015). Ethnography: An introduction to definition and method. In L. Naidoo (Ed.), *An ethnography of global landscapes and corridors* (pp. 1–8). InTech.

Nilssen, T. R. (2019). South Saami cultural landscape under pressure. In H. Hermanstrand, A. Kolberg, T. Nilssen, & L. Sem (Eds.), *The indigenous identity of the South Saami: Historical and political perspectives on a minority within a minority* (pp. 171–186). Springer. https://doi.org/10.1007/978-3-030-05029-0_9

Pourret, J. G. (2002). *The Yao: The Mien and the Mun in China, Vietnam, Laos, and Thailand*. Amarin Printing and Publishing Public.

Rangsiyanan, C., & Naowakarn, L. B. (1925). The Yao. *Journal of the Siam Society, 19*(2), 83–128.

Rungrajatawanich, S. (2023, March 24). Kham khopkhun. (In Thai) [Thanking speech]. Retrieved October 7, 2023, from https://drive.google.com/file/d/1A80jCOVZtG_2Js8O7dB8-jQJ0Yzse9VC/view?fbclid=IwAR15PQoziGVXh8UlJ-dLNJuP2lWlFBW9uJUVITeYJPfQtYYopOP9hZ3Ma_Y

Saeju, A. (2014). *Krabuan kan klaipen sinkha khong hatthakam fimue khong chattiphan Lisu*. (In Thai) [Commoditization of Lisu handicrafts] (Master thesis, Chiang Mai University).

Salmon, E., Chavez, J. F., & Murphy, M. (2022). New perspectives and critical insights from Indigenous peoples' research: A systematic review of Indigenous management and organisation literature. *Academy of Management Annals*. https://doi.org/10.5465/annals.2021.0132

Sasitranon, W. (2017). *Strategic for expanding market opportunity about silverware products in Nan province*. (In Thai) (Master thesis, Naresuan University).

Scott, J. C. (2009). *The art of not being governed: An anarchist history of Upland Southeast Asia*. Yale University Press.

Simpson, L. B. (2017). *As we have always done: Indigenous freedom through radical resistance*. University of Minnesota Press.

SUPPORT Arts and Crafts International Centre of Thailand. (2012). Silver: Kamol Saetern as a master silversmith of Phukha peak. In *The mater artisans of Thailand Vol. 4: Gold, silver, nielloware* (pp. 79–100). SUPPORT Arts and Crafts International Centre.

Takaeng, C. (2017). *Kafae Doi Chaang: Attalak chattiphan lae kan thamhai pen sinkha*. (In Thai) [Doi Chaang coffee: Ethnic identity and commoditisation] (Master thesis, Chiang Mai University).

Trupp, A. (2020). Migration into tourism micro-entrepreneurship: Socioeconomic advancement or mobility trap. In C. Dolezal, A. Trupp, & H. T. Bui (Eds.), *Tourism and development in Southeast Asia* (pp. 188–132). Routledge.

Tsan, L. J., Cushman, R. D., & Jonsson, H. (2016). Highland chiefs and regional networks in Mainland Southeast Asia: Mien perspective. *Southeast Asian Studies, 5*(3), 515–551.

Tuhiwai Smith, L. (1999). *Decolonizing methodologies: Research and Indigenous peoples*. Zed Books.

United Nations. (1967). *Report of the United Nations survey team on the economic and social needs of the opium-producing areas in Thailand*.

Uttaradit Rajabhat University. (2003). *Prawat lae phonngan nai Kamon Seatern parinya witthayasatcbandit kittimasak*. (In Thai) [Autobiography and works of Kamol Seatern, honorary degree graduate in science (Uttaradit Rajabhat University).

Vaddhanaphuti, C. (2005). The Thai state and ethnic minorities: From assimilation to selective integration. In W. Thompson & K. Snitwongse (Eds.), *Ethnic conflicts in Southeast Asia* (pp. 151–166). ISEAS–Yusof Ishak Institute.

Ventresca, M. J., & Mohr, J. W. (2002). Archival research methods. In J. A. C. Baum (Ed.), *Companion to organisations* (pp. 805–828). Blackwell Business.

Winichakul, T. (2000). The Others within: Travel and ethno-spatial differentiation of Siamese subjects 1885–1910. In A. Turton (Ed.), *Civility and savagery: Social identity in Tai States* (pp. 38–62). Curzon Press.

Witthayapak, C., & Baird, I. G. (2018). Communal land titling dilemmas in Northern Thailand: From community forestry to beneficial yet risky and uncertain options. *Land Use Policy, 71*, 320–328.

Yangcheepsutjarit, U. (2021). Kan phayayam sang saphawa yokwen chak kan bangkhap chai amnat khong Hmong nai prathet Thai. (In Thai) [Attempting to build the state of exception from the state's implementation of laws by the Hmong in Thailand]. *Journal of Social Sciences, 32*(2), 71–111.

Yun, M. (2010). *Commercialising Hmong used clothing: The transnational trade in Hmong textiles across the Mekong region* (Research report, Chiang Mai University).

CHAPTER 7

Local Knowledge, Indigenous Entrepreneurship, and Tourism Business Resilience: An Indonesian Micro-Case Study

Kathleen M. Adams and Dirk Sandarupa

Introduction

In recent years, natural disasters, COVID-19, and eruptions of political tumult in Southeast Asia have prompted growing concerns about the unpredictable, precarious nature of small enterprises (e.g. Baker & Coulter, 2007; Biggs et al., 2012; Cohen, 2008). These issues have been

This chapter is a revised and expanded version of Adams and Sandarupa (2018).

K. M. Adams (✉)
SOAS, University of London, London, UK
e-mail: kadams@luc.edu

Loyola University Chicago, Chicago, IL, USA

D. Sandarupa
Hasanuddin University, Makassar, Indonesia

E. L. Eijdenberg et al. (eds.), *Indigenous Entrepreneurship in Southeast Asia*, Palgrave Studies in Equity, Diversity, Inclusion, and Indigenization in Business, https://doi.org/10.1007/978-3-031-54457-6_7

particularly acute in Indonesia, where COVID-19, Severe Acute Respiratory Syndrome outbreaks, terrorism, floods, earthquakes, and volcano eruptions routinely challenge the long-term survival of local businesses. Indigenous-run enterprises catering to tourists and the communities of workers employed in the tourism sector are particularly vulnerable in tumultuous times, hence this chapter focuses on indigenous tourism-sector entrepreneurs in Indonesia.

This chapter has two aims. First, we seek to better understand and highlight how certain indigenous-run businesses manage to thrive, despite numerous local and global challenges. We believe that rather than autopsying failed entrepreneurial endeavours, the analysis of a successful indigenous-run business offers valuable lessons for both business practitioners and scholars. Our project aims to unearth unique, locally honed practices that sometimes run counter to (or are eclipsed/ignored by) Western business approaches.

Second, this chapter aims to contribute to the decolonization of business and tourism studies by highlighting the role of indigenous wisdom and local knowledge in fostering business resilience. In short, we counterbalance tourism and business management's classic emphasis on Western practices, ideologies, and models by presenting a micro-case study of a successful indigenous entrepreneur whose local cultural insights enabled him to grow a thriving business in an unlikely location. In so doing, we underscore the shortcomings of blindly applying Western business models in non-Western locales and suggest the need for greater attention to (and respect for) locally informed, indigenous business models, which can help entrepreneurs foster more circular supply chains, hire more effectively, and ultimately develop more resilient businesses. Like others advocating for more culturally nuanced indigenous-informed approaches (Bruton et al., 2022; Turner, 2003; Vaara & Lamberg, 2015; Van de Ven & Jing, 2012), we emphasize the importance of historical and cultural context-specific theories of entrepreneurship. Additionally, in keeping with efforts to decolonize management literature and the production of knowledge, we have deliberately embraced a collaborative approach to the research presented here (Sandarupa is an indigenous scholar and member of the local community and Adams is a scholar from the United States). As Chambers and Buzinde (2015) underscore, close collaborations with indigenous community members during research design (and beyond) as well as greater reflexivity on the part of outsider researchers are essential for epistemological decolonization. It is only in this fashion that we can discover "a different way of thinking, being and knowing" (Chambers & Buzinda, 2015, p. 1).

Mapping the Landscape

Concerns about the ramifications of crises for vulnerable local Indonesian tourism-based entrepreneurs and their employees have inspired a small but growing flurry of research over the past two decades (e.g. Ferguson et al., 2017; Henderson, 2003; Hitchcock & Putra, 2007). Some have examined avenues for mitigating the vulnerability while others have spotlighted emergent realms for tourism enterprises that capitalize on that very insecurity, including e-commerce, disaster tourism, and danger zone tourism (e.g. Adams, 2001; Coats & Ferguson, 2013; Liu-Lastres et al., 2020; Nazarrudin & Sulaiman, 2013; Tucker et al., 2017).[1] While such studies highlight important potential avenues for addressing the challenges faced by indigenous Southeast Asian entrepreneurs and communities in tumultuous times, we take a different approach and suggest that novel insights into strategies leading to resilience can be gleaned via closely-hewn case studies of indigenous tourism entrepreneurs who have succeeded despite seemingly insurmountable odds.

In this chapter, we offer a micro-case study of an Indonesian indigenous tourism entrepreneur's family business that was established in an unlikely location at a time of political uncertainty and inter-religious violence in Indonesia, when international tourism arrivals were at a low, and domestic tourism was unpredictable. Such dynamics might have frightened outside investors, but this venture has enjoyed tremendous success, blossoming into a restaurant-hotel and recently garnering commendation from district-level government officials for transforming outsider perceptions of the area. We argue that the success of this business was largely due to the indigenous entrepreneur's application of his own "local knowledge"—insights into in situ cultural practices and social and religious concerns—in tandem with other forms of social and cultural capital (Bourdieu, 1977, 1984, 1986).

In spotlighting the underexplored yet critical role of local knowledge in contributing to the cultivation of a successful, resilient business, we hope to offer a modest corrective to some of the classic Eurocentric frameworks

[1] Authors have also explored various factors that foster resilience (Adams, 2018; Cheer & Lew, 2017; Cochrane, 2010; Dahles et al., 2020; Hall et al., 2018).

that have historically dominated industry-oriented tourism and international business scholarship (Boussebaa, 2023; Pritchard & Morgan, 2007, p. 11).[2] Boussebaa's (2022) critique of professional service firm (PSF) scholarship is equally apt for industry-oriented tourism business scholarship as he notes, with the exception of some recent interventions "PSF scholarship is not just empirically/theoretically Western but also generally fails to place (spatial) boundary conditions on its theorizing and, in that sense, assumes universality" (2022, n.p.). This chapter speaks to calls to decolonize tourism and international business theory (Banerjee, 2022; Boussebaa, 2023; Chang, 2015; Hollinshead, 2016; Winter, 2009) by embracing and foregrounding indigenous perspectives and theory (Adams, 2021; Bruton et al., 2022). Ultimately, we hope to foster a richer appreciation of indigenous "ways of knowing about and being [entrepreneurial, (authors' addition)]... that do not privilege Western epistemologies" (Chambers & Buzinde, 2015, p. 5).

While some studies have addressed the role of indigenous knowledge in community-based tourism enterprises or sustainable tourism initiatives (e.g. Butler & Menzies, 2007; Jamal & Stronza, 2009; Rosalina, 2017), fine-grained, ethnographically grounded studies examining how local knowledge figures into indigenous tourism entrepreneurs' strategies and tactics are less common. This case study seeks to enhance our understanding of the ties between successful small-scale tourism entrepreneurship, local knowledge, and resilience.[3]

Indigenous Entrepreneurial Resilience via Local Knowledge

A growing body of research is emerging on indigenous small-scale and micro-tourism entrepreneurs in Southeast Asia, beginning with Dahles and Brass' (1999) landmark edited volume, which presented

[2] Scholars have suggested various avenues as correctives for Eurocentrism in tourism studies. Some advocate paradigm shifts (Winter, 2009), whereas others propose theoretical shifts, such as a focus on post-colonial theory (Chang, 2015).

[3] Resilience, a concept drawn from ecology, concerns the ability to withstand stress. Here, resilience emphasizes the capacity of tourism-dependent indigenous entrepreneurs to endure and withstand unanticipated disruptions in tourism arrivals. Much of the current scholarly work on resilience is either conceptual/theoretical or entails regional or community-level studies rather than studies of individual indigenous tourism entrepreneurs (e.g. Cheer & Lew, 2017; Cochrane, 2010).

case studies of small-scale Indonesian tourism entrepreneurs, ranging from guides, gigolos, and beachside masseuses to pedicab drivers and homestay/budget accommodation entrepreneurs. Studies have highlighted various themes, including motivational factors in local tourism entrepreneurs' decision-making (Ahmad et al., 2014), the relationship between local entrepreneurs and state bureaucracies (Bennett, 2009), the narrative strategies indigenous tourism entrepreneurs employ to foster sales (Causey, 2003), and how indigenous, culturally defined gender activities enable local women to grow resilient tourism microenterprises (Adams, 2018) among other topics.

Certainly, multiple factors can contribute to local tourism entrepreneurs' success. These include the inter-linkages forged between small-scale and larger-scale tourism enterprises (Go, 1997; Tefler & Wall, 1996), personal networks, family labour, and emotional support (Dahles & Brass, 1999; Dahles, 1999; Green & Pryde, 1989)[4] and managerial characteristics, such as training, business skills, and experience (Ibrahim & Goodwin, 1986), among other factors. Numerous studies have stressed the importance of understanding the habits, interests, and tastes of foreign tourists for successful tourism ventures, often suggesting that would-be indigenous entrepreneurs are disadvantaged due to their lack of Western cultural and business knowledge (Bunten & Graburn, 2017, p. 15).[5] While such knowledge gap can certainly factor into the failure of some small-scale, locally operated tourism enterprises oriented towards foreigners, this article highlights the other side of the coin. We argue that local knowledge—a nuanced understanding of in situ socio-cultural practices, including religious, economic, and ecological concerns—is an equally important and under-studied factor in the success of small-scale tourism entrepreneurs.

Local knowledge is rooted in "specific cultural contexts, anchored in local environments, and entails deep, often intuitive appreciations of

[4] However, scholars also caution that extended family and social networks can also "exert leveling pressures on successful individuals to redistribute wealth, instead of reinvesting it in economic ventures" (Ferguson et al., 2017, pp. 173–174).

[5] See Bunten and Graburn's (2017) discussion of "knowledge movements," in the context of changing sensibilities about indigenous traditional knowledge and the information needed to successfully operate a tourism enterprise on their own terms. For the authors, knowledge movements include "the practical know-how needed to run a tourism business, a sense of what tourists want to understand, and how to manipulate touristic desire" (ibid., p. 15).

local practices, rather than analytical understandings "(Butler & Menzies, 2007, p. 18). As Butler and Menzies elaborate, the concept shares terrain with that of "indigenous knowledge" (understandings held by autochthonous peoples): both refer to ways of knowing that "have a subaltern relationship with Western "modern" scientific knowledge" (ibid., p. 17). Moreover, both local knowledge and "traditional knowledge" are dynamic, "long-term, cumulative and contemporary" (ibid., p. 18) (Also see Purcell, 1998). As mentioned above, in recent years, scholars have begun to attend to the important contributions of indigenous and local knowledge to various aspects of tourism enterprises, most frequently in ecotourism and community-based tourism. However, insufficient attention has been devoted to exploring the role of local knowledge in the resilience of small-scale tourism entrepreneurs. This case study represents a step in that direction.

Methodology

This collaborative qualitative study drew on a mixed methods approach (Bernard, 2006) using interviews, participant observation, autoethnography, and photographic documentation. Kathleen Adams has been conducting ethnographic research on tourist and cultural change in the Toraja highlands of Sulawesi since 1984. Her long-term participant observation (Atkinson & Hammersley, 1994) with members of the restaurant's core customer base (tourists and Toraja travellers moving between their ancestral homeland in the mountains and the lowland capital of Makassar) helped inform our understanding of travellers' perceptions of the business and the niche it has come to fill. Dirk Sandarupa is a Toraja social scientist, tourism faculty member at a Sulawesi university, and member of the entrepreneurial family at the core of this case study. His participant observation waiting tables and preparing food alongside the restaurant's employees, and in local Bugis communities (accompanying the restaurant owner when she negotiated with farmers and fishermen for locally sourced food for the restaurant) fostered insights into employees' work relationships, perceptions of their jobs, aspirations, and encounters with the outsiders stopping at the restaurant en route to their ultimate destinations.

We also drew on the critical methodologies of autoethnography and analytic autoethnography (Anderson, 2006; Ellis, 1997, 2004). Morgan and Pritchard (2005) have written persuasively about the interpretive, reflexive methodology of autoethnography, which entails drawing on "one's own lived experience as a resource" (Morgan & Pritchard, 2005, p. 35). Likewise, other scholars note that reflexive methodologies (including autoethnography) can potentially assist in reframing and decolonizing research (e.g. Russell-Mundine, 2012). Both Adams's and Sandarupa's personal experiences of making the nine-hour bus journey between the lowland capital of Makassar and the Toraja highlands on many occasions over thirty years enabled them to appreciate the bodily exhaustion, boredom, hunger, crankiness, unease tingled with excitement that travellers often carry with them as they make their way through the lowlands en route to upland Sulawesi. Understanding these experiences at a visceral level assisted us in making sense of the mindsets of some of the travellers arriving at the restaurant. Anderson (2006, p. 373) further distinguishes this form of "evocative" autoethnography from what he terms "analytic autoethnography." He defines analytic autoethnography as entailing research where the researcher is

> (1) a full member in the research group or setting, (2) visible as such a member in published texts, and (3) committed to developing theoretical understandings of broader social phenomena. (ibid., p. 373)

As the son of the restaurant's Indonesian founders, Dirk Sandarupa has divided the past fifteen years of his life between the restaurant (where he lived and worked) and Makassar (three hours away), where he attended graduate school and now teaches. Dirk Sandarupa witnessed the restaurant's initial conception and planning, participated in, and documented these early phases, and partook in the restaurant's growth, and the planning of the adjacent hotel, which celebrated its grand opening in 2019. His experiences of the early uncertain years, and the slow, careful cultivation of bonds with local community members and officials (who differed in ethnicity and religion), enriched our appreciation of the history and vision behind the restaurant. His analytic autoethnography (together with Adams's interviews of his parents) helped us discern the factors enabling this indigenous-run enterprise to succeed despite seemingly negative odds.

We supplemented data drawn from participant observation and autoethnography with open-ended interviews with 26 of the current employees, as well as customers (both foreign and domestic tourists, most of whom were interviewed at their final destination in the Toraja highlands), and the husband-and-wife team who founded the restaurant. Excluding conversations with foreign tourists, all interviews were conducted in Indonesian or Torajan language, since language and indigenous knowledge are deeply entwined. Observations culled from these research activities were recorded in field notes and analysed to identify emergent themes pertaining to our broader research agenda.

The research also entailed photographic documentation (Feighey, 2003) of hotel construction, employee training, daily work, restaurant operations, and holiday celebrations with the local community, as well as interactions with food vendors from the adjacent community.

Our analysis of the data collected drew on the qualitative methodology of content analysis (Fairclough, 1995). Coding categories were derived inductively from our review of field notes, interview transcripts, and one author's (Sandarupa) autoethnographic account. This enabled us to generate the thematic schema that informed our ultimate analysis, in keeping with grounded theory (Corbin & Strauss, 1990). We felt this approach to data analysis was best equipped to reveal indigenous (emic) strategies, approaches, and theories surrounding entrepreneurship.

Findings

The Road to Arum Pala Restaurant: Local Knowledge of Travelling Toraja (and Tourist) Mindsets and Preferences

Travelling between the South Sulawesi capital of Makassar and the tourist destination of the Toraja highlands entails a long, sometimes bone-rattling eight-hour bus journey. The highway parallels the coast for the first three and a half hours, passing through Bugis county seats, towns, and rural farming areas until it reaches the port city of Pare Pare. There, the road abandons the coast, narrows, winds, and bumps its way north into the hills, ultimately climbing up to the ethnically and religiously distinct Toraja highlands. Known for elaborate funeral rituals, traditional architecture, haunting burial sites, and spectacular scenery, the Toraja highlands are a major international and domestic tourist destination (Adams, 2006). The road carries buses and minivans bearing these tourists, as well as local Indonesian traders, travellers, students, and migrants returning for visits to ancestral villages. Three hours from Makassar, the road hugs the coast, offering sweeping views of calm seas and smaller islands. This stretch of the road, in the Barru District, is less densely populated than the exhaust-choked, dusty portions of the road to the south, where the roadsides are lined with shops, filling stations, and bustling truck-stop restaurants churning out fast food for the passenger-laden vehicles plying the road (Fig. 7.1).

It was on this isolated, seaside stretch of the road that Stanis Sandarupa preferred to stop for picnic lunches with his family when travelling to the highlands to visit the Toraja kin. In the 1990s, when he was supplementing his university lecturer income with guiding work, he also paused

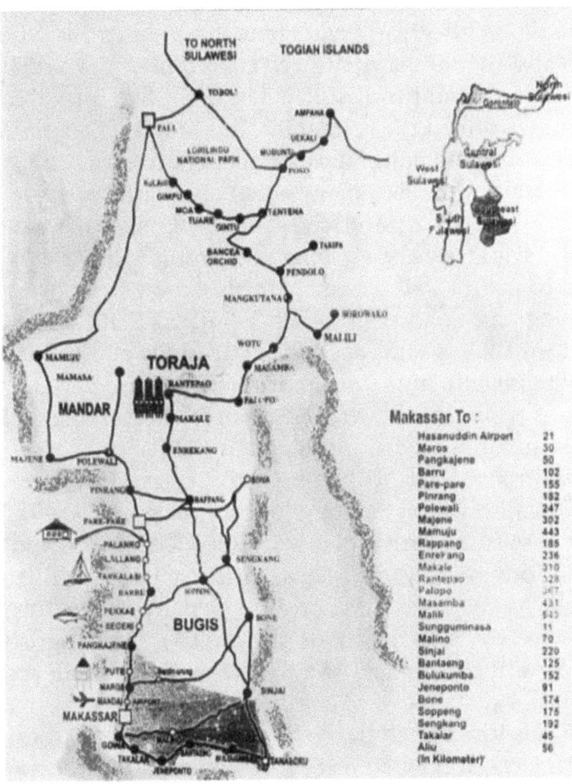

Fig. 7.1 Map of South Sulawesi, indicating the Toraja highlands, Stanis and Katrin's Restaurant and Makassar (Drawn by the late Stanis Sandarupa and used with permission from Dirk Sandarupa)

here with tourists, as the spot satisfied their desires for seascape photos. Despite the inspiring seaside scenery, many South Sulawesi travellers found this section of the road lonely (*sunyi*, Indonesian; or *makarorrong*, Torajan), even eerie. Though the road was dotted with bamboo and plywood stands selling corn or yams and several small villages were nearby (inland from the road), this broader region was home to only three unassuming roadside restaurants, several miles apart. For most, this was a pass-through zone—not a destination, or even a rest stop.

Yet, Stanis Sandarupa remained captivated by the sea views from one particularly isolated Barru restaurant and, in 2000, while passing through the area with a minivan packed with tourists, he discovered the restaurant was for sale. With great excitement, he phoned his wife Katrin and shared his plans to purchase the restaurant. They would need to sell their Makassar house and move their family of five into a cramped two-bedroom home to afford the restaurant, but Stanis was determined. Based on his own personal and cultural experiences (what we term "local knowledge") as a Toraja who, like many other Torajans, had spent a lifetime moving between Makassar and the Toraja highlands, Stanis knew that Toraja travellers and returning migrants would always flow along this road, even in tourism's low seasons. He also knew from his years of experience travelling this road with other Torajans, that Torajans distrusted the food sold in the lowland roadside food stalls and restaurants. In the Toraja popular imagination, lowlanders were presumed to run unsanitary kitchens—reusing barely washed utensils and serving unboiled water and food that had lingered unrefrigerated for far too long. Rather than dine in these "risky" lowland bus rest-stop cafes, Toraja travellers often packed their own meals for the long journey, or purchased only "reliable" snacks at the rest-stops (instant noodles, bottled drinks, and other packaged foods). More broadly, for many Christian Toraja highlanders, riding through the Muslim Bugis lowlands entailed travelling through a zone of vague unease (see Adams, 2006, pp. 12–13). Drawing from this local knowledge—in situ experiences as a Toraja with an innate appreciation of local intercultural dynamics—Stanis instinctively knew that a Toraja-run restaurant on this lowland stretch of the road would draw a steady stream of Toraja travellers, even when international and domestic tourism arrivals dipped.

He also had a sense of international tourists' predilections for sea views, based on his guiding experience as a graduate student and as the owner of a Toraja-focused tourism business (Torindo Tours and Travel) since 1996.

His instincts told him that both tourists and Torajan travellers could one day find it irresistible to stop at this stretch of the road for a rest and meal, before resuming the arduous eight-hour drive between Makassar and the Toraja highlands.

Stanis remained determined to buy the restaurant, despite the disapproval of extended family members, and his friends' cautions against the purchase. As many warned him, Indonesia was in a period of political and economic tumult, with ethno-religious rioting and violence erupting elsewhere on Sulawesi as well as on other islands. Tourism had plummeted and showed little likelihood of regaining traction. Moreover, many voiced concerns about starting a business in a Muslim Bugis area, where his family would be the only Christian Toraja entrepreneurs in the region. Yet Stanis was undeterred. He had spent much of the 1990s pursuing a Ph.D. in linguistic anthropology at the University of Chicago and assured his friends that he had systematically researched situations where ethnic or religious violence had erupted in Indonesia and beyond. His studies suggested that instances of violence were least likely in locales where one group was clearly dominant. His academic knowledge reinforced his instincts (culled from local knowledge) that this would be a good place to plant business roots.

Cultivating Neighbourly Support: Indigenous Knowledge and Rapport-Building

Thus, despite words of caution from others, the couple bought the restaurant from its once-wealthy Bugis owner (who resided in Makassar) whose bankruptcy had obliged the sale. The parcel included the restaurant—a beautifully crafted one-room wooden structure at the edge of the sea—and twelve small open-air picnicking stands (Fig. 7.2).

As soon as the school holidays began, the family relocated to the restaurant, making repairs, and sleeping together in the one-room structure. Their menu was minimal: only two items were offered: Bugis corn porridge (using the prior owner's recipe) and coconut juice. When evening fell, they discovered that the restaurant's lonely setting had not only lent itself to rumours of ghosts but also to nefarious human activities as provocatively clad sex workers (***kupu kupu malam***, Indonesian) showed up along with drunken men and thugs. As they discovered, under the prior owner, the restaurant had been a locally known gathering spot

Fig. 7.2 The restaurant's picnic stands, repainted by the Sandarupa family soon after they purchased the parcel in 2000 (Photo Credit Dirk Sandarupa)

for illicit activities (*kenakalan*, Indonesian[6]). The restaurant's reputation was so dark that even local soldiers and police officers feared the prior owner and turned a blind eye to the restaurant's nocturnal activities. Frightened, Stanis and his wife Katrin began closing the restaurant each evening at ten p.m. However, the activities persisted outside, and they were often awakened by showers of rocks pelted at their windows or, on one occasion, by an attempted break-in. Clearly, the late-night orientation of the prior restaurant was one potentially economically devastating piece of local knowledge they lacked!

Yet, other forms of local knowledge were soon to make up for this oversight. Stanis started approaching the local villagers, as well as the local soldiers and police. Counter to the classic "time is money" approach embraced by most Western businesses, Stanis took time off from the demands of establishing the restaurant and getting his tour company off the ground and began spending hours each day talking informally with the male villagers and local officials, exchanging thoughts, and simply

[6] *Kenakalan* translates as "naughtiness" but entails a far wider range of behaviour than the English term suggests. This Indonesian term covers everything from the antics of a baby, to criminal activities.

spending time together. From his childhood and youth in a rural Toraja village, Stanis understood the cultural importance of informal time spent visiting with neighbours, sipping coffee, or tea, and chatting in non-goal-directed ways, while building trust and rapport. During these ambling conversations, Stanis shared his knowledge of South Sulawesi folklore,[7] astonishing his Bugis neighbours with his rich understanding of their cultural heritage.

Stanis' wife Katrin, in turn, began spending time with women in the village, building rapport and sharing strategies for becoming more economically independent. Some of these women were widows with limited means, others were saddled with heavy child-rearing and household responsibilities, and her suggestions were generally welcomed. As Stanis and Katrin's ties with the local community, local soldiers, and local police developed and they became more accepted despite their different cultural and religious backgrounds, the illicit activities adjacent to their restaurant evaporated. They could now safely keep the restaurant open all night, eventually making it possible to capture business from the night buses that carried travellers between Makassar and the Toraja highlands.

Stanis and Katrin's approach to launching their business contrasts with classic Western approaches, which tend to be more laser-focused and deliberately goal-directed. A Western strategy for addressing the illicit activities might have entailed hiring a fleet of private guards, fortifying the property or confronting local leaders with a set of security demands, yet Stanis and Katrin took an approach that reflected more indigenous values and approaches to problem solving. Although indigenous values and approaches vary from one society to the next (and even within societies), many rural Indonesian indigenous communities (be they Toraja or Bugis) emphasize the importance of indirection and respect, that is, rather than directly pursuing one's own individual needs and goals, one approaches issues indirectly, as it is important to show respect for fellow community members, to engage in rapport-building sociality and to demonstrate one's dedication to the greater community. In taking an indirect approach steeped in indigenous values, Stanis and Katrin's security challenges were effectively resolved.

[7] His Ph.D. dissertation addressed Toraja oral literature and ritual verse: variations of these tales also feature the exploits of Bugis or Makassarese heroes.

"Learn, Listen, and Be a Part of the Process": Labor and Local Knowledge

Although the restaurant initially had little to no income in the early 2000s, the family knew they needed local support and hired a Bugis neighbour and his daughter to keep an eye on the place when they needed to be away in Makassar.[8] By 2006, the Sandarupa family began to expand the restaurant's offerings, adding chicken and fish to their repertoire. By 2008, as more buses and tour groups frequented the restaurant and business grew, they expanded the menu yet again, as well as the staff. Initially, they tried hiring Torajan relatives and high-school students from highland villages, as well as some local Bugis. They knew that both Bugis and Toraja cultural ritual demands would unpredictably pull employees away from work. For the Torajan employees, frequent funeral rituals necessitated their return to highland villages for a week at a time, sometimes several times during a season. For the Bugis employees, it was weddings that required absences of several days. The Sandarupas understood these cultural dictates and made it their business philosophy to "never fire anyone but themselves." Moreover, some of their Bugis employees were attending high school while working at the restaurant. Flexibility became embedded in their scheduling.

Ultimately, it was hard to retain Torajan employees, who found the location too far from home, too far from a large Toraja community, and too lonely. In the beginning, even their own teenaged children complained of the "creepy" locale and pined to return to Makassar. But their parents' mantra was to "learn and listen and open your minds…to be a part of the process." As their son explains:

> What I learned… from my father and mother is never to chase success, but be the mindset, because success has its own limits, but our minds keep expanding, limitless…so we are willing to learn and listen, open our mind [sic]. And that's where our father started to feed our minds through his guiding. We learned to see [respect] other cultures, ethnicities, and religions. What's more important is that our mindset has changed. As we grow older, we get more involved with the local people and help them to grow with us, too… We're not looking for something on top, we're looking for something to live on forever, not just us alone, but togetherness.

[8] There were only two houses on the quiet stretch of the road near the restaurant. The two nearby villages are not immediately adjacent to the restaurant.

In short, according to his parents' imparted philosophy, the business was not centred on profit but on growth, local knowledge, and community. Here, too, we see a non-western, indigenous approach to business, one that is not blindly focused on individualistic "success" but rather attends to the values of community and collaboration.

From early on, Stanis and Katrin were determined to establish not only a restaurant but also to make Arum Pala a tourist destination. The mixture of customers—Indonesians of different ethnicities and religions, as well as occasional European package tour groups (subcontracting with Stanis' company as their local operator)—made for cultural gaps with the rural, generally insular, staff. Stanis and Katrin became de facto cultural brokers, teaching their employees about Western cultural expectations and tastes. They also taught greetings in various foreign languages and demonstrated the preparation of several Western dishes that were incorporated into the menu. They were well situated to serve as cultural brokers, given the cultural capital they had accrued in the earlier decades of their lives (Stanis' decades of guiding foreign tourists, and the years they spent in Chicago when Stanis was pursuing a graduate degree and Katrin was working at a university cafeteria and catering Indonesian meals for graduate events). Stanis' guiding experiences also enabled him to recognize that lunching tourists might be interested in dance. Thus, they arranged for local community members to perform traditional Bugis dances to welcome tour groups to the restaurant (Fig. 7.3).

Katrin also decided that rather than purchasing ingredients for the restaurant's dishes from large businesses or the public market, it was better to work with local fishermen and farmers. In keeping with their philosophy that the restaurant should benefit local people, Katrin began buying vegetables from staff members who had family gardens and sold excess vegetables. Through visits with neighbouring Bugis families, she had become familiar with local sweets and began encouraging staff members to sell their traditional cookies in the restaurant. She approached local fishermen and made daily arrangements for the types of fish she wished to buy from them as they returned from the sea (Fig. 7.4).

Previously, local fishermen and farmers had been obliged to spend time at the three-day-a-week market if they hoped to sell their goods. Since Katrin began buying directly from them, they now only travel to the market once a week, and younger boys and teens are finding it worthwhile to take on fishing as an extra after-school pocket money activity,

Fig. 7.3 Bugis dancers welcoming tourists (Photo Credit Dirk Sandarupa)

Fig. 7.4 Cooks sorting freshly caught fish (Photo Credit Dirk Sandarupa)

something that would have been unthinkable before the restaurant's arrival.

These steps not only mean that more profits are flowing into the local community, but they also enable Katrin to control the food supply ensuring, for instance, that the restaurant's fish are freshly caught and not doused with chemical preservatives, as is increasingly the norm with long-distance fishermen out at sea for several days. As Katrin sums up, "It would probably be cheaper for me to buy food from industrial food producers, but then the food might not be safe. This way, the fishermen know they have a buyer before they do the work, and I know I am serving safe food." In a time of mounting alarm over food safety, and of growing interest in locally sourced food, Katrin's instincts to ensure that locals also profit from the restaurant have paid off, not in terms of profit but in terms of forging bonds with the community and creating a more circular economy that is community inclusive. This indigenous, locally oriented approach that does not centre on maximizing profits as the primary goal has also enabled community members to feel more invested in the restaurant.

Religion, Culture, and Local Knowledge

Although Stanis and Katrin are Catholic, they appreciated the cultural (and social) importance of Muslim Bugis practices. The worn mosaic-paved entry way to the restaurant bears a Bugis greeting written in Lontara-styled script, installed by the prior owner yet carefully maintained by the current owners. The greeting reads, "Ta pada Salama" (Fig. 7.5).

The words bear multiple meanings: most commonly they are translated as a simultaneous welcome and goodbye and as conveying a prayer for those staying and departing to enjoy safety and peace. Stanis always made it a point to indicate the words and their meaning to outsiders arriving for the first time, and his son has posted the image and its unpacking on the restaurant's Facebook page. As many Bugis visitors have commented: "These are beautiful words."

As Catholic Toraja entrepreneurs in a predominantly Muslim area, the family knew that their restaurant would not survive if it served pork, a meat favoured by Torajans. Instead, they serve only halal food, following Islam-certified methods for animal slaughter and food preparation. The family also recognized the social and religious importance of the mosques in the two nearby Muslim Bugis communities. Thus, early on, they joined

Fig. 7.5 Mosaic flooring at the entry way to the restaurant (Photo Credit Dirk Sandarupa)

the mosques in each community (not as converts but as supporters) and began making donations. They also drew on their knowledge of Muslim cultural practices. During Lebaran (the Islamic fasting month), they donate food to the mosques weekly, so that the local communities can gather together inside the mosque to break the fast with the donated food. On the day of Lebaran itself, they make cash donations to the two local mosques. Likewise, on their own Catholic holidays, they make food contributions to their neighbouring Muslim communities. On Easter, for instance, they distribute rice to all their Muslim employees. Their 2018 Easter Facebook entry explains their views (translated from Indonesian):

> What we believe does not need to be believed by others. Every religion teaches its members how to celebrate their great day. We are imperfect as human beings, but we believe there are two important things in life. First, all humans are the same (we all have thoughts, hearts, and souls). We only appear different on the outside, in skin colour, culture, ethnicity, religion, or nationality. Second, we believe that every religion teaches one thing: Love... As always, every year, whatever holiday we celebrate, we always share what we have with one another.

Stanis and Katrin's engagements with the local mosques and their respect for Muslim religious practices have earned them local Muslim clients (Bugis local officials and residents), who have been key to enabling them to maintain a baseline revenue in times when tourism has stalled. In fact, the restaurant has become a destination for local (predominantly Muslim) government officials hosting visiting dignitaries. And, in recent years, local Muslims are starting to regard the restaurant as an attractive location for family events, such as birthdays and wedding receptions.

Stanis and Katrin's local knowledge—their understanding of the religious lay of the land culled from their lived experience in rural and urban areas of South Sulawesi—fuelled their approach to successfully navigating potentially explosive inter-religious relations. Whereas a Western approach to business might see monetary and time investment in religious activities and rituals as superfluous (or even wasteful of business resources), Stanis and Katrin's approach, born from their own community-oriented indigenous values and wisdom, has helped fuel their success.

From Restaurant to Hotel

In 2012, as part of their long-term plan to make the spot a tourist destination (rather than simply a tourist lunch stop), Stanis and Katrin began constructing a small hotel. The first overnight guests arrived at the hotel in the summer of 2012, when the first eight rooms were completed. Work continued intermittently since that time, interrupted for a period by Stanis' unexpected death in early 2016. The hotel's grand opening occurred in April 2018, when eight additional rooms and an expansive new lobby and multipurpose room were completed (Fig. 7.6).

The hotel and restaurant enterprise now has 27 employees—all Bugis from the local area—and currently draws domestic tourists, government officials, as well as Muslim and Christian religious leaders. Moreover, the enterprise has recently received official commendation from Barru Regency leaders for positively transforming perceptions of the area. In short, despite the enterprise's unlikely location (on what was an eerie, lonely stretch of road known for criminal activity), the inauspicious timing of the restaurant purchase (in a period of bloody inter-ethnic and inter-religious conflicts), and the risks that are associated with being ethnic and religious minority entrepreneurs, Stanis and Katrin's efforts to launch their Barru enterprise as a tourist destination have met with success. While their cultural capital (education abroad and tourism-related experiences)

Fig. 7.6 The newly expanded hotel in 2018 (Photo Credit Dirk Sandarupa)

and social capital (connections with European tour operators and Toraja travellers) certainly played important roles, we contend that their local knowledge and indigenous wisdom were essential for their success as indigenous entrepreneurs.

Discussion and Conclusion

As this micro-case study illustrates, indigenous wisdom offers a valuable lens for insights into better understanding how locally run business can grow and thrive despite seemingly impossible odds. Stanis and Katrin's dedication to learning about and building bridges with the local Bugis community, carefully cultivating relationships and engagements with the local mosques, neighbouring farmers, and fishermen, entailed a distinctly different path than those commonly advocated by Western tourism and business schools. Implicit in their activities and actions is an approach that foregrounds local knowledge as an important ingredient in forging a resilient tourism business. Also underlying their indigenous approach is a perspective that does not place economic profit above all else, but rather features broader community well-being in the calculus. For scholars, this micro-case study offers affirmation of the value of researching indigenous approaches to entrepreneurial activities. For business practitioners elsewhere in the world, we hope our discussion of Stanis and Katrin's enterprise reaffirms the potential value of local wisdom and indigenous perspectives on how best to manage and grow a business. Clearly, what constitutes indigenous wisdom varies from one locale to the next, and the strategies embraced by Stanis and Katrin are not one-size-fits-all. However, in presenting this detailed, grounded case study we sought to offer a model for uncovering indigenous knowledge and wisdom elsewhere. For, as this case study suggests, local knowledge can be the under-recognized factor responsible for fostering business resilience.

A second argument in this chapter concerns the broader issue of decolonizing business and tourism studies. Our study offers a lens into the biases and limitations of Western business models and theories, which have long enjoyed pre-eminence in academic training programmes. As our case study suggests, a Western business approach would not have enabled Stanis and Katrin's business to survive and thrive in tumultuous times. Likewise, a classic Western-rooted approach to research would not have uncovered the role of indigenous wisdom in their business success. Ultimately, drawing from our experiences with this case study, we suggest that interdisciplinary and international research collaborations between indigenous community members, local scholars (and those with long-term experiences and rapport with community members, as well as language competency, such as anthropologists), and business researchers are essential if we are to unearth new strategies for local business resilience in tumultuous times. It is only through such collaborations that we can hope to avoid what we term "indigenous washing." Indigenous washing is closely related to "cosmetic indigenization," which Bastien et al. define as "the superficial appropriation of indigenous identities and knowledge to enhance...the image of a colonial organizer" (2023, p. 668). With "indigenous washing," the researcher's starting point is rooted in Western-based theories, which are subsequently given an indigenous hue via superficial, formal interviews with local knowledge bearers collected with the aid of translators on short-term visits. In short, it is only via deep, long-term grounding in the community, data collection in the local language, and an established history of respect and rapport, that mutually beneficial knowledge production can happen. Thus, interdisciplinary, intercultural collaborations are essential if we hope to advance our efforts to decolonize business and tourism studies.

References

Adams, K. (2021) What Western tourism concepts obscure: Intersections of migration and tourism in Indonesia. *Tourism Geographies*, 1–26. 23(4): 678–703. https://doi.org/10.1080/14616688.2020.1765010

Adams, K. (2001). Danger zone tourism: Potentials and problematics for tourism in tumultuous times. In P. Teo, H. Chong, & T. Chang (Eds.), *Interconnected worlds: Southeast Asia tourism in the 21st century* (pp. 267–281). Pergamon Press.

Adams, K. (2006). *Art as politics: Re-crafting identities, tourism and power in Tana Toraja, Indonesia* . University of Hawaii Press.

Adams, K. (2018). Local strategies for economic survival in touristically volatile times: Micro-vendors, gendered cultural practices and resilience in Indonesia. *Tourism, Culture, Communication, 18*(4), 287–301. https://doi.org/10.3727/109830418X15369281878422

Adams, K., & Sandarupa, D. (2018). A room with a view: Local knowledge and tourism entrepreneurship in an unlikely Indonesian locale. *Asian Journal of Tourism Research, 3*(1), 1–27. https://doi.org/10.1080/14616688.2020.1765010

Ahmad, S., Jabeen, F., & Khan, M. (2014). Entrepreneurs choice in business venture: Motivations for choosing home-stay accommodation businesses in Peninsular Malaysia. *International Journal of Hospitality Management, 36*, 31–40. https://doi.org/10.1016/j.ijhm.2013.08.006

Anderson, L. (2006). Analytic autoethnography. *Journal of Contemporary Ethnography, 35*(4), 373–395. https://doi.org/10.1177/08912416052804

Atkinson, P., & Hammersley, M. (1994). Ethnography and participant observation. In N. K. Denzin & Y. S. Lincoln (Eds.), *Handbook of qualitative research* (pp. 248–261). Sage.

Baker, K., & Coulter, A. (2007). Terrorism and tourism: The vulnerability of beach vendors' livelihoods in Bali. *Journal of Sustainable Tourism, 15*(3), 249–266. https://doi.org/10.2167/jost643.0

Banerjee, S. (2022). Decolonizing management theory: A critical perspective. *Journal of Management Studies, 59*(4), 1074–1087. https://doi.org/10.1111/joms.12756

Bastien, F., Coraiola, D. M., & Foster, W. M. (2023). Indigenous Peoples and organization studies. *Organization Studies, 44*(4), 659–675. https://doi.org/10.1177/01708406221141545

Bennett, J. (2009). The development of private tourism business activity in the transitional Vietnamese economy. In M. Hitchcock, V. King, & M. Parnwell (Eds.), *Tourism in Southeast Asia: Challenges and new directions* (pp. 146–164). NIAS Press.

Bernard, H. R. (2006). *Handbook of methods in cultural anthropology: Qualitative and quantitative methods*. AltaMira Press.

Biggs, D., Hall, M., & Stoeckl, N. (2012). Resilience of formal and informal tourism enterprises to disasters: Reef tourism in Phuket, Thailand. *Journal of Sustainable Tourism, 20*(5), 645–665. https://doi.org/10.1080/09669582.2011.630080

Bourdieu, P. (1977). *Outline of a theory of practice*. Cambridge University Press.

Bourdieu, P. (1984). *Distinction: A social critique of the judgment of taste* (R. Nice, Trans.). Harvard University Press.

Bourdieu, P. (1986). The forms of capital. In J. Richardson (Ed.), *Handbook of theory and research for the sociology of education* (pp. 241–258). Greenwood.

Boussebaa, M. (2022). Unsettling West-centrism in the study of professional service firms. *Human Relations*. https://doi.org/10.1177/00187267221128262

Boussebaa, M. (2023). Decolonizing international business. *Critical Perspectives on International Business*. https://doi.org/10.1108/cpoib-12-2022-0121

Bruton, G. D., Zahra, S. A., Van de Ven, A. H., & Hitt, M. A. (2022). Indigenous theory uses, abuses, and future. *Journal of Management Studies, 59*(4), 1057–1073. https://doi.org/10.1111/joms.12755

Bunten, A., & Graburn, N. (2017). *Indigenous tourism movements*. University of Toronto Press.

Butler, C. F., & Menzies, C. R. (2007). Traditional ecological knowledge and indigenous tourism. In R. Butler & T. Hinch (Eds.), *Tourism and indigenous peoples: Issues and implications* (pp. 15–27). Elsevier.

Causey, A. (2003). *Hard bargaining in Sumatra: Western travelers and Toba Bataks in the marketplace of souvenirs*. University of Hawai'i Press.

Chambers, D., & Buzinde, C. (2015). Tourism and decolonization: Locating research and self. *Annals of Tourism Research, 51*, 1–16. https://doi.org/10.1016/j.annals.2014.12.002

Chang, T. C. (2015). The Asian wave and critical tourism scholarship. *International Journal of Asia Pacific Studies, 11*(1), 83–101.

Cheer, J., & Lew, A. (2017). *Tourism resilience and sustainability: Adapting to social, political, and economic change*. Routledge.

Coats, A., & Ferguson, S. (2013). Rubbernecking or rejuvenation: Post-earthquake perceptions and the implications for business practice in a dark tourism context. *Journal of Research for Consumers, 23*(1), 32–65. http://www.jrconsumers.com/Academic_Articles/issue_23/

Cochrane, J. (2010). The sphere of tourism resilience. *Tourism Recreation Research, 35*(2), 173–185. https://doi.org/10.1080/02508281.2010.11081632

Cohen, E. (2008). Tourism and disaster: The tsunami waves in Southern Thailand. In E. Cohen (Ed.), *Explorations in Thai tourism* (pp. 23–51). Emerald.

Corbin, J. M., & Strauss, A. (1990). Grounded theory research: Procedures, canons, and evaluative criteria. *Qualitative Sociology, 13*(1), 3–21. https://doi.org/10.1007/BF00988593

Dahles, H. (1999). Tourism and small entrepreneurs in developing countries: A theoretical perspective. In H. Dahles & K. Bras (Eds.), *Tourism and small entrepreneurs: Development, national policy and entrepreneurial culture: Indonesian cases* (pp. 1–19). Cognizant Communication Corporation.

Dahles, H., & Brass, K. (Eds.). (1999). *Tourism and small entrepreneurs: Development, national policy and entrepreneurial culture: Indonesian cases.* Cognizant Communication Corporation.

Dahles, H., Prabawa, T. S., & Koning, J. (2020). Local tourism businesses in Indonesia: A pathway to crisis resilient development? *Austrian Journal of South-East Asian Studies, 13*(1), 17–33. https://doi.org/10.14764/10.ASEAS-0027

Ellis, C. (1997). Evocative autoethnography: Writing emotionally about our lives. In W. Tierney & Y. Lincoln (Eds.), *Representation and the text: Re-framing the narrative voice* (pp. 115–142). State University of New York Press.

Ellis, C. (2004). *The ethnographic I: A methodological novel about autoethnography*. AltaMira Press.

Fairclough, N. (1995). *Critical discourse analysis*. Addison Wesley.

Feighey, W. (2003). Negative image? Developing the visual in tourism research. *Current Issues in Tourism, 6*(1), 76–85. https://doi.org/10.1080/13683500308667945

Ferguson, J., Dahles, H., & Prabawa, T. (2017). The Indonesian tourism industry under crisis: A Bourdieuan perspective on social boundaries among small-scale business owners. *Asia Pacific Business Review, 23*(2), 171–191. https://doi.org/10.1080/13602381.2017.1281640

Green, S., & Pryde, P. (1989). *Black entrepreneurship in America*. Transaction Publishers.

Go, F. (1997). Entrepreneurs and the tourism industry in developing countries. In H. Dahles (Ed.), *Tourism, small entrepreneurs and sustainable development: Case studies from developing countries* (pp. 5–22). Atlas.

Hall, M., Prayag, G., & Amore, A. (2018). *Tourism and resilience: Individual, organizational and destination perspectives*. Channel View Publications.

Henderson, J. C. (2003). Terrorism and tourism: Managing the consequences of the Bali bombings. *Journal of Travel and Tourism Marketing, 15*(1), 41–58. https://doi.org/10.1300/J073v15n01_03

Hitchcock, M., & Putra, N. (2007). *Tourism, development and terrorism in Bali.* Ashgate.

Hollinshead, K. (2016). Postdisciplinarity and the rise of intellectual openness: The necessity for "plural knowability" in tourism studies. *Tourism Analysis, 21*(4), 349–361. https://doi.org/10.3727/108354216X14600320851613

Ibrahim, A., & Goodwin, J. (1986). Perceived causes of success in small businesses. *American Journal of Small Business, 11*(2), 41–50. https://doi.org/10.1177/104225878601100204

Jamal, T., & Stronza, A. (2009). Collaboration theory and tourism practice in protected areas: Stakeholders, structuring and sustainability. *Journal of Sustainable Tourism, 17*(20), 169–189. https://doi.org/10.1080/09669580802495741

Liu-Lastres, B., Mariska, D., Tan, X., & Ying, T. (2020). Can post-disaster tourism development improve destination livelihoods? A case study of Aceh, Indonesia. *Journal of Destination Marketing & Management, 18*. https://doi.org/10.1016/j.jdmm.2020.100510

Morgan, N., & Pritchard, A. (2005). On souvenirs and metonymy: Narratives of memory, metaphor and materiality. *Tourist Studies, 5*(1), 29–53. https://doi.org/10.1177/1468797605062714

Nazaruddin, D. A., & Sulaiman, R. (2013). Introduction to "tsunami tourism": Notes from Aceh, Indonesia. *International Journal of Sciences, 2*(March), 71–81. http://www.ijsciences.com/pub/pdf/V2-201303-16.pdf

Pritchard, A., & Morgan, N. (2007). De-centring tourism's intellectual universe, or traversing the dialogue between change and tradition. In I. Ateljevic, A. Pritchard, & N. Morgan (Eds.), *The critical turn in tourism studies: Innovative research methodologies* (pp. 11–28). Elsevier.

Purcell, T. W. (1998). Indigenous knowledge and applied anthropology: Questions of definition and direction. *Human Organization, 57*(3), 258–272. https://doi.org/10.17730/humo.57.3.qg0427ht23111694

Rosalina, P. D. (2017). The implementation of Hindu philosophy "tri kaya parisudha" for sustainable tourism in Munduk Village, North Bali. *Jumpa, 3*(2), 223–237.

Russell-Mundine, G. (2012). Reflexivity in indigenous research: Reframing and decolonising research? *Journal of Hospitality and Tourism Management, 19*(1), 85–90. https://doi.org/10.1017/jht.2012.8

Tefler, D., & Wall, G. (1996). Linkages between tourism and food production: An Indonesian example. *Annals of Tourism Research, 23*(3), 635–653. https://doi.org/10.1016/01607383(95)00087-9

Tucker, H., Shelton, E. J., & Bae, H. (2017). Post-disaster tourism: Towards a tourism of transition. *Tourist Studies, 17*(3), 306–327. https://doi.org/10.1177/1468797616671617

Turner, S. (2003). *Indonesia's small entrepreneurs: Trading on the margins*. Routledge.

Vaara, E., & Lamberg, J. (2015). Taking historical embeddedness seriously: Three historical approaches to advance strategy process and practice research. *Academy of Management Review, 41*(4), 633–657. https://doi.org/10.5465/amr.2014.0172

Van de Ven, A., & Jing, R. (2012). Indigenous management research in China from an engaged scholarship perspective. *Management and Organization Review, 8*(1), 123–137. https://doi.org/10.1111/j.1740-8784.2011.00281.x

Winter, T. (2009). Asian tourism and the retreat of anglo-western centrism in tourism theory. *Current Issues in Tourism, 12*(1), 21–31. https://doi.org/10.1080/13683500802220695

CHAPTER 8

Indigenous Entrepreneurship in Thailand: The Case of Gaia Ashram and Lazyman Coffee

Naida Culshaw, Natalie Limwatana, and Thao Ngo

Introduction

Operating at the intersection of social and economic entrepreneurship, Indigenous entrepreneurship "incorporates both social and economic entrepreneurial activity and explicitly acknowledges the particular historical and cultural context from which they arise" (Tapsell & Woods, 2008,

N. Culshaw (✉)
Grenoble Ecole de Management, Grenoble, France
e-mail: naida.culshaw@grenoble-em.com

N. Limwatana
Global Ecovillage Network Oceania and Asia, Chiang Mai, Thailand

T. Ngo
Global Ecovillage Network Oceania and Asia, Hanoi, Vietnam
e-mail: ngothao.kin@ecovillage.org

E. L. Eijdenberg et al. (eds.), *Indigenous Entrepreneurship in Southeast Asia*, Palgrave Studies in Equity, Diversity, Inclusion, and Indigenization in Business, https://doi.org/10.1007/978-3-031-54457-6_8

2010; as cited in Overall et al., [2010, p. 150]). Indigenous entrepreneurship is a process of drawing value from community-based resources (people, land, capabilities, culture, etc.) and contributing value back that is responsive to a community's particular set of socio-economic conditions (Colbourne, 2017; Jack & Anderson, 2002; Kenney & Goe, 2004; Peredo & Anderson, 2006; as cited in Colbourne et al., 2023).

There are underlying challenges in developing an ideal approach to entrepreneurship literature in an indigenous context (Anderson & Giberson, 2003; as cited in Molina-Ramírez & Barba-Sánchez, 2021, p. 19) due to the differences in "communal values, the link between entrepreneurship and land, achievements without economic profitability, decisions based on common benefit (Dana & Smyrnios, 2013; Peredo et al., 2004) and others. However, it is a fertile field for contributions that current researchers can provide" (Hindle, 2005).

William Bygrave (2007; as cited in Hindle, 2010, p. 605) expresses a longstanding lament:

> that entrepreneurship as a discipline is sadly astray in overemphasising reductionist quantitative approaches to knowledge creation in a kind of 'physics envy'. Steyaert (2007, p. 16) echoes this sentiment and asks the field of entrepreneurship to be more focused on local context in both its choice of methodologies and its choice of units of analysis and, thereby, to start creating a relevant identity of its own 'instead of pursuing a nervous search' for the spurious 'progress' of over-generalisation.

By taking a contextualized perspective on entrepreneurship, Welter et al. (2019, p. 321) "encourages us to see, consider, and analyse varieties of entrepreneurship that too often remain invisible to us." Following this thread, Padilla-Meléndez et al. (2022, pp. 17–19) noted six different thematic groups for future lines of research including a call to "expand the fields of research with added cases studied" as well as those which explore the "*entrepreneurial spirit* ... [as well as] analyse the causes and motivations that encourage entrepreneurship."

This chapter embraces the above aim grounded in the experiences of two Indigenous entrepreneurs (Bastien et al., 2023, p. 661). We'll highlight how context influences venture design which in turn is informed by an Indigenous Innovative approach. This is guided by the following research question: How do embeddedness and an Indigenous approach to innovation inform the initiative(s) of an Indigenous entrepreneur?

Literature Review

In this section, we present the literature providing context for the two cases which are elaborated in Findings and Discussion.

Dismembering Entrepreneurship

There have been active attempts to dismember and reconstruct the concepts around entrepreneurship to address the "limitations of the fundamental constructs" Tengeh et al. (2022, p. 7). Banerjee (2022, p. 1079) elaborates further noting that:

> when ways of knowing become hegemonic, epistemic blindness inevitably leads to forms of *epistemic erasure* that negate or subjugate alternate knowledges through discursive processes that construct them as 'traditional', 'superstition', or 'ethnoscience' (Sharma, 2021). After centuries of colonial domination that subjugated Indigenous knowledge, Western science in the last few decades appears to have recognized the potential for Indigenous knowledge to address global problems of climate change, land management, conservation, and habitat loss. (Mistry & Berardi, 2016)

With the emerging challenges around environmental and social issues, as well as the desire to transition towards more sustainable approaches, there has been an increase in studies on Iindigenous people and Indigenous entrepreneurship. Dana (2015, p. 166) observes that "Indigenous entrepreneurship is usually environmentally sustainable; this often allows indigenous people to rely on immediately available resources, and consequently, work in indigenous communities is often irregular." Salmon et al. (2022, p. 439) offer an overview of this trend, noting that:

> Indigenous perspectives have significantly contributed to academic discussions on the values and epistemological assumptions that inform management practice and research (Gregg & Wishart, 2012; Mika & O'Sullivan, 2014; Seremani & Clegg, 2016) ... [noting that] these perspectives have revealed a landscape populated by organizational forms that persist over time, but are underrepresented in mainstream management and organization scholarship as they differ in purpose (Anders & Anders, 1986; Ponting et al., 2015), governance structures (Kingi & Kompas, 2010), and their (inter)relationships with the social and ecological systems in which they are embedded. (Stephen, 1991; Valente, 2012; Whiteman & Cooper, 2000)

However, despite the growing interest in Indigenous entrepreneurship, which reveals "cultural values [that] are incompatible with the basic assumptions of mainstream theories of entrepreneurship" (Tengeh et al., 2022, p. 7), there is an overwhelming dominance of Western colonial thought whose normative convictions and ideas are antithetical to the worldviews for many Indigenous peoples (Bastein et al., 2023, p. 666). While theories developed in North America and/or Europe are founded in their own business contexts, those same theories "lack explanatory power with regards to local phenomena" (Tsui, 2007; as cited in Filatotchev et al., 2022, p. 1037) when applied in other situations or contexts. The authors go on to suggest that by contextualizing research, it has the "potential to increase the probability of management scholarship yielding viable results that can inform future research."

Considering the context of Thailand, this chapter travels in good yet sparse company. Studies ranging from Phiphatsērītham and Yoshihara (1983) highlighting the various business groups in Thailand, to Swierczek and Jatusripatak (1994) exploring more generally the entrepreneurship cultures in Southeast Asia, to more recent research focused on the Thai government's "One Tambon (Village) One Product (OTOP)" project intended to boost the household income for Thai villagers (Chouichom, 2021), as well as one on the Hmong community's Indigenous tourism business success factors (Chartrungruang et al., 2022). We follow these and other academic forebears, building a case for seeing Indigenous entrepreneurs not "apart" from the mainstream but as an influential component of the Thai entrepreneurial ecosystem.

Indigenous Innovation and "Entrepreneuring"

For Indigenous entrepreneurs, the act of entrepreneurship can fulfil aspirations for community self-determination and sustainable development (Mika et al., 2017, as cited in Mika, 2020, p. 23) while "incorporating Indigenous values, culture, language and institutions—forms of cultural and spiritual capital—into the identity and nature of their firms, their products and services and contributions to Indigenous communities" (Mika, 2020, p. 23).

Cahn (2008, p. 1) notes that "in Indigenous societies throughout the world 'business' and economic activities are embedded in cultural and social aspects, creating unique styles of entrepreneurship, which are often community-oriented, and with diverse livelihood outcomes." In Walters and Takamura's (2015, pp. 77, 78–79) essay they presented a decolonized model of entrepreneurship which is "grounded in acknowledging the past, but more importantly has the potential to create sustainable indigenous/tribal economies in the immediate future." They go on to describe the framework stating (Picture 8.1).

> This framework is based on the combination of *Community, Spirituality, Sustainability,* and *Entrepreneurship,* factors unique to indigenous peoples, and is used for sustainable enterprise creation. The overlap or combinations of each of these four factors leads to a subset of *Cultural, Social, Economic,* and *Environmental* factors, also very much focused on indigenous perspectives. The overlapping factors located at the epicentre of the quadruple bottom line result in the creation of *Indigenous Innovation.*

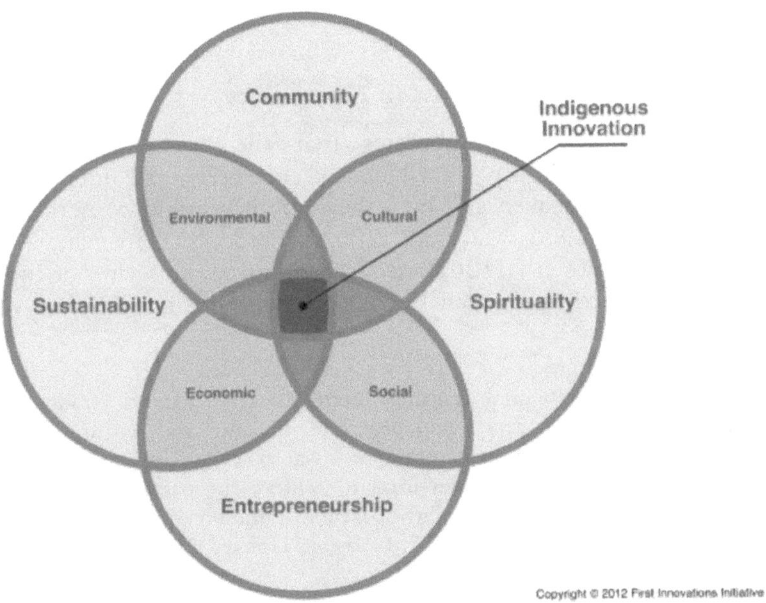

Picture 8.1 Quadruple bottom line, 2012 (Courtesy First Innovations Initiative; copyright 2012; Walters and Takamura ([2015, p. 79])

In this chapter we're also taking a turn towards the conceptualization of "entrepreneurIng" (Steyaert, 2007, p. 472) which offers a more expansive way to see the act of "being" an entrepreneur which "increase[s] the connections with new theoretical perspectives that so far have been kept outside the strongly policed disciplinary boundaries of entrepreneurship studies." The author further suggests that:

> the ultimate idea is to uproot entrepreneurship studies and to envision it as a field of creative efforts that unfold along a rhizomatic logic (Steyaert, 2005). … Taking more practice-based and relational-materialist approaches, which have been the least used in entrepreneurship studies, hold the greatest potential for those who conceive of entrepreneuring within a creative process view beyond its current, mostly interpretive, social constructionist and pragmatist use … bring[ing] the field of entrepreneurship studies away from methodological individualism and closer to a social ontology of relatedness.

Embedded in Community

Hindle (2010, p. 602) elaborates that the "community context profoundly influences both what kinds of entrepreneurial initiatives can and should be undertaken and how they are and should be performed" (Anderson et al., 2006; Mazzarol, 2007; Peredo & Chrisman, 2006). Agreeing, Henriques et al. (2020, p. 320) point to the review of Indigenous entrepreneurship research by Peredo and Anderson (2006) which noted that:

> Indigenous entrepreneurial ventures often reflect the values, traditions, traditional knowledge, access and proximity to lands and resources, and these understandings in turn influence what is viewed as an opportunity and how a venture is structured to achieve the particular blend of social, cultural, environmental and economic value creation important to the community. (Colbourne, 2017; Curry & Donker, 2009; Dana, 2007; Spiller et al., 2011; Wuttunee, 2004)
>
> [It is also] a process of drawing value from community-based resources (people, land, capabilities, culture, etc.) and contributing value back that is responsive to a community's particular set of socio-economic conditions. (Colbourne, 2017; Jack & Anderson, 2002; Kenney & Goe, 2004; Peredo & Anderson, 2006)

In the case of an Indigenous entrepreneur, being embedded both in community and land affords access to Indigenous knowledges and ways of knowing, the distinctive connection to the natural world seen through an Indigenous worldview which "is [a] contract with animals, land and the cosmos (Cajete, 2000) ... which [also] emphasize(s) and encourage(s) reciprocal relationships between variables that are often nonlinear (Taagepera, 2008), complex, related and seemingly circular" as cited in Bastien et al. (2023, p. 663).

Welter et al. (2019, p. 323) note the elevation of "contexts" as a consideration "is rooted, in part, in the increasing influx of entrepreneurship scholars from—or at least studying phenomena outside of—the mainly Western contexts that generated the standard model of so much prior work. This mirrors what happened in some of the broader organizational scholarly communities a decade earlier." This chapter aims to contribute to these ongoing conversations.

Research Strategy

To better understand the "existence, nature and character of entrepreneurial activity, expressed in written and oral language and associated interpretations" (Patton, 1990; Bourgeois, 1979; Denzin & Lincoln, 2005; Groenland & Dana, 2019; as cited in Mika, 2020, pp. 4–5) qualitative and inductive research "*with* indigenous peoples as co-researchers or collaborators" (Kwame, 2017, p. 3) was employed. Two interpretive case studies were developed with the aim of contributing rich insights, as well as descriptions of broader and more diffused implications (Walsham, 1995, p. 80). As noted by Ponelis (2015, p. 537) "the defining feature of case study research is its focus on 'how' and 'why' questions (Myers, 2009) and is appropriate for descriptive and exploratory studies (Mouton, 2001)."

Research Methodology

In choosing qualitative research, a purposive sampling technique was used to identify participants in the appropriate contexts who could address the research question under study, helping to articulate or explain their experience connected to the research focus. Taking a cue from Bastien et al. (2023, pp. 667–668) we employed an Indigenous research methodology involving the participants, which included hosting an informal gathering to open the process collectively, as well as reviewing emerging thematic choices. Guided by a reflective interviewing approach (Nardon et al., 2021), primary data was gathered by hosting two "conversational" interviews. The first using a guide with semi-structured questions that encouraged participants to describe their inner world symbolically and in greater detail (Tosey et al., 2014; Nardon et al., 2021). During the second interview, participants were invited to reflect on excerpts selected from the first interview for further exploration, with additional questions where needed.

It is important to note that two of the authors are practitioners who have lived and worked within the region for a combined total of 23 years, have worked closely with the two entrepreneurs featured in this chapter, and actively participated in the interviewing process. Benefiting from these personal connections offered a pathway to developing rich contextualized cases. In the case of Om Sunisa Jamwiset Deiters, at-a-distance interviews were co-facilitated by two of the authors via Zoom. In the case of Siwakorn Odochao, the interviews, using the same guide, were conducted in person by one of the authors at the location of the entrepreneur. Conversations were recorded and then transcribed, with the transcription shared for validation.

Analytic Approach

Adopting the approach of Miles et al. (2013; as cited in Weatherbee and Sears (2024, pp. 8–9) our "analysis process was both iterative and grounded in a qualitative interpretation" of the datasets collected. During the first preliminary examination of the transcripts, the focus was on identifying the stories and narratives found in their individual entrepreneurial journeys considering cultural contexts, personal and professional learnings, as well as the influence of external factors including governmental policies. Then a cross-case comparative approach was used to identify both common and unique themes. We then centred our analysis on the emerging themes to find "linkages, complementarity, or conflict" (Weatherbee & Sears, 2024, p. 9) among them, ending the process by aligning and connecting those themes to the research question. Prior to discussing our findings, the next sections will present the case contexts.

Findings

In this section we present the results of qualitative analysis beginning with contextual descriptions for both cases, followed by thematic findings.

Gaia Ashram: Wisdom in Land and Spirit

Founded in 2012 by Om Sunisa Jamwiset Deiters and her husband Tom Deiters in the Udon Thani province, near the border of Nong Khai, Gaia Ashram is an eco-learning centre and regeneration project, inspired by deep ecology and the ecovillage movements, bridging between inner and outer ecology. The dream of Gaia Ashram was nourished in Wongsanit Ashram, a socially engaged spiritual community where Sunisa lived for nine years and worked as a facilitator (Picture 8.2).

In the history of Thailand, you'll find environmental activism interconnected with Buddhist perspectives from the "forest conservation monks" (*phra anurak pa*) to contemporary scholar-monk P. A. Payutto, and social activist and environmentalist Sulak Sivaraksa who "devoted his life to the pursuit of economic and educational reform, social and environmental justice, human and civil rights" (Swearer, 2014, p. 53). The embodiment of this philosophy can be found in Wongsanit Ashram, founded in 1984 by Sivaraksa and colleagues, where personal and social transformation (Swearer, 2009) informs a model of sustainable living connecting spirituality, cultural diversity, and environmental integrity exemplifying "the ideal of simple living close to nature or, as he fondly quotes Gandhi,

Picture 8.2 Sunisa and Gaia Ashram, Gaia Ashram

'living simply so that others may simply live'" (as cited in Swearer, 2014, p. 54).

In Wongsanit Ashram, teachings were grounded in the "Buddhist concept of *pratitya-samutpada* (Sanskrit)"—dependent co-arising—which posits that all phenomena constituting individual existences are interdependent and mutually condition each other. Joanna Macy (1983, p. 33; as cited in Pyles, 2005), a Buddhist practitioner and activist, describes it this way:

> One's personal awakening (*purushodaya*) is integral to the awakening of one's village (*gramodaya*), and both play integral roles in *deshodaya* and *vishvodaya*, the awakening of one's country and one's world. Being interdependent, these developments do not occur sequentially, in a linear fashion, but synchronously, each abetting and reinforcing the other through multiplicities of contacts and current, each subtly altering the context in which other events occur.

Working alongside her teachers, Sunisa began to see how spiritual practice could serve as a response to injustice through resistance, collective action, and the creation of new cultural forms (Hunt-Perry & Fine, 2000; Pyles, 2005). Here a deepening connection to land and spirit commingled:

> What brought me into the work of regeneration, apart from the sense of gratitude and the sense of responsibility, I feel the sense of magic and wonder like feeling that this planet earth is really special, although I haven't seen other planet(s), but it is special for me enough to feel like blessed to be here. And knowing that learning that the earth has the magic of regenerating herself because from her history, she's just passed through many crises of the earth, period, different period of the earth.

Gaia Ashram is an embodiment of the Isaan community where Sunisa grew up. Before the influence of capitalism and globalism, these communities lived harmoniously with nature, were deeply connected to spirit, and operated as "a miniature society with a production system, resource management, a health system, a knowledge and learning system, a judicial system, self-governance, and an economic system run by each family and the community" (Mungmachon, 2012, p. 176). Sunisa left Wongsanit Ashram and spent one year living and working at the Panya project, a permaculture-based community in Northern Thailand, then became involved in NextGEN (Next Generation of the Global Ecovillage

Network) and continued to teach and facilitate courses such as Ecovillage Design Education (part of Gaia Education), Socially Engaged Buddhism/ Spirituality and Training of Trainers. She facilitated courses for NGO workers, young Buddhist activists, international students, children, and teachers using participatory teaching (Picture 8.3).

Upon returning home to open Gaia Ashram in her community, Sunisa reflected on that time, stating:

> I came to the land of Gaia Ashram at the moment ... and (i)n those days when I look at it, that land was quite degraded, bare land and doesn't look like there's a lot of life there. It was, oh, I feel so, I was with a sense of both gratitude, sense of responsibility and also the excitement to know that, knowing that I could be part of this self-regeneration of the earth and that meaning that I have to learn how she do(es) it and then being part of it.

For Isaan, an important value is to have knowledge and to use it wisely, a philosophical stance reflected in numerous local proverbs that put value on working smartly and wisely. Local wisdom is adapted to the new society and economy, created, and developed by the people within the community. Na Thalang (2001; as cited in Mungmachon, 2012, p. 176) further explains these characteristics (Picture 8.4).

Picture 8.3 Returning home, Gaia Ashram, Google Map Image 2013 and Aerial Photo 2024

Picture 8.4 On the land in the Issan Community (Gaia Ashram), Work That Reconnects (WTR) framework, Global Ecovillage Network (right)

> Many Isaan leaders encourage the ideal of "Hedkin, Hedyoo" (living simply, and being self-reliant) through the use of traditional ways of Integrated Farming and thereby increase the number of self-sufficient farmers. This has given birth to an agricultural network based on local traditions. From the painful lessons of industrial agriculture, many have come to embrace subsistence farming. This includes growing rice, fruits, vegetables, and raising animals for their own consumption, and to share with others in the community. Planting a variety of crops together is sometimes called Integrated Farming and is a manifestation of their traditional wisdom.

When asked to describe why she created Gaia Ashram and what was the spirit of the place, Sunisa offered these words:

> … I think … what Gaia Ashram is doing is creating a holistic living, a holistic sustainable living that includes all the different aspects of the eco village dimension(s) and … at the personal level - the head, the heart, the hand and the spirit. We are trying to make it well integrated and so then people can come and experience this, this is a new story … It is possible.

Lazyman Coffee: Maintaining Community and Connection

Lazyman Coffee was founded by Siwakorn Odochao in the Karen pgak'yau community in Ban Nong Tao, Northern Thailand, where his family has lived for five generations.

The term "Karen" or "Kariang" or "Yang" is used by the people outside of their community, shifting over time from Karen (*yaang*) as forest people (*chaw paa*) to Karen (Kariang) as hill tribe (*chaw khaw*), then to Karen (*pga k'nyau*) as indigenous people (Hayami 2006 as cited in Phongchiewboon, 2016, p. 102). The terms Karen and Pga K'Nyau will be interchangeably used to refer to the same group of people. However, as Odochao self-identified as Karen pgak'yau, this term will appear in his quotes or when the authors refer to his community (Picture 8.5).

Odochao grew up in a Karen pgak'yau village with nine brothers and sisters, learning local wisdom and traditional knowledge from elders. To situate both the village and the context, Phongchiewboon (2016, pp. 61, 64) notes that:

> (t)hese Indigenous hill tribe communities have their own cultures, languages, customs, and styles of dress, and belief systems, which are distinct from the majority of Thai people who are lowland settlers (IMPECT & FPP, 2006). They have unique systems of natural resource management that are centred on their traditional knowledge, which has been passed down from one generation to the next. The Kariang (Karen) are ... acknowledged as having a strong background in sustainable natural resource management, and recognised as employing practices that protect the environment. (Buergin, 2000; Forsyth & Walker, 2008; Santasombat, 2004; Walker, 2001)

Odochao completed a Masters degree from the Open University. Then in 2009, he attended the Asian Rural Institute (ARI) where he learned about the impacts of globalization and the influence of local movements.

Picture 8.5 Siwakorn Odochao (left), Karen pgak'yau village, Lazyman Coffee

Through community-based learning, the institute encourages participants in their nine-month "Rural Leaders Training Program" to "become independent learners who think critically and learn to ask questions that are relevant to their home community" (ARI, 2023). Participants explore how to leverage local resources, including their individual and collective abilities, discover the power of small-scale farming, and how these could help alleviate poverty and lead to more sustainable development.

In 2011, he started Lazyman Coffee against the imposing approach of mono-cropped corn, introducing coffee as part of the alternative farming approach in his Karen pgak'yau village, then marketing the resulting coffee crops directly to people in Thailand. The "Lazyman" of Lazyman Coffee was inspired by the folk tale "The Lazy Boy Who Became an Ox" where being lazy "makes space for embodied, relational, and spiritual ways of being, learning, and existing" (Ng 1998; as cited in Thomas & Carvajal-Regidor, 2021, p. 3) (Picture 8.6).

This seemingly contradictory sense of the word is woven into the conceptual position of their coffee—both a way to be slow and to work smarter, as Odochao elaborates:

> At the beginning, we don't know how to present this idea now. But then later we turn to realise that, oh we have the story of the person in the folk story. He is mentioned, the person in the men's story is lazy, but the lazy can be a hero and the important person of the story. How can it be? And then we start because we already know that story and then we try to

Picture 8.6 The "Lazy Boy" and Lazyman Coffee

present (it). ... the reason behind the coffee. That's why we try to present Karen pgak'yau culture through the story of the lazy man.

Thematic Findings

Becoming Entrepreneuring

In Poldner's (2020) Inaugural speech "Entrepreneuring a regenerative society," she presented entrepreneuring "as a process consisting of practices enables a more inclusive perspective and allows business to become a form of art, activism and even spirituality. ... It is an open invitation to become a change agent or angel of change, not as that lonely hero at the top, but as the unique embodiment of a larger social movement towards a regenerative society." This formulation of *entrepreneuring* as a verb (where a sense of relationality is restored) resonates with how Odochao and Sunisa connected as an Indigenous entrepreneur to their ventures, closer to an ontology of relatedness where embeddedness and the dynamics of being and becoming are centred. Here "there is a common belief in something greater than ourselves, that our humanity is part of a wider cosmic order, and that spirituality is a search for inner identity, meaning, connectedness, and transcendence" Tackney et al. (2017, p. 2):

> I think my learning about Engaged Buddhism at Wongsanit Ashram really lays the foundations ... for me to be able to take the concept of Deep Ecology because they are quite aligned... for example ... the concept(s) of interconnectedness and interdependence ... that is kind of the main teaching in Buddhism. Engaged Buddhism and Deep Ecology are aligned because Deep Ecology is also about knowing who you are, finding yourself and finding your place and your role in this whole system. Sunisa, personal communication, May 19, 2023

> In respect of the Lazy man coffee farmer, we are a very very small part in the world but we also try to bring people back to harmony with the land and nature. I believe that small-scale farming with thousand millions that are moving around the world will hold on to sustainability development in the future. Odochao (2017, p. 23)

Embedded in Community

According to Molina-Ramírez and Barba-Sánchez (2021, p. 5), the "Indigenous entrepreneurial spirit is closely related to the economic development base in the community (Barba-Sánchez & Molina-Ramirez, 2016), as well as cultural values, where work is involved in every moment of communal life accomplished in the communal assembly through a decision (Meza-Bernal, 2012); furthermore, it is motivated by the family and land to which it belongs (Wennecke et al., 2019)." Harris and Wasilewski (2004, p. 494) expand on this point defining Indigeneity as:

> rooted in core values based on communal life handed down from our many grandfathers and many grandmothers. Indigenous peoples see everything through the filter of community. This common Indigenous worldview and its associated 'deep logic' has an asset base arising out of the intangibles of cultural identity, communal wisdom, values, philosophies, and their resulting alternative worldviews. … Indigeneity is, thus, a very ancient global paradigm of sustainability, spiritual interconnectedness, and coexistence — of *convivencia* — of living together. This is a worldview that up until now has been undervalued.

It is in this worldview, in community, where Sunisa found inspiration for her projects, saying:

> we're going to start a business that supports local farmers who grow, who do agroforestry and then buy their crops make into products (for) sales (to) customer and the money - the profit we have, they will continue to support local farmers or buy more land so then we can regenerate the biodiversity. So, I think this intention is clear as throughout the years of experience.

Sunisa's efforts align with those observed by Baba and Fortin-Lefebvre (2021, p. 9) where there is a "(p)luralistic conception of entrepreneurial objectives: economic viability, contribution to the well-being of the community, its political project of self-determination and self-sufficiency, preservation, and development of local cultures and traditions."

Connecting the Karen pgak'yau worldview and the importance of forest conservation, Lazyman Coffee provides a way for the community to stay in the forest to continue conservation of the forest and connect to the wider world. Sanpa (2020) researched coffee production among the rural people of Chatpinat Pu Kakayo in the Hm Ban Nong Tao area, Mae Ni sub-district, Mae Wang district, Chiang Mai province. Sanpa (2020, p. 97, 108,) noted that:

1. "organic coffee is a tool for community movement to show Karen identity: preserve and take care of natural resources.
2. these entrepreneurs didn't have the typical "individual way" but in connection to the problems of the community and other resolutions for community development, and
3. the practice of K'nyau for growing and making coffee uses a diverse blend of planting processes instead of a single crop. That is, for both the rehabilitation of the land and a way of life of Pga K'nyau."

In describing his community Odochao shared these observations:

> So, I think the structure of the culture is everything that is in a social structure, maybe there are some people who stay at a position of command or maybe a control. In Karen pgak'yau culture, the highest command is not people. The high command is spirit. Spirit that we don't know exactly how it looks, but everywhere in a tree, live in a tree, live in a water, live in a mountain, live in a stream. And we also have a traditional belief culture and that mention we drink water, we need to be taking care of water, we use the soil, we need to take care of the land, we breathe from the air, we need to take care of the air, is something very basic but is connected.

Indigenous wisdom traditions (Pio et al., 2013) are intimately connected to the systems of life and place, where the relationship with Earth is one of interdependence and relationality between ourselves and the natural world (Salmón, 2000). These traditions embrace the complex ecosystems that they are rooted in. They incorporate an ethos of adaptability and change, elevating reciprocity and regeneration, and a sense of connection to the whole (Harris & Wasilewski, 2004), while remaining in balance and harmony with their surroundings. As Sunisa recounted:

> One of the reasons that motivated me to do the Gaia Ashram project back in my home village is that this sense of community, the sense of belonging to the land, I mean when I grew up in this village ... seeing ... how the village takes care of me, I mean at the school that my teachers were the elders from the village... I was quite inspired by the sense of community that that experience was quite deep. But when I learned about

> the eco village principles and then used that principle, looking back to my experience in my hometown, I understood.
>
> It's like we are, I am made by the whole universe, by all people around me, by the experience I interact with everyone there, my wisdom also coming from others. So is it not just mine.

Odochao works with the people of his community to ensure the continued protection of their ancestral forests and traditional ways of life by creating a livelihood aligned with their culture. Comparing their conservation approach to the more dominant Western approach, he frames their worldview in these words:

> We cannot say *here* is a conservation area and *here* is for humans, we are living together. But modern ideas. So if the idea is said this is conservation, there are no people, no, it's like maybe they draw a very big area and then they don't put humans inside, if they don't put humans in, they don't conserve that area. So it's kind of a separation. This is a modern idea. But in Karen culture we are living together. Sometimes it's like we are holding this. Sometimes we have people, sometimes we have nature and sometimes we are together.

There is also an intergenerational aspect to Lazyman Coffee, linked to the concept of temporality and the importance of the long-term and the consideration of future generations (Baba & Fortin-Lefebvre, 2021). For Odochao, Lazyman Coffee wasn't a project for today, it was one that allows the community's cultural past to persist and shows the new generations possibilities to continue traditions in the modern world.

Visioning Through Venturing

Rindova et al. (2009) refer to the motives for entrepreneurship as being more than merely wealth creation. They bring attention to the emancipatory aspects, "intended not only to create new wealth but also to bring about new states in relevant economic, social, institutional, and cultural environments" as cited in Henry and Dana (2016, p. 3). In the case of Lazyman Coffee, it acts as a vehicle to encourage the recovery of, use of, and access to their traditional lands. Swae expanded on this point saying (Picture 8.7).

> At that time what inspiration and strong in my mind was like, oh we need to stop corn. ... And then we start to have an idea and introduce it, and we say to people, if you have coffee, I will buy all just brought to me and then we will buy all. But that idea. But not if you have coffee you brought to me, we can set the price together .... and that is the beginning idea. And then it is time coming now have citizen coming, and people brought many coffee. Oh, so money where? And then we have to borrow... money from the relative, from some organisation that we know before. And then we start collecting money. So we have to pay cash. Yes. Because people live with cash. No, we cannot say next year I will pay. No, people will not do it this way.
>
> "So that's why we start collecting money, borrow money, and then we pay cash, we borrow money. ... We could expand to another village in this area. We work together, we are involved in the co coffee projects in more than 15 villages. We receive all the coffee cherries from 15 villages.

Families in Ban Nong Tao and neighbouring villages farm Arabica coffee using their Indigenous forestry techniques, which are then collected, processed, and roasted on-site. When asked "Did you understand how it would change how your village and how you are?" Odochao offered a picture of what impact within his community looked and felt like:

> I never expected, no, because I think I just continued and could stop corn. I feel very satisfied. Yeah. That's what my aim and my target was at that time we could stop corn because many people involved like more than 250 families interested in coffee. And then this idea of the corn and coffee, we work with the people with the thinking way idea. So we could stop corn at that time 12 years ago. And then, but coffee is, you still need to run and

Picture 8.7 Coffee Harvesting, Lazyman Coffee

> continue. … and when asked "Do people now that contribute to Lazyman Coffee, do they grow corn?" Odochao replied: No. Yeah, they don't grow. … It worked! It works! You can see there's no in this area!

For Sunisa it was the later years at Wongsanit Ashram Om and the exploration of Deep Ecology philosophy, where personal change and social change are seen as one. Nandram (2016, p. 70) has observed that entrepreneurship requires the individual to have a "strong will and the capacity to see, believe and imagine things others don't see or believe in. … leav(ing) behind certainty, be it material or immaterial, to engage in following a vision through venturing, no matter how intangible or ephemeral it may initially seem" (Picture 8.8).

As noted by Walters and Takamura (2015) "spirituality as the fourth bottom line … [is] a means to bridge knowledge from the past to the present and from the scientific to other ways of knowing." This intersectionality of the Indigenous entrepreneurial experience is evident for Sunisa who stated:

Picture 8.8 Sunisa teaching, Gaia Ashram

I feel even more rooted in the uniqueness of my individual self as I see how important it is that it plays its part in the greater whole. When I experience this sense of oneness I feel proud and pride of my existence as it feels I really belong here. I am needed here, and I meant to be here on this earth. I am here with life, and I am going to stand with it no matter what. Because I am part of this living system called earth. This is the force of my actions for social change.

Discussion

"Being" an Indigenous Entrepreneur

The motivation in both cases for starting a business and being "entrepreneuring" is driven by the interest to serve the community, including both human and non-human elements of their ecosystems. Welter (2011, p. 170) notes that "community entrepreneurship and similar concepts such as heritage and tribal entrepreneurship highlight social commitment, non-profit goals, and benefits for the wider community as (additional) drivers for entrepreneurship besides calculated and self-interested individual behaviour."

For both Odochao and Sunisa, making profit and/or managing profit was a by-product or resulting necessity of these initiatives, not a driver or reason why these efforts were undertaken. As informal change agents, they focused on a form of value creation that, according to Henriques et al. (2020, p. 324) "de-centers economic value creation in favor of social, cultural, spiritual or other relevant values in order to address intractable social problems in a sustainable and scalable manner." For Sunisa, being an entrepreneur is an act deeply rooted in her Indigenous identity, one is not separate from the other. So, her challenge has been how to embrace the "entrepreneurial" aspects of her emerging identity:

My heart in the first few years feels like we are going on the path of capitalism and all that. So, then it's hard to think and put myself in the same position (of an entrepreneur). And then I think recently that what we transformed is actually that idea. I think I become, through … practical experience, I think I become my vision and my spirit becomes more grounded and solid in clarity in what I'm doing... So then I feel open and confident that okay this is a game, I'm going to play this game – the business game, I'm going to play the game…

When considering Sunisa's words, a question came to mind—Is being an "entrepreneur" seen as a good thing? Baba and Fortin-Lefebvre (2021, p. 9) allude to this tension in defining oneself with the dominant "Silicon Valley" imaginary. Sunisa sees instead the opportunity to bring to the community an initiative centring relationality and symbiotic benefits which connect to her identity as the "mother of the land" while only recently connecting her work linked to the *idea* of entrepreneur:

> Before I would see myself as earth, … what you'd call earth steward (or) stewardship. And I see that these terms of entrepreneur are just within that context of earth steward. It's just one aspect of my role. And then I start to see myself as an entrepreneur, just to make it clear what role am I playing. I realize that it is more effective. I realize clearly what role am I playing, what action I'm doing.

Connecting the Karen pgak'yau worldview and the importance of forest conservation, Lazyman Coffee provided a way for the community to remain in the forest, continue the conservation of the forest, and connect to the wider world. When asked about these liminal connections, Odochao shared this thought:

> We already have clean air, we need to drink clean water. We already have what our ancestors already prepared for us. We need to see this pride, proud. And then we need to see the soil. Everything has life and even the small things, they are also work hard to make another life survive. So if we are proud in this way, that is just a smart thing we need to overcome. And then I also proud of myself that I can continue even very small things, but I can keep going for more than 10 years. I am also thanks for [me] not giving up on the way… And we are inspired, really inspired by a new generation. Now you can see a lot of coffee, new brands in Karen pgak'yau village. Nice.

Pangriya (2019, p. 8) noted that "entrepreneurs with prosocial motives create value in the community by establishing social ventures, which helps people who face challenging circumstances (Moroz et al., 2018)." There are four motivational factors identified by Pangriya (2019, p. 15) for social entrepreneurs which could apply in these cases, including (1) self-transcendence where one reorients from self to something which is more valued than oneself, (2) unique ideas and innovation to solve pain points, (3) inspiration, and (4) personal experience. Odochao and Sunisa became a valuable component of the human capital in their communities, serving as an active agent leveraging "creativity, flexibility, cognitive complexity and intercultural effectiveness" (Tretiakov et al., 2020, p. 195) where their Indigenous values affected the strategy and design of their ventures.

Limitations and Implications

This chapter is based on interviews of two Indigenous entrepreneurs located in Thailand. Increasing the number of interviews or incorporating Indigenous entrepreneurs with other projects or possible perspectives might influence the findings, offering a broader or more in-depth view. Additionally, due to the locations of the authors, in-person and on-site interviews were limited. Having the opportunity to be on-site for a longer period of time or having time for further themed conversations would have enriched the data gathered. Due to time and access constraints, opportunities to locate, identify, and gather relevant secondary data were also limited. The analysis of the data was based on the authors' own interpretations, whereas others could have interpreted the data differently. However, considering these limitations, the case findings do contribute to conversations related to both the practice and research.

Following Steyaert (2007, p. 472) who encouraged researchers to use "entrepreneuring as a conceptual attractor to adopt a relational turn and to move entrepreneurship towards a social ontology of becoming" the cases of Sunisa and Odochao are examples of entrepreneurial processes which:

1. "are embedded in and sensitive to the streams of the past and the present and [are] making a creative and critical difference in the realm of the possible,
2. break with a dualist world where object and subject are disconnected and ... situate process in the lived world and experience and,
3. connect to lived and observable experience[s] ... that emphasize the connection to ... cultural, political, and social forces."

As a contribution, this chapter echoes the importance of an Indigenous approach to innovation which considers a form of growth that also nurtures the full ecosystem, supporting the community's culture and place. Both Odochao and Sunisa see themselves as a part of something bigger—be it their community, the land they are on, the ecosystem, or the Earth. The "business" they have created, nurtured, and grown serves the larger whole.

These cases also point to the interconnections between an entrepreneur's cultural worldview, their approaches to venture design considerations, and the vision setting that was informed by something higher than themselves. Opportunity discovery and creation, as well as the entrepreneurial process itself, is non-linear and emergent. It operates within the mental framing or "logic" of the entrepreneur which influences what is envisioned or enacted as possible futures.

For Odochao and Sunisa their learning journeys, which centred "being" in parallel to "doing," played a key role in their approach to learning that "involves moving beyond epistemic and ontological assumptions embedded in modern western culture, particularly with respect to human relations to the more-than-human, or nature" (Barrett et al., 2017, p. 132). Additionally, Mirvis (2008) also analysed the ripple effects these experiences created, considering how, at a collective scale, they transformed the participants and de facto the systems they affect. He does flag that, depending on the "readiness" of the individual, the impact and effect of consciousness-raising varies, reminding the reader of Weick's (1995) commentary that "Experiences are not what happen to us, but what we do to what happens to us" (as cited in Mirvis, 2008, p. 176).

Conversely, we also encourage Indigenous practitioners to look beyond the walls of traditional academia and consider as valid other forms of learning and knowing gleaned in the field and in community. In the case of Sunisa and Odochao respectively, Wongsanit Ashram and Asian Rural Institute (ARI) served an important role, not only providing the necessary skills, but additionally the mental and spiritual grounding from which to build. There is a connection, if we see entrepreneuring as an "in-between" sensemaking effort to remain connected to being "human" within an economically informed process.

Moving from *homo economicus* to *zoon politikon* "who is intrinsically motivated to self-actualize and serve humanity through what they do" (Pirson & Lawrence, 2010, pp. 554–555) asks entrepreneurs to navigate the realms between, looking inside themselves not only for ideas but also for guidance. Traditional entrepreneurial educational approaches are bumping up against their limits as it is no longer just a case of looking at all the knowledge that's out there, it's having the ability to transcend the equivalent state and inhabit a different place/space.

Regarding future research, it would be interesting to expand the inquiry to include different worldviews and approaches, with a larger more varied dataset. Which form of educational support helps them to thrive while keeping their traditional/indigenous values? What might a shift in education do to positively influence the work of Indigenous entrepreneurs? Lastly, building on the Indigenous Innovation Framework and the conceptualization of "entrepreneuring" has the potential for further development within the field.

Acknowledgment We would like to thank our brother Swae and sister Sunisa for manifesting the collective efforts of their human and non-human communities, and for contributing their knowledge and experiences in conversation with us. Their perseverance and continued work to heal the land, regenerate their ecosystems, and re/connect spirit, place, and people is inspiring. By doing so, we re/member and are forever grateful.

References

Anders, G. C., & Anders, K. K. (1986). Incompatible goals in unconventional organization: The politics of Alaska Native corporations. *Organization Studies, 7*(3), 213–233.

Anderson, R. B., Honig, B., & Peredo, A. M. (2006). Communities in the global economy: Where social and indigenous entrepreneurship meet. *Entrepreneurship as Social Change, 5*, 3.

Asian Rural Institute. (2023, July 19). *Rural Leaders Training Program – Asian Rural Institute*. https://ari.ac.jp/en/trainingprogram/

Baba, S., & Fortin-Lefebvre, E. (2021). *Indigenous entrepreneurship, marginal ontologies and sustainable development goals*. https://doi.org/10.1007/978-3-319-71059-4_152-1

Banerjee, S. B. (2022). Decolonizing management theory: A critical perspective. *Journal of Management Studies, 59*(4), 1074–1087.

Barba-Sánchez, V., & Molina-Ramirez, E. (2016). Social entrepreneurship in Mexico. In R. Laratta (Ed.), *Social enterprise—Context-dependent dynamics in a global perspective* (pp. 59–78).

Barrett, M. J., Harmin, M., Maracle, B., Patterson, M., Thomson, C., Flowers, M., & Bors, K. (2017). Shifting relations with the more-than-human: Six threshold concepts for transformative sustainability learning. *Environmental Education Research, 23*(1), 131–143.

Bastien, F., Coraiola, D. M., & Foster, W. M. (2023). Indigenous peoples and organization studies. *Organization Studies, 44*(4), 659–675.

Bourgeois III, L. J. (1979). Toward a method of middle-range theorizing. *Academy of Management Review, 4*(3), 443–447.

Buergin, R. (2000). *Hill tribes and forests: Minority policies and resource conflicts in Thailand*. OAIster.

Cahn, M. (2008). Indigenous entrepreneurship, culture and microenterprise in the Pacific Islands: Case studies from Samoa. *Entrepreneurship & Regional Development: An International Journal, 20*(1), 1–18. https://doi.org/10.1080/08985620701552413

Cajete, G. (2000). *Native science: Natural laws of interdependence*. Clear Light Publishers.

Chartrungruang, B., Wattanalaungarun, W., Sa-Ingthong, K., & Hanafiah, M. H. M., & Zamzuri, N. H. (2022). Factors of indigenous community tourism business success for the Mhong entrepreneurs in Thailand. *Journal of Tourism, Hospitality and Culinary Arts, 14*(3), 152–164. ISSN 1985-8914; 2590-3837

Chouichom, S. (2021). Readiness of entrepreneurs towards group performance development of OTOP product: A case study in northeastern Thailand. In M. Behnassi, M. B. Baig, M. El Haiba, & M. R. Reed (Eds.), *Emerging challenges to food production and security in Asia, Middle East, and Africa: Climate risks and resource scarcity* (pp. 317–328). Springer.

Colbourne, R. (2017). Indigenous entrepreneurship and hybrid ventures. In A. Corbett & J. Katz (Eds.), *Perspectives and approaches to blended value entrepreneurship: Advances in entrepreneurship, firm emergence and growth* (Vol. 19). Emerald.

Colbourne, R., Peredo, A. M., & Henriques, I. (2023). Indigenous entrepreneurship? Setting the record straight. *Business History*, pp. 1–23.

Cooper, M. (2017, September 25). *The Work that Reconnects—Global Ecovillage Network*. Global Ecovillage Network. https://ecovillage.org/solution/the-work-that-reconnects/

Curry, J. & Donker, H. (2009). Development corporations in aboriginal communities: The Canadian experience. *Journal of Developmental Entrepreneurship, 14*(1), 1–19.

Dana, L. P. (2007). Toward a multidisciplinary definition of indigenous entrepreneurship. In L. P. Dana & R. Anderson (Eds.), *International handbook of research on indigenous entrepreneurship* (pp. 3–7). Edward Elgar.

Dana, L. P. (2015). Indigenous entrepreneurship: An emerging field of research. *International Journal of Globalisation and Small Business, 14*(2), 158–169.

Dana, L. P., & Smyrnios, K. (2013). The push-pull of indigenous Sámi family reindeer herding enterprises: A metaphor for sustainable entrepreneurship. In *Handbook of research on family business* (2nd edn, pp. 588–606). Edward Elgar Publishing.

Denzin, N. K., & Lincoln, Y. S. (2005). *The sage handbook of qualitative research* (3rd edn). Sage.

Filatotchev, I., Ireland, R. D., & Stahl, G. K. (2022). Contextualizing management research: An open systems perspective. *Journal of Management Studies, 59*(4), 1036–1056.

Forsyth, T., & Walker, A. (2008). *Forest guardians, forest destroyers: The politics of environmental knowledge in northern Thailand*. University of Washington Press.

Gregg, M. T., & Wishart, D. M. (2012). The price of Cherokee removal. *Explorations in Economic History, 49*(4), 423–442.

Groenland, E., & Dana, L. (2019). *Qualitative methodologies and data collection methods: Toward increased rigour in management research*. World Scientific Publishing Co. Pte. Ltd.

Harris, L. D., & Wasilewski, J. (2004). Indigeneity, an alternative worldview: Four R's (relationship, responsibility, reciprocity, redistribution) vs. two P's (power and profit). Sharing the journey towards conscious evolution. *System Research, 21*, 489–503. https://doi.org/10.1002/sres.631

Henriques, I., Colbourne, R., Peredo, A. M., & Anderson, R. B. (2020). Relational and social aspects of Indigenous entrepreneurship: The hupacasath case. In *Indigenous wellbeing and enterprise* (pp. 313–340). Routledge.

Henry, E. Y., & Dana, L. P. (2016). Social and cultural capital: Enhancing emancipatory Indigenous entrepreneurship. In *Academy of Management Proceedings* (Vol. 2016, No. 1, p. 14414). Briarcliff Manor, NY 10510: Academy of Management.

Hindle, K. (2005). Contrasting Indigenous entrepreneurship in Australia and Canada: How three applied research perspectives can improve policy and programs. *Small Enterprise Research, 13*(1), 92–106.

Hindle, K. (2010). How community context affects entrepreneurial process: A diagnostic framework. *Entrepreneurship & Regional Development, 22*(7/8), 599–647. https://doi-org.grenoble-em.idm.oclc.org/10.1080/08985626.2010.522057

Hunt-Perry, P., & Fine, L. (2000). All Buddhism is engaged: Thích Nhất Hạnh and the order of interbeing. In C. S. Queen (Ed.), *Engaged Buddhism in the west* (pp. 35–66). Wisdom Publications.

IMPECT (Inter Mountain Peoples Education and Culture in Thailand Association) & FPP (Forest Peoples Programme). (2006). *Indigenous knowledge, customary use of natural resources and sustainable biodiversity management: Case study of Hmong and Karen communities in Thailand*. Retrieved from Chiang Mai, Thailand: 224 http://www.forestpeoples.org/sites/fpp/files/publication/2010/08/10cthailandimpectjun06eng.pdf

Jack, S. & Anderson, A. R. (2002). The effects of embeddedness on the entrepreneurial process. *Journal of Business Venturing, 17*(5), 467–487.

Kenney, M. & Goe, W. R. (2004). The Role of social embeddedness in professorial entrepreneurship: A comparison of electrical engineering and computer science at UC Berkeley and Stanford. *Research Policy, 33*(5), 691–707.

Kingi, T. T., & Kompas, T. (2010). Rural reform and Fiji's indigenous sugarcane growers: An application of stochastic frontier analysis. *Pacific Economic Bulletin, 25*, 42–61.

Kwame, A. (2017). Reflexivity and the insider/outsider discourse in indigenous research: My personal experiences. *AlterNative: An International Journal of Indigenous Peoples, 13*(4), 218–225.

Mazzarol, T. (2007). Different strokes for different folks: Stimulating entrepreneurship in regional communities. In L.-P. Dana & R.B. Anderson (Eds.), *International handbook of research on indigenous entrepreneurship* (pp. 494–507). Edward Elgar.

Meza Bernal, I. (2012). Lengua y cosmovisión. Elementos de resistencia y comunalidad en tres comunidades mayas: macehuales de Quintana Roo. *Cultura y representaciones sociales, 7*(13), 96–153.

Mika, J. P. (2020). Indigenous entrepreneurship: How Indigenous knowing, being and doing shapes entrepreneurial practice. In D. Deakins & J. M. Scott (Eds.), *Entrepreneurship: A contemporary & global approach* (pp. 1–32). Sage.

Mika, J. P., & O'Sullivan, J. G. (2014). A Māori approach to management: Contrasting traditional and modern Māori management practices in Aotearoa New Zealand. *Journal of Management & Organization, 20*(5), 648–670.

Mika, J. P., Warren, L., Foley, D., & Palmer, F. R. (2017). Perspectives on indigenous entrepreneurship, innovation and enterprise. *Journal of Management & Organization, 23*(6), 767–773.

Mirvis, P. (2008). Executive development through consciousness-raising experiences. *Academy of Management Learning & Education, 7*(2), 173–188.

Mistry, J., & Berardi, A. (2016). Bridging indigenous and scientific knowledge. *Science, 352*(6291), 1274–1275.

Molina-Ramírez, E., & Barba-Sánchez, V. (2021). Embeddedness as a differentiating element of Indigenous entrepreneurship: Insights from Mexico. *Sustainability, 13*(4), 2117. https://doi.org/10.3390/su13042117

Moroz, P. W., Branzei, O., Parker, S. C., & Gamble, E. N. (2018). Imprinting with purpose: Prosocial opportunities and B Corp certification. *Journal of Business Venturing, 33*(2), 117–129.

Mouton, J. (2001). *How to succeed in your Master's and Doctoral studies: A South African guide and resource book*. Van Schaick Publishers.

Mungmachon, M. R. (2012). Knowledge and local wisdom: Community treasure. *International Journal of Humanities and Social Science, 2*(13), 174–181.

Myers, M. D. (2009). *Qualitative research in business and management*. Sage.

Nandram, S. S. (2016). How do spirituality, intuition and entrepreneurship go together? *Philosophy of Management, 15*(1), 65–82. https://doi.org/10.1007/s40926-016-0029-7

Nardon, L., Hari, A., & Aarma, K. (2021). Reflective interviewing—Increasing social impact through research. *International Journal of Qualitative Methods, 20*, 16094069211065232.

Overall, J., Tapsell, P., & Woods, C. (2010). Governance and indigenous social entrepreneurship: When context counts. *Social Enterprise Journal, 6*(2), 146–161.

Padilla-Meléndez, A., Plaza-Angulo, J. J., Del-Aguila-Obra, A. R., & Ciruela-Lorenzo, A. M. (2022). Indigenous entrepreneurship. Current issues and future lines. *Entrepreneurship & Regional Development, 34*(1–2), 6–31.

Pangriya, R. (2019). Hidden aspects of social entrepreneurs' life: A content analysis. *Journal of Global Entrepreneurship Research, 9*, 1–19.

Patton, M. Q. (1990). *Qualitative evaluation and research methods*. SAGE Publications, inc.

Peredo, A. M. & Anderson, R. (2006). Indigenous entrepreneurship research: Themes and variations. In C. S. Galbraith (Ed.), *Developmental entrepreneurship: Adversity, risk, and isolation* (Vol. 5, pp. 253–273). Emerald.

Peredo, A. M., & Chrisman, J. J. (2006). Toward a theory of community-based enterprise. *Academy of Management Review, 31*(2), 309–328.

Peredo, A. M., Anderson, R. B., Galbraith, C. S., Honig, B., & Dana, L. P. (2004). Towards a theory of indigenous entrepreneurship. *International Journal of Entrepreneurship and Small Business, 1*(1–2), 1–20.

Phiphatsērītham, K., & Yoshihara, K. (1983). *Business groups in Thailand* (Vol. 41). Institute of Southeast Asian.

Phongchiewboon, A. (2016). *Livelihood strategies and environmental management practices in Northern Thailand National park communities*. A dissertation presented in partial fulfilment of the requirements for the degree of Doctor of Philosophy in Natural Resource Management at Massey University, Palmerston North, New Zealand (Doctoral dissertation, Massey University). https://mro.massey.ac.nz/handle/10179/9901

Pio, E., Waddock, S., Mangaliso, M., McIntosh, M., Spiller, C., Takeda Ho, M., & Syed, J. (2013). Pipeline to the future? Seeking wisdom in indigenous, eastern and western traditions. In J. Neal (Ed.), *Handbook of faith and spirituality in the workplace: Emerging research and practice* (pp. 195–222). Springer. https://doi.org/10.1007/978-1-4614-5233-1_13

Pirson, M. A., & Lawrence, P. R. (2010). Humanism in business–towards a paradigm shift? *Journal of Business Ethics, 93*, 553–565.

Poldner, K. A. (2020, April 16). *Entrepreneuring a regenerative society: Introductory speech by Kim Poldner* at The Hague University of Applied Sciences for the Research Group Circular Business. De Haagse Hogeschool.

Ponelis, S. R. (2015). Using interpretive qualitative case studies for exploratory research in doctoral studies: A case of Information Systems research in small and medium enterprises. *International Journal of Doctoral Studies, 10*, 535–550. http://ijds.org/Volume10/IJDSv10p535-550Ponelis0624.pdf

Ponting, S. S. A., Ponting, J., & Spilde, K. (2015). Developing tribal casino employees as conduits for tribal government messaging. *Journal of Business Research, 68*(10), 2140–2145.

Pyles, L. (2005). Understanding the engaged Buddhist movement: Implications for social development practice. *Critical Social Work, 6*(1), 1–12. https://doi.org/10.22329/csw.v6i1.5721

Rindova, V., Barry, D., & Ketchen, D. J., Jr. (2009). Entrepreneuring as emancipation. *Academy of Management Review, 34*(3), 477–491.

Rural Leaders Training Program. Asian Rural Institute. (2023, July 19). https://ari.ac.jp/en/trainingprogram/

Salmón, E. (2000). Kincentric ecology: Indigenous perceptions of the human–nature relationship. *Ecological Applications, 10*(5), 1327–1332.

Salmon, E., Chavez, J. F., & Murphy, M. (2022). New perspectives and critical insights from Indigenous peoples' research: A systematic review of Indigenous management and organization literature. *Academy of Management Annals.* https://doi.org/10.5465/annals.2021.0132

Santasombat, Y. (2004). Karen cultural capital and the political economy of symbolic power. *Asian Ethnicity, 5*(1), 105–120. https://doi.org/10.1080/1463136032000168925

Sanpa, P. (2020). Ethnic coffee: Ethnic entrepreneurization with cultural capital. *PSDS Journal of Development Studies, 3*(1), 95–137. https://so05.tci-thaijo.org/index.php/gvc-tu/article/view/246041

Seremani, T. W., & Clegg, S. (2016). Postcolonialism, organization, and management theory: The role of "epistemological third spaces". *Journal of Management Inquiry, 25*(2), 171–183.

Sharma, A. (2021). Decolonizing international relations: Confronting erasures through Indigenous knowledge systems. *International Studies, 58*, 25–40.

Spiller, C., Pio, E., Erakovic, L., & Henare, M. (2011). Wise up: Creating organizational wisdom through an ethic of Kaitiakitanga. *Journal of Business Ethics, 104*(2), 223–235.

Stephen, L. (1991). Culture as a resource: Four cases of self-managed indigenous craft production in Latin America. *Economic Development and Cultural Change, 40*(1), 101–130.

Steyaert, C. (2005). Entrepreneurship: In between what? On the "frontier" as a discourse of entrepreneurship research. *International Journal of Entrepreneurship and Small Business, 2*(1), 2–16.

Steyaert, C. (2007). 'Entrepreneuring' as a conceptual attractor? A review of process theories in 20 years of entrepreneurship studies. *Entrepreneurship and Regional Development, 19*(6), 453–477.

Swae (Siwakorn Odochao), Karen pgak'yau. (2017, November 11–17). Message from Lazyman. [Speaker Abstract, p. 23]. Economics of Happiness World Forum, Japan, Tokyo. https://www.localfutures.org/past-conference/economics-of-happiness-world-forum-tokyo-japan/

Swearer, D. K. (2009). *Religion and globalization from the historical pespective of Thai Buddhism* (pp. 1000–1018).

Swearer, D. (2014). Environmental ethics: Thai Buddhist perspectives. *The Journal of Oriental Studies, 24*, 49–55.

Swierczek, F. W., & Jatusripatak, S. (1994). Exploring entrepreneurship cultures in Southeast Asia. *Journal of Enterprising Culture, 2*(2), 687–708.

Taagepera, R. (2008). *Making social sciences more scientific: The need for predictive models*. Oxford University Press.

Tackney, C. T., Chappell, S., Harris, D., Pavlovich, K., Egel, E., Major, R., Finney, M., & Stoner, J. (2017). Management, spirituality, and religion (MSR) ways and means: A paper to encourage quality research. *Journal of Management, Spirituality & Religion, 14*(3), 245–254.

Tengeh, R. K., Ojugbele, H. O., & Ogunlela, O. G. (2022). Towards a theory of Indigenous entrepreneurship: A classic? *International Journal of Entrepreneurship and Small Business, 45*(1), 1–15.

Thomas, M., & Carvajal-Regidor, M. (2021). From "slow" to "being 'lazy' and slowing down" and the impact on student learning. *Teaching and Learning Inquiry, 9*(2). https://doi.org/10.20343/teachlearninqu.9.2.12

Tosey, P., Lawley, J., & Meese, R. (2014). Eliciting metaphor through clean language: An innovation in qualitative research. *British Journal of Management, 25*(3), 629–646. https://doi.org/10.1111/1467-8551.12042

Tretiakov, A., Felzensztein, C., Zwerg, A. M., Mika, J. P., & Macpherson, W. G. (2020). Family, community, and globalization: Wayuu indigenous entrepreneurs as n-Culturals. *Cross Cultural & Strategic Management, 27*(2), 189–211.

Valente, M. (2012). Indigenous resource and institutional capital: The role of local context in embedding sustainable community development. *Business & Society, 51*(3), 409–449.

Walsham, G. (1995). Interpretive case studies in IS research: Nature and method. *European Journal of Information Systems, 4*(2), 74–81.

Walters, F., & Takamura, J. (2015). The decolonized quadruple bottom line: A framework for developing indigenous innovation. *Wicazo Sa Review, 30*(2), 77–99.

Weatherbee, T. G., & Sears, D. (2024). Circuits of organizational stories: Wineries, history, and the performance of place. In *A world scientific encyclopedia of business storytelling set 1.* Corporate and Business Strategies of Business Storytelling Volume 2: History and Business Storytelling (pp. 1–27). https://doi.org/10.1142/13336-vol1

Weick, K. E. (1995). *Sensemaking in organizations.* Sage.

Welter, F. (2011). Contextualizing entrepreneurship—Conceptual challenges and ways forward. *Entrepreneurship Theory and Practice, 35*(1), 165–184.

Welter, F., Baker, T., & Wirsching, K. (2019). Three waves and counting: The rising tide of contextualization in entrepreneurship research. *Small Business Economics, 52*, 319–330.

Wennecke, C. W., Jacobsen, R. B., & Ren, C. (2019). Motivations for Indigenous island entrepreneurship: Entrepreneurs and behavioral economics in Greenland. *Island Studies Journal, 14*(2), 43–60.

Whiteman, G., & Cooper, W. H. (2000). Ecological embeddedness. *Academy of Management Journal, 43*(6), 1265–1282.

Wuttunee, W. (2004). *Living rhythms: Lessons in aboriginal economic resilience and vision* (Vol. 37). McGill-Queen's Press.

CHAPTER 9

Indigenous Entrepreneurship in Myanmar: The Role of Community-Based Enterprises in Sustainable Human Development

Oliver S. Crocco, Omaima Hajjami, and Bethany Hager

Introduction

Various forms of entrepreneurship have existed throughout all of humankind and across communities around the world (Hébert & Link, 2009). Given the economic, cultural, and political diversity of Southeast Asia (Crocco, 2021), it is no surprise that countries such as Myanmar (Burma) with its 135 officially recognized ethnic groups across eight "major national ethnic races" (Myanmar Government, 2018, para 2)

O. S. Crocco (✉) · O. Hajjami · B. Hager
Louisiana State University, Baton Rouge, LA, USA
e-mail: olivercrocco@lsu.edu

O. Hajjami
e-mail: ohajja1@lsu.edu

B. Hager
e-mail: bfran46@lsu.edu

E. L. Eijdenberg et al. (eds.), *Indigenous Entrepreneurship in Southeast Asia*, Palgrave Studies in Equity, Diversity, Inclusion, and Indigenization in Business, https://doi.org/10.1007/978-3-031-54457-6_9

includes a variety of manifestations of indigenous entrepreneurship. The word "indigenous" primarily refers to groups of people who reflect the "earliest known inhabitants of a place and especially of a place that was colonized" but it also refers to a legal status afforded certain people groups (Merriam-Webster, n.d.). According to the International Labour Organization's (1989) Indigenous and Tribal Peoples Convention, indigenous people self-identify as a group with traditional ways of living that occur historically in a particular area with their own ways of organizing and self-governing and a "culture and way of life different from other segments of the national population, e.g. in their ways of making a living, language, customs" (ILO, 2003, p. 7). The term indigenous may not be the most appropriate term in the Myanmar context given that some countries describe indigenous peoples in other ways, "such as first peoples/nations, aboriginals, ethnic groups, etc." (UNESCO, n.d., para 5). In Myanmar, groups of people who could be described as indigenous peoples are commonly referred to as ethnic groups, which is the term this chapter adopts. However, it is worth noting that the official decision to use the term "ethnic groups" in Myanmar instead of indigenous groups may also be related to the desire to avoid granting the rights and responsibilities associated with indigenous groups such as those found in the United Nations Declaration on the Rights of Indigenous Peoples (United Nations, 2007).

The Emergence of Contemporary Indigenous Entrepreneurship in Myanmar

To understand indigenous entrepreneurship in Myanmar, one must first examine the context in which contemporary indigenous entrepreneurship has emerged. This is also vital because indigeneity is inextricably tied to the idea of place and the historical residence of people groups in certain locations. Myanmar is a country of 54 million people who live across over 650,000 square kilometres with a GDP per capita (current US$) of 1,096 (World Bank, n.d.). Thus, even though Myanmar is the second largest country in terms of size after Indonesia and the fifth most populous country in Southeast Asia after Indonesia, the Philippines, Vietnam, and Thailand, it remains the poorest country in the region (Crocco, 2021). In fact, Cambodia, which is the second poorest country in Southeast Asia, boasts a GDP per capita 63% higher than Myanmar's at 1,786 US$ (World

Bank, n.d.). In 1987, Myanmar was designated the status of "Least Developed Country" by the United Nations; a status it has been unable to "graduate" from (United Nations Conference on Trade and Development, n.d., para 7). In terms of human development, Myanmar currently ranks 149th on the Human Development Index and saw a decrease of nearly 10% in 2021 (United Nations Development Programme, 2022). The majority of the country belongs to the ethnic race of Bamar located primarily in the geographic and political centre of the country.

Myanmar's colonial legacy, in particular the British colonialization of Myanmar, led to the shift away from vital societal and community structures, such as Buddhist temple schools, which provided vocational education, and local leadership systems, which provided structure and ensured rights of community members (Odaka, 2016). This legacy as well as post-colonial realities have led to "social fissures" in Myanmar's society across a variety of dimensions, including ethnicity (Aung-Thwin, 2018, p. 15). In Myanmar, ethnic identity represents "a hierarchical means of social organisation and a normative struggle for emancipation..." as well as "a claim to particularly histories, a demand for citizenship and a share of power and resources" (Cho, 2018, p. 49). In post-colonial Myanmar, there is a long history of violent and oppressive military rule recently punctuated by a 2021 military coup and subsequent junta that has led to the increased persecution of Myanmar's ethnic minorities (Stokke, 2023). It is vital to explore this colonial legacy in relation to the development of indigenous entrepreneurship in Myanmar to avoid "epistemic blindness" that would come from excluding this important history in the analysis (Banerjee, 2022, p. 1074).

The lack of government support for health, education, and business in ethnic minority areas as well as ongoing conflict has necessitated the rise and importance of community-based organizations (CBOs). These CBOs take a variety of shapes and serve a host of functions in society. According to Takeda (2023), there are over 200,000 CBOs operating in Myanmar at varying degrees of formality. Some function more as volunteer organizations while others are civil society organizations promoting the rights of citizens (Takeda, 2023), and some function as community-based enterprises (CBEs). These CBEs represent a form of indigenous entrepreneurship that has emerged out of necessity and survival but also as a result of recent technological and economic advancements. For example, entrepreneurship has grown due to increased access to financial institutions or mobile-money-service providers, which has jumped from 23% of the population in 2014 to 48% in 2021 (World Bank, n.d.). Even access to cell phones in Myanmar came relatively late compared to other emerging economies. Until the mid-2000s, SIM cards sold for as much as $2500 and were not widely available until after the government held semi-democratic elections in 2010 (McCarthy, 2018). According to the International Telecommunication Union (n.d.-a), Myanmar had the lowest rate of mobile-cellular telephone subscriptions in 2011 among the 237 countries listed. While increased access has been achieved, only 44% of individuals in the country have access to the Internet as of 2021, which puts Myanmar in the bottom 15% of countries around the world and second only to Timor-Leste in Southeast Asia (International Telecommunications Union, n.d.-b).

In their analysis of social entrepreneurship in Myanmar and Thailand, Meallem and Herpich (2022) highlight key threats to entrepreneurs, i.e., lack of government support and collaboration with the public sector, little or no access to financial resources such as loans, and lack of a skilled workforce. In fact, this last point is borne out in the fact that only 28% of Myanmar's labour force can be considered skilled labour (Crocco, 2021). Other contextual variables include the fact that the nation's technical and vocational education and training (TVET) system is largely ineffective at generating skilled workers (Win, 2022) and no universities in Myanmar have achieved international rankings in the world's top universities (Crocco, 2021). As a result of its political, economic, and technological conditions, it is not surprising that Myanmar welcomed only 76,446 migrants in 2020 but saw over 3.7 million of its citizens emigrate, 60% of whom went to other Southeast Asian countries (Crocco, 2021; United Nations, 2020). These variables differentiate the case of Myanmar from its Southeast Asian neighbours such as Thailand and Malaysia, which have experienced stronger economic development, more stable political institutions, and more access to technology. In particular, Myanmar stands in stark contrast to Thailand, whose strong monarchy allowed it to avoid colonization and whose relatively homogenous cultural society meant that indigenous entrepreneurship was relegated to the hill tribes and not a central component of its economic development. It is noteworthy, however, that many of the hill tribes in Thailand, such as the Karen (Kayin), are the same ethnic groups persecuted across the border in Myanmar (Hortsmann, 2016).

Fuelled by these forces, indigenous entrepreneurship has seen progress in Myanmar. However, it is noteworthy to distinguish between

Fig. 9.1 People sell items on the side of the road outside Yangon, Myanmar (*Source* Oliver S. Crocco)

community-based indigenous entrepreneurship and state-sponsored indigenous entrepreneurship, the latter of which is exemplified in the military's program for "national entrepreneurs" which were "indigenous big businesspeople who would be loyal and useful to the state" (Jones, 2018, p. 185). CBEs in Myanmar represent a form of non-state indigenous entrepreneurship that seeks to meet the needs of sustainable human development (Fig. 9.1).

Purpose

Given the call for more indigenous research in the field of human resource development and management studies (Bruton et al., 2022; Ghosh et al., 2023; Kuchinke et al., 2022), the purpose of this chapter is to highlight the role of CBEs as a form of indigenous entrepreneurship in promoting human development in Myanmar. This chapter builds on the empirical work of Crocco and Cseh (2021) and Crocco (2017) on CBEs in Myanmar as well as a review of the literature to describe illustrative cases of CBEs in the Myanmar context, particularly those related to training and development. Methodologically, this chapter is a conceptual analysis. Conceptual articles are non-empirical papers that can accomplish a variety of purposes such as to "further develop a concept… illuminate issues and problems" and/or "suggest a new approach to research" (Rocco et al., 2022, p. 119).

This chapter is situated primarily within the literature on CBE (Peredo & Chrisman, 2006, 2017), indigenous entrepreneurship (Mika et al., 2017), and human resource development (McLean & McLean, 2001), particularly in the Southeast Asian context (Crocco & Tkachenko, 2022; Tkachenko et al., 2022). It concludes with implications for research and a discussion on the challenges of conducting research in Myanmar to further understand and support this work in Myanmar and comparable contexts. This chapter contributes to the literature in a few ways. First, according to a systematic literature review of indigenous entrepreneurship, most of the research on indigenous entrepreneurship occurs in countries such as Canada, New Zealand, and Australia (Padilla-Meléndez et al., 2022), and thus this chapter offers an introductory analysis into the case of Myanmar, which has received less attention in the scholarship. Second, it reviews relevant and complementary examples of both community-based indigenous enterprises and social enterprises in the Myanmar context. Last, it presents a robust research agenda, which includes key considerations for scholars seeking to further this work in Myanmar and the challenges they will likely face.

The Phenomenon of Community-Based Enterprise

A CBE occurs when a community seizes on an entrepreneurial activity to serve its collective good (Peredo & Chrisman, 2006, 2017). In CBEs, "the community acts as an entrepreneur when its members, [act] as owners, managers, and employees" and thus become sustainable economically and socially (Peredo & Chrisman, 2006, p. 315). CBEs emerge as the result of four major influences: (a) economic and social hardship from isolation or lack of opportunity, which leads to "the desire of communities to gain or regain control of their own local development"

(Peredo & Chrisman, 2006, p. 317); (b) collective learning through experiences in the community that has led it to recognize and take advantage of an entrepreneurial opportunity; (c) a dependence on social resources and social capital in the community "on the bases of collectively owned cultural, social, and ethnic endowments" (p. 318); and; (d) the existence of a large enough community to support the initiatives of the CBE but not too large that social networks are lost. Peredo and Chrisman (2006) go on to establish three core characteristics of a CBE including access to skills and resources, a "multiplicity of goals" that reflect the diverse needs of the community, and a dependence on the involvement of the community (p. 319). The concept of CBE has received increased attention since its introduction and shows enduring usefulness in explaining community entrepreneurship (Pradhan & Samanta, 2022). Thus, CBEs represent a subset of the larger social entrepreneurship movement in Myanmar. As Dale and Samuel-Nakka (2018) assert, "The promise of social enterprises in Myanmar lies in their capacity to address social inequality in ways that deepen democracy" (p. 332).

In many ways, CBEs are inextricably tied to processes of learning and change. According to Merriam and Bierema (2014), "adults are motivated by wanting to improve their situation in adult life, whether that situation is work-related, personal (such as improving their health, dealing with family issues), or social/community-related" (p. 12). A key mechanism by which adults can achieve this is learning. Broadly speaking, adult learning consists of "activities intentionally designed to bring about learning among those whose age, social roles, or self-perception, define them as adults" (Merriam & Brockett, 2007, p. 8). Thus, many of CBEs in the Myanmar context revolve around adult learning and training initiatives that support the development of individuals and their communities.

Examples of Community-Based Indigenous Entrepreneurship and Social Enterprise in Myanmar

There are limited studies that strictly employ the concept of CBE as a theoretical framework (e.g., Crocco & Cseh, 2021); however, the idea of community-based indigenous entrepreneurship is more widely applied in the scholarly discourse. In their study of social entrepreneurship in

Myanmar, Meallem and Herpich (2022) report that 57% of respondents agreed or partially agreed that conditions are favourable for social entrepreneurs to start and grow businesses; however, only 43% similarly agreed that social entrepreneurs in Myanmar could make a living on their work.

Community-based enterprises are often rooted in intangible aspects that are not easily measurable. CBEs are formed and maintained based on emotional links between community members, which encompass a strong sense of belongingness and attachment to the community. Four key factors drive the sense of community including membership, influence, shared emotional connection, and needs fulfilment (McMillan & Chavis, 1986). These factors also serve as the foundation for CBEs. In Myanmar, several community-based forms of indigenous entrepreneurship have emerged in various regions of the country, serving different populations and operating in diverse sectors. This section highlights several of these organizations while demonstrating the different manifestations of indigenous entrepreneurship in Myanmar.

The CBE explored by Crocco and Cseh (2021) was founded in 2005 in Southeast Myanmar and "prepares young adults to be effective their next stages of life whether that is higher education or participation in the workforce" (p. 440). Students pay a monthly fee of 30,000 Kyats (US$22.20), which covers the operating budget (i.e., rental fee, trainer pay). The trainers come from the community and feel a sense of obligation to serve the trainees, who are young adults in the community by filling in the educational and skills gaps that the formal educational system lacks. These training courses are offered in nine subjects: "English language, computer, religion (which included topics such as ethics and personal development), civic education, guitar, international music notation, physical education, speech and debate and management (which included topics such as project management and leadership)" (Crocco & Cseh, 2021, p. 440). Other members of the community serve as key stakeholders that formally and informally influence the operations of the enterprise. One of the core processes explored in this study was the role of social learning in cultivating organizational development and change.

In a recent qualitative study, Crocco and Rockett (2023) explored the role that community-based education and training enterprises play in supporting community development in a variety of rural areas in Myanmar. To protect the identity of the participants in a heightened time of vulnerability after the military coup, names and specific details about these organizations have been left out. These organizations offered training to community members in a variety of areas and used a tuition/fee structure to remain financially viable. These training areas included skill development in the areas of healthcare, sustainable agriculture, religion, and general leadership development. In all cases, the leaders took the weight of the community on their shoulders and implemented a social enterprise that both supported the human development of individuals but also brought about positive benefits for the communities as a whole (Fig. 9.2).

There are also related examples of social enterprise that often emerge in communities but then extend beyond them. The following examples of indigenous entrepreneurship in Myanmar are those that are more established and formalized including websites and research conducted about them. Plan Bee, a social enterprise operating in South Shan, Myanmar, aims to promote and sustain the apiculture (i.e., beekeeping) sector

Fig. 9.2 A community-based enterprise focused on sustainable agricultural training, Myanmar (*Source* Oliver S. Crocco)

(Plan Bee, n.d.). Their primary focus is to train community members as beekeepers and buy their honey products at fair-trade prices (Plan Bee, n.d.). Their mission is to support young people "to establish successful beekeeping enterprises by providing start-up capital, beekeeping equipment, and ongoing mentorship (Tag Development, n.d.). Through training and mentoring programs, Plan Bee has successfully trained "over 300 beekeepers in 18 villages from 2013 to 2018" (Plan Bee, n.d.). In addition, it has empowered women within the community to lead microenterprises, producing and selling beeswax candles and natural cosmetic products. These products are marketed both locally throughout Myanmar supermarkets and internationally in Mainland China, Hong Kong, and Japan while currently under FDA review for export to the United States. Looking ahead, Plan Bee's goal is to help beekeepers achieve sustainable income levels and establish a research development centre and beekeeping farms (Plan Bee, n.d.).

In agriculture, Proximity Design focuses on providing affordable, user-friendly, and durable products and services to rural farmers (Proximity Design, n.d.). Founded by Debbie Aung Din and partner Jim Taylor, their lab-based unit gains insights into the challenges the local farmers face through case studies and interviews and design solutions that meet their needs (Proximity Design, n.d.). An example of the products they have designed is a gravity-fed drip irrigation system, which has helped improve water access and facilitate irrigation practices for smallholder farmers. Other services include farm advisory services and small loan opportunities. Their efforts have led to serving over 250,000 farm customers annually, with an average increase in farmers' income amounting to $275 per year (Proximity Design, n.d.). This represents a 25% increase in the aforementioned GDP per capita (current US$) of 1,096 (World Bank, n.d.).

In the tourism sector, social enterprises like Precious Lady in Rakhine State, Myanmar, play a vital role in supporting women by helping them generate income and improve their livelihoods (Community Partners International, 2022). Precious Lady achieves this by offering training programs, sewing machines, and raw materials to enable women to create various items like handbags, purses, and necklaces, which are then sold in the Precious Lady's shop to tourists (Community Partners International, 2022). To ensure sustainable development, Precious Lady made a strategic shift from producing high-end bags primarily for international tourists to targeting the local and national markets. This decision proved beneficial during the COVID-19 lockdown crisis when international tourist numbers were low, as the enterprise could maintain a steady income (Community Partners International, 2022).

By focusing on the local market and providing valuable skills training, Precious Lady not only empowers women to enhance their livelihoods but also contributes to broader sustainable development goals in the region. An example of this impact is seen in a participant who took part in the enterprise's soap training program. Through this program, this participant learned how to make soap, manage production costs, identify potential markets within hotels and resorts, and expand her sales (Community Partners International, 2023). As a result, she was able to save enough of her income to attend university. Another beneficiary of Precious Lady participated in a sandal-making program, which enabled her to generate income and support her family. Producing around 10 pairs of sandals daily, she has earned 350,000 Kyats (approximately $166) per month (Community Partners International, 2023).

In the same industry, Myanmar Adventure Outfitters (MAO) functions as a social enterprise that offers tour packages in remote communities for visiting tourists. However, with the onset of the COVID-19 pandemic in Myanmar and the subsequent military coup, the tourism sector experienced a significant downturn, severely impacting tour and adventure guiding services. In response to this challenging situation, MAO made a strategic decision to realign its social mission towards providing training and health education (Hartzler, 2021). The training programs introduced by MAO now focus on mental health support for those caring for COVID-19 patients, offering guidance on how to care for individuals in a home environment, and providing instruction on administering medication for minor cases as well as severe cases where patients experience difficulty breathing (Hartzler, 2021). Additionally, MAO initiated relief efforts, such as food aid for communities with limited cultivatable land, and organized grassroots clothing drives across Myanmar to support these communities. These initiatives are made possible through community donations, showcasing MAO's commitment to making a positive impact on the affected regions beyond its traditional tourism operations allowing sustainable solutions (Hartzler, 2021).

Community-based enterprises have played a significant role in supporting various segments of Myanmar's population. A notable example is Pan Nann Ein, which has a primary focus on empowering individuals with physical disabilities to explore their creative potential.

Through training programs, participants acquire the skills to handcraft various products such as journals, cards, and recycled plastic baskets (Pann Nann Ein, n.d.). To continually innovate, the enterprise also provides additional training to diversify its product range. In addition, to promote with team inclusivity, members of Pan Nann Ein have taken the initiative to learn sign language, enabling effective communication with deaf team members, and fostering a stronger sense of belonging within the group.

Pan Nann Ein's influence has transcended borders, as they have expanded their market internationally through the establishment of online pop-up shops in various countries. This has led to a growing demand for their products within Myanmar, resulting in the increasing recognition of the PNE brand. Consequently, the enterprise has achieved self-sufficiency as a social enterprise. Moreover, some group members have become the primary income earners in their households, highlighting the positive impact of Pan Nann Ein's initiatives on individuals and their families (Pann Nann Ein, n.d.).

There are also examples of community-based entrepreneurship that have thrived due to the vision and support of outsiders of the community who have leveraged the community's resources and vision to support their needs. One example of this in the agricultural sector is the organization Impact Terra (Impact Terra, n.d.). To address the issue of the lack of agricultural information available for farmers (Thant et al., 2020), this social enterprise designed a mobile application to support local farmers in their activities. With the wide use of smartphones among farmers, Impact Terra has bridged its community population by bringing a mobile app that offers access to valuable information such as weather forecasts, crop market prices, and financial opportunities (Impact Terra, n.d.). The application service is customized based on types of crops and includes advice to improve agricultural practices and increase productivity. The enterprise has raised $3 million through support from various sources including financial services firms, the Ministry of Agriculture, and venture philanthropy (Sparling, 2018).

Implications for Research

While no definitive catalogue of implications for research can be established by a cursory overview such as this chapter, several directions for future research in this vital area of entrepreneurship exist, especially considering the lack of scholarly literature on this topic. These must also be discussed within the context of challenges related to researching indigenous entrepreneurship in Myanmar.

While authors such as Bartlett et al. (2002) explored indigenous firms and multinational affiliates in Southeast Asia, more research could be done regarding indigenous social enterprises in rural areas to understand how they interface and interact with multinational affiliates, if at all. Similarly, one commonality of some of the forms of community-based indigenous entrepreneurship mentioned above involved an outsider to the community or an outsider to the country who catalysed the enterprise. More research could explore the role of outsiders, in particular in the Myanmar context, in forming these community-based firms. From a cursory overview, it appears these outsiders offer idea generation and technological savvy around an idea that is then used to empower local community members.

Although Crocco and Cseh (2021) identified the role of social learning in fostering organization development and change in a community-based organization focused on training and development, more research could explore how social learning unfolds in the multitude of other contexts where these organizations occur. In particular, the Myanmar indigenous entrepreneurial ecosystem among and between its ethnic groups warrants further study. What are the success factors and stumbling blocks for extension beyond one's ethnic group or community into other areas? Case study research into some of the aforementioned enterprises could prove illustrative.

From a macro perspective, there are visible initiatives in the regional organization the Association of Southeast Asian Nations (ASEAN) to promote human resource development (HRD) in general (e.g., Tkachenko et al., 2022) and entrepreneurship in particular (e.g., ASEAN, 2012) in its member states. One organization that focuses on this is the ASEAN Human Development Organization, which represents a macro form of regional indigenous HRD as discussed by Kuchinke et al. (2022). Attempts to do this from a Regional HRD perspective in Southeast Asia were Crocco and Tkachenko (2022) and Crocco (2021) who analysed mechanisms and processes involved in multi-country HRD among ASEAN's ten member states; however, indigenous entrepreneurship was not a primary focus of those studies.

Lastly, while there are challenges to do so, longitudinal designs that would allow researchers to understand the lifecycle of indigenous entrepreneurship and how those enterprises evolve over time would be valuable in furthering our understanding of how to support them at various stages. Furthermore, while studies such as Crocco and Rockett (2023) explored the views of leaders in overcoming challenges, it would be important to understand community perspectives on the resilience of community-based enterprises in the face of the unique challenges faced by minority ethnic groups in Myanmar.

While these areas of future research may rely on mainstream theories and research practices in organizational studies, it is important when considering indigenous entrepreneurship for future research to flexibly depart from typical conventions. This includes "creating an intellectual space that can enable a fruitful exchange of ideas and perhaps collaboration between mainstream and heterodox approaches to research" (Banerjee, 2022, p. 1083).

Decolonizing Indigenous Entrepreneurship in Myanmar

To begin creating this space, it is prudent to describe some of the challenges associated with decolonizing indigenous entrepreneurship in Myanmar. In particular, the following section was informed by the experiences of the first author (Crocco) in previous work (e.g., Crocco, 2017; Crocco & Cseh, 2021) as well as a recent study he conducted on leaders of community-based training and education organizations in Myanmar (Crocco & Rockett, 2023). The study explored the challenges faced by these leaders in facilitating their programs in post-coup and post-pandemic Myanmar.

Misapplication of Western/Global North Theory

Studying indigenous entrepreneurship in Myanmar relies on eschewing, at least partially, familiar theories and research practices associated with mainstream research. This is especially salient for quantitative studies where theory is employed deductively to test whether core propositions can be confirmed, disconfirmed, or extended (Creswell & Creswell, 2018). To do so requires defining and employing pre-existing variables that may not be applicable in all contexts. Indigenous theories, on the contrary, are "context specific" and are "especially attentive to the complex motives of different actors and the related power dyanmcis and underlying forces" (Bruton et al., 2022, p. 1058). Thus, more qualitative approaches such as ethnography or grounded theory will likely better support scholars in this endeavour. However, given the commonly cross-cultural nature of indigenous research, scholars cannot simply employ qualitative methods in a new cultural context and expect to unearth and understand indigenous theory. Rather, researchers must seek to develop a global mindset for their work that appreciates the epistemological and paradigmatic differences among cultures (Cseh & Crocco, 2020) and avoids "the myth of universalism" commonly held both in scholarly research and in business practice (Boussebaa, 2023, p. 556).

Access

As mentioned above, most of the research on indigenous entrepreneurship occurs in countries such as Australia, Canada, and New Zealand (Padilla-Meléndez et al., 2022). This is likely due, in part, to the difficulty of gaining access to countries with indigenous populations such as Myanmar. The Myanmar government has restricted access of tourists to many parts of the country due to armed conflict, which would make it difficult to access ethnic areas where indigenous entrepreneurship is occurring. At the time of writing, the United States Department of State (2023) has issued its most serious travel warning of Level 4: Do Not Travel due to "civil unrest and armed conflict" (para 5), "land mines" (para 7), and that the "military regime arbitrarily enforces local laws, including carrying out random and wrongful detentions without due process" (para 8). Even if researchers decided to travel there, tourist visas are limited in time, and it is unlikely that a visa to study anything related to ethnic groups (which are in conflict with the de facto government) would be approved. While physical travel to ethnic areas in Myanmar is limited, there are other ways of conducting research, i.e., through audio-visual digital conference software such as Zoom. This has only recently become a possibility due to advances in internet and digital infrastructure mentioned above. Zoom was used to conduct the semi-structured interviews in the Crocco and Rockett (2023) study mentioned above.

Participant Security

A core challenge to conducting research in ethnic minority areas in Myanmar relates to ensuring the safety and protection of participants who have reasonable reasons to fear military backlash. This also means that indigenous participants may have doubts about participating in a study or sharing openly about anything that relates to the challenges they face with regard to the junta, which is the de facto government at the time of writing. This can also make it difficult to gain approval from research ethics boards at universities. In fact, to conduct a study with leaders of organizations in Myanmar about the challenges they face, Crocco and Rockett (2023) had to promise to take out any direct mention of the government or military for the study to be approved by Louisiana State University's Institutional Review Board. This dramatically influenced the extent of the data we could include but was likely the best way to ensure the safety of participants. Crocco and Rockett (2023) took additional measures to mask the identity of the participants by excluding any tabulation of demographic information or descriptive vignettes that could have been used to narrow down the possibility of the organizations being studied.

Participant Recruitment

As a result of these security concerns, participant recruitment continues to be a challenge for conducting studies of indigenous entrepreneurs in Myanmar. While some ethnic groups readily cooperate with outsiders, others are more sceptical and hesitant to do so. This has elevated the importance of personal relationships and connections as a means of participant recruitment. Crocco and Rockett (2023) managed to recruit participants for their study by having a local contact in the region who has worked extensively in Myanmar with hundreds of organizations sharing the participant recruitment message with people who potentially fit the selection criteria. It also helped that one of the authors (Crocco) has worked in the region for many years with dozens of organizations and is known in some circles among organizational and community leaders. However, the use of personal networks has its downsides as well, especially that this has the potential to limit research (and thus introduce bias) to populations predisposed to interacting with foreigners and potentially seeking particular gain from such relationships.

Conclusion

Indigenous knowledge is vital to sustainable development in Myanmar, in particular in rural areas (Matsuda, 2016). Given that most of the scholarship on indigenous entrepreneurship occurs in countries with more direct connections to the West (e.g., Canada, Australia), scholarship illuminating the context of Myanmar is vital, especially given its vast population of ethnic minorities. This type of research involves a kind of scholarly "wandering *away* from existing paradigms, explanations, and wandering *into* the breadth and depth of voices, perspectives, and experiences" (Crocco & Grenier, 2021, p. 62). It is difficult to balance the desire to fit new inquiries into current frames of reference while still being critical of the ways Western/Global North perspectives have influenced current understandings. As scholars move forward in seeking to study the many forms of indigenous entrepreneurship in Myanmar, they will need to immerse themselves in the historical, cultural, economic, and political context of the research site as well as practice researcher reflexivity to identify the ways that ethnocentrism and Western/Global North biases subsist.

References

Association of Southeast Asian Nations. (2012). *Common curriculum for entrepreneurship in ASEAN*. https://asean.org/wp-content/uploads/2012/05/8.-Common-Curriculum-for-Entrepreneurship-in-ASEAN.pdf

Aung-Thwin, M. (2018). The state. In A. Simpson, N. Farrelly, & I. Holliday (Eds.), *Routledge handbook of contemporary Myanmar* (pp. 15–24). Routledge.

Banerjee, S. B. (2022). Decolonizing management theory: A critical perspective. *Journal of Management Studies, 59*(4), 1074–1087. https://doi.org/10.1111/joms.12756

Bartlett, K. R., Lawler, J. J., Bae, J., Chen, S. J., & Wan, D. (2002). Differences in international human resource development among Indigenous firms and multinational affiliates in East and Southeast Asia. *Human Resource Development Quarterly, 13*(4), 383–405. https://doi.org/10.1002/hrdq.1040

Boussebaa, M. (2023). Decolonizing international business. *Critical Perspectives on International Business, 19*(4), 550–565. https://doi.org/10.1108/cpoib-12-2022-0121

Bruton, G. D., Zahra, S. A., Van de Ven, A. H., & Hitt, M. A. (2022). Indigenous theory uses, abuses, and future. *Journal of Management Studies, 59*(4), 1057–1073. https://doi.org/10.1111/joms.12755

Cho, V. (2018). Ethnicity and identity. In A. Simpson, N. Farrelly, & I. Holliday (Eds.), *Routledge handbook of contemporary Myanmar* (pp. 43–52). Routledge.

Community Partners International. (2022). *Making ends meet: Helping women in Myanmar build artisan livelihoods.* https://www.cpintl.org/field-notes--updates/making-ends-meet-helping-women-in-myanmar-build-artisan-livelihoods

Community Partners International. (2023). *International women's day: Helping women in Myanmar to achieve financial independence.* https://www.cpintl.org/field-notes--updates/international-womens-day-helping-women-in-myanmar-to-achieve-financial-independence

Creswell, J. W., & Creswell, J. D. (2018). *Research design: Qualitative, quantitative, and mixed methods approaches* (5th ed.). Sage.

Crocco, O. S. (2017, June 7–9). *Community-based enterprise in Myanmar: An exploratory pilot study.* The 18th International Conference on Human Resource Development across Europe, Lisbon, Portugal.

Crocco, O. S. (2021). *Developing human resources in Southeast Asia: A holistic framework for the ASEAN community*. Palgrave Macmillan. https://doi.org/10.1007/978-3-030-79697-6

Crocco, O. S., & Cseh, M. (2021). Learning, development, and change in a community-based enterprise in Myanmar. *European Journal of Training and Development, 45*(4/5), 436–448. https://doi.org/10.1108/EJTD-12-2019-0198

Crocco, O. S., & Grenier, R. S. (2021). Not all those who wander are lost: Critically reflective research for a new HRD landscape. *Advances in Developing Human Resources, 23*(1), 55–65. https://doi.org/10.1177/1523422320973425

Crocco, O. S., & Rockett, A. (2023, June 7–9). *Challenges on all sides: A qualitative study of leaders of training and education organisations in post-coup Myanmar.* The 22nd International Conference on Human Resource Development and Practice Across Europe, Dublin, Ireland.

Crocco, O. S., & Tkachenko, O. (2022). Regional human resource development: The case of Southeast Asia and ASEAN. *Human Resource Development International, 25*(1), 40–58. https://doi.org/10.1080/13678868.2020.1858261

Cseh, M., & Crocco, O. S. (2020). Globalizing HRD academic practice: Developing a global mindset for teaching and research. *Advances in Developing Human Resources, 22*(1), 51–71. https://doi.org/10.1177/1523422319886288

Dale, J., & Samuel-Nakka, S. (2018). International law and inter-governmental organisations. In A. Simpson, N. Farrelly, & I. Holliday (Eds.), *Routledge handbook of contemporary Myanmar* (pp. 324–334). Routledge.

Ghosh, R., Nachmias, S., & McGuire, D. (2023). Indigenous research in HRD: Reflections from HRDI & call for contributions. *Human Resource Development International, 26*(1), 1–6. https://doi.org/10.1080/13678868.2022.2162675

Hartzler, B. (2021, October 6). *Opportunities in a post-tourism Myanmar.* Myanmar Adventure Outfitters. https://myanmaradventureoutfitters.com/journal

Hébert, R. F., & Link, A. N. (2009). *A history of entrepreneurship.* Routledge.

Hortsmann, A. (2016). The culture and landscape of the humanitarian economy among the Karen (Kayin) in the borderland of Southeast Myanmar and Northwest Thailand. In S-A. Oh (Ed.), *Myanmar's mountain and maritime border scapes: Local practices, boundary-making and figured worlds* (pp. 171–190). ISEAS Publishing.

Impact Terra. (2023). *Farmer platform.* Retrieved July 19, 2023, from https://www.impactterra.com/farmer-platform

International Labour Organization. (1989). *ILO convention on indigenous and tribal peoples 1989 (No. 169).* Retrieved August 1, 2023, from https://www.ilo.org/dyn/normlex/en/f?p=NORMLEXPUB:12100:0::NO::P12100_ILO_CODE:C169

International Labour Organization. (2003). *ILO convention on Indigenous and tribal peoples, 1989 (no. 169): A manual.* Retrieved July 31, 2023, from https://www.pro169.org/res/materials/en/general_resources/Manual%20on%20ILO%20Convention%20No.%20169.pdf

International Telecommunications Union. (n.d.-a). *Mobile-cellular subscriptions (excel).* Retrieved July 17, 2023, from https://www.itu.int/en/ITU-D/Statistics/Pages/stat/default.aspx

International Telecommunications Union. (n.d.-b). *Percentage of individuals using the internet (excel).* Retrieved July 17, 2023, from https://www.itu.int/en/ITU-D/Statistics/Pages/stat/default.aspx

Jones, L. (2018). Political economy. In A. Simpson, N. Farrelly, & I. Holliday (Eds.), *Routledge handbook of contemporary Myanmar* (pp. 181–191). Routledge.

Kuchinke, K. P., Cho, Y., Cseh, M., Han, H., McLean, G. N., & Crocco, O. S. (2022). Indigenous research in HRD: Perspectives and a call for contributions. *Human Resource Development Review, 21*(4), 371–373. https://doi.org/10.1177/153448432211258

Matsuda, M. (2016). Sustainable farming systems in Myanmar: The implications of findings from field surveys in the 2000s. In K. Odaka (Ed.), *The Myanmar economy: Its past, present and prospects* (pp. 131–154). Springer.

Mika, J. P., Warren, L., Foley, D., & Palmer, F. R. (2017). Perspectives on indigenous entrepreneurship, innovation and enterprise. *Journal of Management & Organization, 23*(6), 767–773. https://doi.org/10.1017/jmo.2018.4

McCarthy, G. (2018). Cyber-spaces. In A. Simpson, N. Farrelly, & I. Holliday (Eds.), *Routledge handbook of contemporary Myanmar* (pp. 92–105). Routledge.

McMillan, D. W., & Chavis, D. M. (1986). Sense of community: A definition and theory. *Journal of Community Psychology, 14*(1), 6–23. https://doi.org/10.1002/1520-6629(198601)

Meallem, M. J., & Herpich, S. (2022). An exploration of social entrepreneurship ecosystems in Thailand and Myanmar. *Social Entrepreneurship Review, 1*, 44–62. https://doi.org/10.15678/SER.2022.1.04

Merriam, S. B., & Bierema, L. L. (2014). *Adult learning: Linking theory and practice*. Jossey-Bass.

Merriam, S. B., & Brockett, R. G. (2007). *The profession and practice of adult education: An introduction*. Jossey-Bass.

Merriam-Webster. (n.d.). Indigenous. In *Merriam-Webster.com dictionary*. Retrieved July 17, 2023, from https://www.merriam-webster.com/dictionary/indigenous

McLean, G. N., & McLean, L. (2001). If we can't define HRD in one country, how can we define it in an international context? *Human Resource Development International*, *4*(3), 313–326. https://doi.org/10.1080/13678860110059339

Myanmar Government. (2018). *People & society*. https://www.myanmar.gov.mm/web/guest/people-society

Odaka, K. (2016). A new light to shine? Historical legacies and prospects for Myanmar's economy. In K. Odaka (Ed.), *The Myanmar economy: Its past, present and prospects* (pp. 1–28). Springer.

Padilla-Meléndez, A., Plaza-Angulo, J. J., Del-Aguila-Obra, A. R., & Ciruela-Lorenzo, A. M. (2022). Indigenous entrepreneurship. Current issues and future lines. *Entrepreneurship & Regional Development, 34*(1–2), 6–31. https://doi.org/10.1080/08985626.2021.2011962

Pann Nann Ein. (n.d.). *Our story so far: Crafting a better life*. Retrieved July 19, 2023, from https://pannnannein.com/pages/contact

Peredo, A. M., & Chrisman, J. J. (2006). Toward a theory of community-based enterprise. *Academy of Management Review, 31*(2), 309–328. https://doi.org/10.5465/amr.2006.20208683

Peredo, A. M., & Chrisman, J. J. (2017). Conceptual foundations: Community-based enterprise and community development. In M. van Ham, D. Reuschke, R. Kleinhans, C. Mason, & S. Syrett (Eds.), *Entrepreneurial neighbourhoods: Towards an understanding of the economies of neighbourhoods and communities* (pp. 151–178). Edward Elgar Publishing.

Plan Bee. (2022). *Behind the beehive: The plan bee story.* Retrieved July 19, 2023, from https://www.my-planbee.com/about

Pradhan, S., & Samanta, S. (2022). Global research on community-based enterprise: A bibliometric portrait. *Journal of Enterprising Communities: People and Places in the Global Economy*, Vol. ahead-of-print No. ahead-of-print. https://doi.org/10.1108/JEC-01-2022-0010

Proximity Design. (n.d.). *This is us: The power of being proximate.* Retrieved July 19, 2023, from https://proximitydesigns.org/who-we-are/

Rocco, T. S., Plakhotnik, M. S., & Silberman, D. (2022). Differentiating between conceptual and theory articles: Focus, goals, and approaches. *Human Resource Development Review, 21*(1), 113–140. https://doi.org/10.1177/15344843211069795

Sparling, N. (2018, March 19). *Social enterprise raises $3m to digitally support smallholder farmers in Myanmar.* AFN. https://agfundernews.com/impact-terra-social-enterprise-myanmar-seed

Stokke, K. (2023). Civil society and the contentious politics of democratisation and autocratisation in Myanmar. In E. Hansson & M. L. Weiss (Eds.), *Routledge handbook of civil and uncivil society in Southeast Asia* (pp. 118–138). Routledge.

Tag development. (n.d.). *Plan bee: Some have plan A; Tag has plan bee.* The Tag Foundation for Social Development. Retrieved July 19, 2023, from https://www.tagdevelopment.org/plan-bee

Takeda, M. (2023). Ethnic children at the Thai-Burma border: Community-based organizations promoting the rights and equality. In M. Takeda & C. Yamahata (Eds.), *Myanmar's changing political landscape: Old and new struggles* (pp. 113–132). Springer.

Thant, P. S., Espino, A., Soria, G., Myae, C., Rodriguez, E., Bardon, W. J., & Gonsalves, J. (2020). Myanmar local food systems in a changing climate: Insights from multiple stakeholders. *Environmental and Sustainability Indicators, 14*, 100170. https://doi.org/10.1016/j.indic.2022.100170

Tkachenko, O., Crocco, O. S., Nguyen, L. A., & Jonathan, V. (2022). Regional human resource development in ASEAN: An institutional theory perspective. *Human Resource Development Review, 21*(2), 225–248. https://doi.org/10.1177/15344843221083190

UNESCO. (n.d.). Indigenous peoples. In *UNESCO World Heritage Convention glossary.* Retrieved July 27, 2023, from https://whc.unesco.org/en/glossary/275/

United Nations. (2007). *Declaration on the rights of Indigenous peoples.* Retrieved August 1, 2023, from https://www.un.org/esa/socdev/unpfii/documents/DRIPS_en.pdf

United Nations. (2020). *International migrant stock 2020*. Retrieved July 27, 2023, from https://www.un.org/development/desa/pd/content/international-migrant-stock

United Nations Conference on Trade and Development. (n.d.). UN list of least developed countries. Retrieved July 27, 2023, from https://unctad.org/topic/least-developed-countries/list

United Nations Development Programme. (2022). *Human development reports: Myanmar*. Retrieved July 27, 2023, from https://hdr.undp.org/data-center/specific-country-data#/countries/MMR

United States Department of State. (2023). *Burma (Myanmar) travel advisory*. Retrieved July 31, 2023, from https://travel.state.gov/content/travel/en/traveladvisories/traveladvisories/burma-travel-advisory.html

Win, W. H. (2022). The status of perspectives and challenges of TVET for the national human development (NHRD) in Myanmar. *Human Resource and Organization Development Journal, 14*(2), 116–146.

World Bank. (n.d.). *World Bank open data*. https://data.worldbank.org

CHAPTER 10

Gender and Credit Access for Indigenous Rural Self-Employed Businesses: A Case Study in Vietnam and Thailand

Chung Thanh Phan, Diem Thi Hong Vo, Daniel Borer, and Thuy Minh To

Introduction

In rural areas, indigenous people usually see entrepreneurship as a method of improving their quality of life and socio-economic circumstances while preserving traditional cultures. However, to kick-start or grow entrepreneurship in these communities, there are often significant barriers

C. T. Phan (✉) · D. T. H. Vo · D. Borer · T. M. To
RMIT University, Ho Chi Minh City, Vietnam
e-mail: Chung.Phan@rmit.edu.vn

D. T. H. Vo
e-mail: diem.vo@rmit.edu.vn

D. Borer
e-mail: daniel.borer@rmit.edu.vn

E. L. Eijdenberg et al. (eds.), *Indigenous Entrepreneurship in Southeast Asia*, Palgrave Studies in Equity, Diversity, Inclusion, and Indigenization in Business, https://doi.org/10.1007/978-3-031-54457-6_10

in accessing capital for each gender, and potential gender discrimination in accessing financial services.

Entrepreneurship is especially promising for indigenous women, with initial expectations of strengthening their families and contributing to their community's development, which are commonly seen as women's priorities. It can also provide a path towards financial independence, which is initiated as women's leadership. However, gender-based disparity remains a persistent social problem given long-lasting social norms regarding gender roles.

Many empirical studies show the importance of gender differences in financial access in various countries. For example, studying indigenous women entrepreneurs, Witbooi and Ukpere (2011) found gender discrimination challenges in accessing finance in South Africa. Aterido et al. (2013) in the Sub-Saharan Africa context found that there is an unconditional gender gap, as financial services are more abundantly used by males rather than females. In Vietnam, Pham and Talavera (2018) estimates do not provide evidence for discrimination against female-owned enterprises in the formal lending market. Brock and De Haas (2019) in the context of Turkey showed that discrimination mainly affected female loan applicants in male-dominated industries, indicating how financial frictions can perpetuate entrepreneurial gender segregation across sectors. Morsy et al. (2019) found the gender gap in access to financial services in Africa to be driven by women entrepreneurs' own self-perception. In a recent study with data from Bangladesh, Shoma (2019) explored the significant gender gap that currently exists in regard to power relations in the Small and Medium Enterprise (SME) sector.

In our study, we examine gender-based discrimination in accessing financial services for rural household entrepreneurs, focusing on Vietnam and Thailand—two developing and neighbouring countries in Southeast Asia. There is a need for more indigenous entrepreneurship scholarship, especially in geographical areas like Southeast Asia. Vietnam and Thailand, in particular, have large rural populations where entrepreneurship can significantly improve living standards. However, research into gender-based discrimination in financial access is lacking.

Vietnam and Thailand have their own unique geopolitical and eco-social status in the region and play important roles in regional cooperation and development. Both countries share some similarities: both have a large rural population (about 60% in Vietnam and almost 50% in Thailand, according to World Bank data for 2021). Hence, encouraging entrepreneurship development in rural areas will significantly contribute to the eradication of poverty, which is a national priority.

More importantly, according to the Gender Inequality Index (GII) by the United Nations Development Programme (UNDP), Thailand and Vietnam rank within the 70's band out of 191 countries in terms of gender inequality. Countries with a low Gender Inequality Index (GII) ranking have smaller gaps between women and men in terms of health, education, and economic status. Countries with a high GII ranking have wider disparities between women and men across these dimensions. Hence, both countries still have substantial room for improvement in terms of gender equality. Furthermore, according to the World Bank, the female labour force participation rates in Thailand and Vietnam were 59% and 69%, respectively, in 2022. These rates are relatively high compared to global standards. Some barriers that stop women from participating full-time at work are gender norms and mobility, gender-based violence, girls' education level in rural areas, etc. An in-depth analysis from aggregated scales of both countries can reveal if gender discrimination towards credit access is limiting work participation, which then, could be addressed by policy recommendations and potentially lead to strengthening rural entrepreneurship.

This study aims to help decolonize entrepreneurship and management literature by examining rural entrepreneurship through an indigenous lens in Vietnam and Thailand. We investigate household and entrepreneur characteristics and compare differences/similarities between the two countries regarding financial access. Further, we examine the effects of gender-based discrimination and suggest policies to improve credit access.

Using a large sample panel dataset of household levels, we employ statistical tests, instrumental variables, and Heckman techniques to empirically study financial access. The results will reveal insights into gender discrimination in credit access in Vietnam and Thailand. Recommendations can then strengthen indigenous entrepreneurship in these developing Southeast Asian countries.

Literature Review

Gender and Discrimination

Overall, economist's studies emphasized two main branches of conscious discrimination: "statistical" theory of racism and sexism (Phelps, 1972) and the economics of discrimination called "taste-based" discrimination (Becker, 2010). Initially, the theory of statistical discrimination was approached by Phelps (1972): when making hiring decisions, employers use statistical information about a group to which applicants belong to infer their job productivity. Elborgh-Woytek et al. (2013) used such theory and found that female-led enterprises may face disadvantages when accessing credit due to gender discrimination. They found that female-related loans could result in lower credit availability and higher borrowing costs. Besides, Brock and De Haas (2019) tested the statistical theory and showed that lenders use the information on the average creditworthiness of women-led companies as a basis to decide on specific loan applications. This led to reduce the costs of collecting more direct information about borrowers.

Being developed later, the economic theory of "taste-based" discrimination was presented by Becker (2010). This economic model studied labour market discrimination and suggested that negative hiring outcomes for minority workers can result from employers' prejudices or dislikes which are rooted on unlawful grounds within an organizational culture. In other words, these employers can be said to have a "taste for discrimination". For example, in the context of financial access, lenders discriminate against women because of their personal preferences or beliefs. The lender's dislike for female borrowers would possibly lead them to set higher credit standards for women to access formal bank credit compared to male borrowers.

Furthermore, an alternative rationale for discrimination was studied by Bertrand et al. (2005) using a psychological rather than economics basis. This study showed that explicit and implicit attitudes and their impact on human behaviour led to this form of discrimination. According to this theory, implicit discrimination may occur outside of the discriminator's awareness. For example, despite explicit claims of the contrary, there may exist an implicit bias favouring male entrepreneurs in the context of credit markets. Women may perceive a higher threshold when their businesses are being assessed in comparison to male-led enterprises, leading to a reduced likelihood of women seeking loans. This implicit discrimination arises when female managers encounter inadequate information and perceive loan procedures as complex and lacking clarity regarding the request for the lenders' history.

Gender and Financial Access

There are important challenges that prevent entrepreneurs' credit access for both genders. Two main research strands that were discussed are the lending behaviours (demand side) and failure of credit markets as well as the complexity of the country's financial institutions (supply side). Both strands of research focus on explaining financial assessment and trying to figure out how to improve the quality of credit assessment.

According to the first strand, credit demand may differ based on differences of the two genders' viewpoints. For example, women may be more likely than men to save informally. Also, women may have a greater distaste for risk and patience. In these cases, women entrepreneurs would not be discouraged from applying for credit due to the complexity of application procedures or unfavourable loan and credit terms. Rather, their self-selection persists even in the absence of discriminatory lending practices and does not relate to the observed creditworthiness of their firms. Studies on the woman credit access by Ghosh (2004) and Gugerty (2007) indicated that women-led firms are often small and operate in the informal sectors, where the information is unavailable, inconsistent, and noisy. Later, Morgan and Trinh (2020) found that women have a lower degree of financial literacy compared to men and this simultaneously affects their default possibility and the taste of risk. These theoretical and empirical studies suggest that credit-promoting programs from governments to support the financially marginalized groups are needed (Hoff & Stiglitz, 1997; Stiglitz & Weiss, 1981).

According to the second strand, both, credit markets (specifically) and financial institutions (in general), can hinder people from both genders to access formal financial services. This can be due to a variety of factors such as lack of infrastructure, limited access to technology, or lack of financial literacy among the population. For example, inquiring into the reason for African banks typically recording low lending (Andrianova et al., 2015) found that low quality in institutions is a major factor inhibiting bank's lending. Similarly (Galor & Zeira, 1993) stipulated that the financial institution would rather stay liquid if there is no preventive approach or legal warranty assuring their investment's capital safety. Besides, formal institutions are struggling to validate small-scale businesses, due to bookkeeping malpractice and lack of un-auditability by credible parties. Therefore, the reason for the limited credit access may be due to the poor quality of the institutions that govern the financial system.

Gender and Indigeneity

Both gender issues and indigenous knowledge are critically discussed by the emerging debate on pre- and post-coloniality literature on entrepreneurship and management. The debate revolves around decolonizing the, still mostly Western, entrepreneurship and management literature.

Recent studies highlight the value of indigenous perspectives. Banerjee (2022) showed how indigenous business draws on local non-Western knowledge, distinct from Western political economies. Bastien et al. (2022) recommend shifting from colonialism to indigenous business scholars to end discrimination. Filatotchev et al. (2022) advocate contextualized management research using an open systems perspective. Bruton et al. (2022) developed a theory on indigenous knowledge and local contexts. Boussebaa (2022) found an absence of decolonizing perspectives in international business research. All the aforementioned authors offer a postcolonial critique of studies on professional service firms, seen as bearing universal validity without local nuance.

A need for more indigenous entrepreneurship scholarship remains, especially from the geographical areas of Vietnam and Thailand. As Padilla-Meléndez et al. put it, the research field of indigenous entrepreneurship in the specificity of geographical and social-cultural context is needed for future efforts both from empirical and theory building (Padilla-Meléndez et al., 2022). Also, the few literature addressing this field is still dispersed and fragmented (Salmon et al., 2022). Scholarly efforts in this field would help to decolonize literature by examining entrepreneurship through an indigenous lens which will lead to more culturally relevant and impactful business and entrepreneurial frameworks, ultimately leading to economic growth in regions direly needing it.

Our study contributes to raise awareness of the aforementioned lack in literature by investigating rural entrepreneurship and financial access in Vietnam and Thailand. We compare differences and similarities between the two countries regarding gender-based discrimination. The results will provide indigenous insights into credit barriers, informing policies to support entrepreneurship in these developing Southeast Asian contexts.

Our Contribution

In our study, we focus on gender discrimination in credit access of non-farm self-employed household businesses in two Southeast Asian countries Thailand and Vietnam, to fill two, main research gaps that we identified: first, we found a lack of studies comparing two countries at the same time. This may be due to lack of data, complexity when comparing two different countries, missing information, knowledge, and/or imperfection of data collection. Second, previous studies focused on the enterprise level, mostly on small and medium-sized businesses, disregarding the household level. Our study not only analyses the enterprise level but also the household level. Besides, our research focuses only on rural environment as the entrepreneurs surveyed are non-farming and self-employed nature. These entrepreneurs can also be viewed as indigenous enterprises due to their locality nature. Therefore, our study aims to investigate gender discrimination of rural, self-employed, household businesses from Thailand and Vietnam.

With regard to the theoretical framework, we analysed gender discrimination in the credit market using both taste-based and statistical discrimination-related theories (Becker, 2010; Phelps, 1972). These two economic theories are employed as we aim to provide insights that are meaningful to microcredit practitioners and policymakers. Besides, our study focuses on entrepreneurs who applied for formal loans (rather than informal ones) to eliminate the influences of the money-demand side. To explain, indigenous people from rural areas in both countries can receive financial support from informal sources such as money lending from kinship or other indigenous relations, or formally from financial mainstream sources such as banking and venture funds. Informal financing can be important for indigenous entrepreneurs who may not have access to traditional banking services or who may face other barriers to accessing formal financing. Still, informal financing can be riskier. Mainstream financial sources are more stable and reliable but may require more stringent requirements for creditworthiness assessment and other factors. Besides, informal lending among family, friends, or neighbours may not be subject to gender discrimination. Hence, our study focuses only on formal credit.

Research Methodology

Data Source and Variable Description

Our study employs the dataset "Thailand Vietnam Socio Economic Panel" (TVSEP). This is a long-term panel project from 2015 to 2024 in the two countries that was financed by a German research funding organization named Deutsche Forschungsgemeinschaft. The data comprised data from 3 provinces from North-eastern Thailand (Nakhon Phanom, Ubon Ratchathani and Buriram) and 3 provinces from North Central Coast Vietnam (Ha Tinh and Thua Thien Hue) and the Central Highlands (Dak Lak). These surveyed provinces all share borders with Laos and/or Cambodia's neighbouring countries—also Southeast Asian economies. TVSEP originally aimed to promote research in the context of rapidly transforming rural areas to better understand income development and poverty reduction. Using this comprehensive dataset for our specific research targets, we collect only 6 out of 9 available panel waves in total and then select supportive data for further analysis purposes. The completed and cleaned dataset for our study is displayed in Table 10.1.

The differences found in statistics from 3901 observations of Vietnam compared to Thailand are generally not significant. Loan applications and approval rates in both countries are more than 66%, which shows the popularity and importance of formal loan access in rural areas. The annual interest rate of Thailand is around 4% while Vietnam's is slightly higher at 5% on average. In contrast, the average loan duration of Thailand is hardly lower than Vietnam's—the difference is about 2 months longer. However, collaterals of loans differ significantly between the two countries in both average ($3,387 in Vietnam and $6,697 in Thailand) and standard deviation indexes ($16,62 in Vietnam and $30,79 in Thailand). This can be explained by another variable of a household characteristic that is plot size: Thailand's average land area is roughly triple the size than Vietnam's in the relevant dataset. Besides, the annual income from agricultural activities of Thailand is, on average, double the value compared to Vietnam.

Besides, with regard to the gender differences, the percentage of female household heads in Thailand is higher than Vietnam's (26.3% and 16.6%, respectively). Interestingly, the rate of female business heads in Thailand is lower than that of Vietnam (55.1% and 67.9%, respectively). This controversy can be explained by the fact that Vietnam is one of the countries that has the highest shares of women in work globally. Besides,

Table 10.1 Descriptive statistics and variable definition

Variables	*Vietnam*		*Thailand*		*Definition*
	Mean	*Std.Dev*	*Mean*	*Std.Dev*	
Loan					
Apply	0.716	0.451	0.803	0.398	One if the household applied for a loan, zero otherwise
Loan approval	0.660	0.474	0.754	0.431	One if the household got at least one loan, zero otherwise
Interest	5.170	6.260	4.307	4.272	Annual interest rate (%)
Duration	18.480	15.340	16.030	12.070	Loan maturity (in months)
Collateral	3,387	16,62	6,697	30,79	Value of collateral (2005 PPP$)
Gender					
Female household head	0.166	0.372	0.263	0.440	One if the household head is female, zero otherwise
Female manager	0.679	0.467	0.551	0.497	One if the household business manager is female, zero otherwise
Business					
Business age	10.030	8.049	11.280	11.060	Age of the household business (in years)
Business labours	1.994	2.286	2.640	4.139	Number of average main labourers in last 12 months (people)
Business revenue	26,559	126,771	30,731	112,673	Business revenue (2005 PPP$)
Household head					
Age	50.6	11.89	56.89	12.91	Age of the household head (in years)
Literacy	0.945	0.228	0.938	0.241	One if the household head can read and write, zero otherwise
Household					
Independence	3.705	1.715	3.752	1.654	The number of household members with age ranging 15 to 64
Size	5.44	1.831	5.488	2.181	Number of members in the household

(continued)

Table 10.1 (continued)

Variables	*Vietnam*		*Thailand*		*Definition*
	Mean	*Std.Dev*	*Mean*	*Std.Dev*	
Official network	0.707	0.455	0.077	0.267	One if the household is a member of a socio-political organization
Plot size	4.737	19.3	11.01	21.92	Land size of the household (1000 m^2)
Income	7,337	8,706	15,653	34,999	Annual income from agricultural activities of the household (2005 PPP$)
Instrument variables					
Savings	1,107	3,936	2,122	24,095	The amount of household savings at the time surveyed (2005 PPP$)
Loan for business	0.371	0.483	0.487	0.500	One if the loan applications are for business purposes, zero otherwise
Number of loans rejected	0.057	0.242	0.052	0.233	Number of loans rejected

Notes N = 3091

Thailand has a longer average age of business and number of labourers which may be caused by a more developed market economy history than Vietnam's. Furthermore, Thailand was never colonized by any European power, hence, having a long history of independence while Vietnam is a younger state, having declared its independence in 1945. On the other hand, though both countries have many similarities in their population in rural areas, Thailand's whole economy is still larger than that of Vietnam in terms of GDP, leading to a considerable, noteworthy gap in economic ranking towards Vietnam.

Hypothesis Development and Empirical Models

To analyse the first two research questions, our study proposes the following hypothesis: a loan taken by female leader entrepreneur is more expensive, shorter maturity, and/or more collateral demanding than one taken by a man (H0). In a separate note, given that, de jure legal ownership of indigenous entrepreneurs in rural areas can sometimes be, de facto, incorrect, we further classify two possible scenarios based on the available datasets: (1) female is the head of a rural household and (2) female is the leader of a business. According to the hypothesis, the primary model of or study is as below:

$$P(Y_{it} = 1|Female = 1, X) = \Phi(Female_{it}\psi + X_{it}\beta) \quad (10.1)$$

To explain model (10.1), on the left-hand side, Y_{it} is a binary variable: 1 meaning enterprise ith at time t has a loan, whereas 0 is otherwise. Also, $Female_{it}$ is a binary and also a control variable: 1 means enterprise ith at time t is led by a woman, whereas 0 is otherwise. Besides, $X_{it} = (x_{1it}, x_{2it}, \ldots, x_{kit})$ is the $(1 \times k)$ vectors of other control variables presented for borrowers' characteristics. On the right-hand side, Φ is assumed to follow a normal distribution for model (10.1). So, if the coefficient ψ of $Female_{it}$ is found to be significant, this would mean that gender discrimination is present in the context of conditions for credit approval in the studied country.

Model (10.1) is the main model in our study; however, it may suffer statistical errors, mostly selection bias and endogeneity, which may lead to further errors in statistical inference and hypothesis testing. Therefore, to eliminate such risk, Model (10.2), applies a Heckman function together with instrument variables (IV) to fit a maximum-likelihood model with sample selection and endogeneity. Model (10.2) shows the probability based on common characteristics of the dataset and enterprises that apply for a loan.

$$P(Y_{it} = 1|Female_i, X_{it}, Z_{it}) = \Phi(X_{it}\beta + Female_i\psi, Z_{it}\gamma, \boldsymbol{\Sigma}) \quad (10.2)$$

Model (10.2) includes $Z_{it} = (z_{1it}, z_{2it}, \ldots, z_{k'it})$ with the $(1 \times k')$ vectors that affect an entrepreneur to enter the credit market when applying for a loan. Z_{it} indicates the level of household savings, representing an instrumental variable (IV). Savings are considered a valid IV in this context, as a household not having sufficient savings to cover their business needs would ultimately need to seek a loan. Furthermore, in a study on household finances, Myers (2000) found that a household typically relies firstly on internal financial sources like savings and, if these are insufficient, only then on external sources such as microcredit. More importantly, from the viewpoint of the lender, the decision-making process for a loan application is not impacted by the household's savings as it is assumed that the lender has no means of knowing it with certainty. Thus, considering savings as IV is valid in this study as savings make a real impact on a household's decision (internal party) while unobservable to credit lender (external parties). Besides, Model (10.2) incorporates an assumption of the auto-covariance matrix ($\boldsymbol{\Sigma}$): each element of diagonal entries of the auto-covariance matrix is equal to 1, while being itself the correlation of another random variable. Similarly, the coefficients β and γ are $(k \times 1)$ and $(k' \times 1)$ vectors, respectively.

To validate the hypothesis Ho, our study uses different regression functions for loan application (with dummy variable *Loan_application*) and other supporting variables for loan application as Model (10.3) indicates:

$$Y_{it} = \alpha + Female_{it}\beta + X_{it}\theta + Loan\_approved_{it}\pi + \varepsilon_{it} \quad (10.3)$$

Here, Y_{it} represents the dependent variables, $Female_{it}$ is either female-headed household or entrepreneur, X_{it} represents money borrowers' characteristics, and ε_{it} stands for errors. Besides, the new variable $Loan\_approved_{it}$ is based on by $Z_{it} = [z_{1it}, z_{2it}]$ which is taken from model (10.2). $Loan\_approved_{it}$ can be number of rejected loans (IV2) or loan's business purposes (IV3). These two new IVs are created to eliminate a possible selection bias caused by a potential correlation between dependent and independent variables. The case being addressed is if a firm has formerly been qualified to receive a loan by a moneylender, meaning that this household has a low credit risk. Therefore, if there are omitted variables that are crucial to the lending decision of both formal and informal lenders, the two new IVs are employed to improve the robustness of the regression process.

Empirical Results

Mean Differences Test

First, tests of mean differences between four categories classified by two genders (male, female) of two countries (Thailand, Vietnam) are performed. Specifically, the null hypothesis of such tests is that the mean values of the variables are statistically the same for women as for men in each country, i.e., no difference would exist when comparing the two genders. Table 10.2 displays preliminary results after testing 3295 households from Vietnam and 3091 from Thailand.

Table 10.2 The difference in mean tests for two groups of business

	Vietnam (N = *3295)*			*Thailand* (N = *3091)*		
	μ_1 *(Female)*	μ_2 *(Male)*	t	μ_1 *(Female)*	μ_2 *(Male)*	t
Loan application	0.72	0.71	0.49 (0.63)	0.82	0.79	2.87*** (0.00)
Loan approved	0.66	0.65	0.55 (0.58)	0.76	0.75	3.13*** (0.00)
Interest	5.36	4.27	3.82*** (0.00)	4.43	4.21	2.31** (0.02)
Duration	18.5	18.4	0.21 (0.83)	16.80	15.40	3.70*** (0.00)
Collateral	3740.5	1622.3	4.48*** (0.00)	7567.74	5987.35	3.36*** (0.00)
Firm age	10.12	9.58	1.46 (0.14)	11.31	11.25	1.55 (0.12)
Labour	2.03	1.79	2.84*** (0.00)	2.85	2.47	4.74*** (0.00)
Revenue	28,680	15,881	4.36*** (0.00)	35,381.61	26,945.7	2.51** (0.02)
Age of business leader	49.31	57.06	−12.17*** (0.00)	56.09	57.54	−8.17*** (0.00)
Literacy	0.97	0.84	8.00*** (0.00)	0.95	0.93	7.65*** (0.00)

(continued)

Table 10.2 (continued)

	Vietnam (N = *3295)*			*Thailand* (N = *3091)*		
	μ_1 *(Female)*	μ_2 *(Male)*	t	μ_1 *(Female)*	μ_2 *(Male)*	t
Household size	5.57	4.80	8.10^{***} (0.00)	5.43	5.54	−1.32 (0.19)
Linkage with political party	0.71	0.70	0.20 (0.84)	0.07	0.08	4.53^{***} (0.00)
Land area (1000 m2)	5.05	3.14	3.69^{***} (0.00)	11.74	10.42	0.27 (0.78)
Income (household)	7642.1	5802.7	5.21^{***} (0.00)	16,550.90	14,922.39	1.52 (0.13)
Saving (household)	1207.8	600.2	4.96^{***} (0.00)	2649.80	1693.17	1.96^{*} (0.05)
Purpose of loan	0.38	0 0.33	2.31^{***} (0.02)	0.51	0.47	1.95^{*} (0.05)
No loans rejected	0.06	0.06	−0.31 (0.75)	0.05	0.05	−0.99 (0.32)

Notes P-values are reported in parentheses. *, **, ***, respectively, denote the statistical significance at 10, 5, 1%. μ_1, μ_2 stand for the mean of the two subgroups

The results show that women-led enterprises are more likely to apply for loans and also receive approvals for loans compared to man-led enterprises in both countries. From rural Thailand, 82% of enterprises led by women applied for at least one loan with an average maturity of 16.8 months and 76% were approved by formal lending institutions, while these three figures are smaller for their male counterparts (79%, 15.4 months and 75%, respectively). Interestingly, these preliminary results indicate a male rather than female discrimination as women had better credit access. The t-test in such gender differences was found statistically significant at 1% in Thailand. However, similar tests in Vietnam resulted in the means not being significantly different among genders. Also, Vietnamese statistics show smaller figures in the loan application as well as approvals and higher loan maturities than in Thailand. This can be interpreted as a more developed and attractive credit market as well as lower risks in Thailand's rural regions.

In addition, with regard to interest rate per annum, women managers in Vietnam suffer the highest rate among four other classes (5.36% on average) and at the same time show a statistically significant difference compared to their male counterparts from Vietnam. Besides, women are often asked for a higher collateral than men when applying for loans. In Vietnam, the mean collateral is more than double for female to male, while in Thailand it is 1.3 times higher. With respect to interest rate and collateral, both countries show a statistically significant mean difference suggesting female discrimination.

Other characteristics of businesses in Vietnam and Thailand, such as labour number, revenue, age of business leader, literacy capability, household size, saving, and loan purposes show significant differences between two gender leaders. The biggest difference is in the business leader's age: the average female leader is 49 years old while the male leader is 57 in Vietnam (Thailand: 56 and 58). There are two possibilities that can explain this: first, women-owned, non-farm businesses are often informal and home-based, and tend to be concentrated in small-scale entrepreneurship and traditional sectors such as retail and service. Second female entrepreneurs may tend to have lower growth ambitions than their male counterparts. Interestingly, in Vietnam, linkage with a political party also shows no difference from both genders given the fact that Vietnam is a one-party Communist state while there are many political parties in Thailand.

Heckman and Instrument Variable Estimations

Next, our study applies the analytical framework of the Heckman model (Heckman, 1979) to eliminate the selection bias risk in large-scale panel data. Besides, the three IVs are also implemented in these estimations to reduce endogenous-related risk. The regression results are shown in Tables 10.3 and 10.4. Four determinants of each loan including approval rate, interest rate, duration, and collateral are, respectively, treated as dependent variables in each model of female-led enterprises and female-led households.

Overall, surprisingly, no clear gender discrimination towards female in the context of credit access in Vietnam and Thailand was found. So, the null hypothesis is rejected. A possible reason to explain this is that moneylenders systematically do consider gender of their borrowers when deciding on loan approvals. So, regardless of the gender of an enterprise leader or a household, the chance to receive a formal loan is not reduced for women compared to men.

However, the results do suggest a slight gender discrimination. Specifically, women-led entrepreneurs in Thailand have a 1% higher probability of having a loan approved compared to men. Similarly, the results also suggest male discrimination as women-led businesses receive longer maturity for loans, and women-led households require lower collaterals in Thailand compared to their male counterparts. This is in line with the preliminary findings when comparing means. Therefore, a robust conclusion on gender discrimination towards female cannot be determined as there might be other invisible and non-quantifiable factors that cannot be accessed via this dataset. For example, as the panel data was processed for a longer period, interest rate fluctuations may play a role; or there are differences between the regulations and preferable options between different moneylenders; or case-by-case study cannot be accessed given some statistics assumptions (e.g., maximum likelihoods, normal distributions, etc.). Besides, the other three loan determinants do also not display statically significant discrimination in gender, from both female-led enterprises and female-led households (Table 10.3).

Table 10.3 Impact of business characteristics on credit access in Vietnam

	Loan approve	*Loan approve*	*Interest (%)*	*Interest (%)*	*Duration*	*Duration*	*Collateral*	*Collateral*
Household head	0.004		−1.335*		1.658		−1.005***	
	(0.007)		(0.717)		(1.045)		(0.348)	
Business head		0.029		−0.225		0.689		−0.196***
		(0.021)		(0.211)		(0.752)		(0.051)
Firm age	−0.001	−0.001	0.037***	0.041***	0.0157	0.008	0.011	0.015*
	(0.001)	(0.001)	(0.012)	(0.009)	(0.078)	(0.081)	(0.009)	(0.009)
Total labour	−0.003	−0.003	0.084	0.080	−0.238**	−0.226***	0.172***	0.168***
	(0.005)	(0.004)	(0.063)	(0.066)	(0.093)	(0.073)	(0.019)	(0.023)
Revenue	0.005	0.004	−0.035	−0.024	−0.395***	−0.421***	0.206	0.216
	(0.007)	(0.006)	(0.080)	(0.101)	(0.102)	(0.138)	(0.147)	(0.161)
Age of head	−0.001	−0.001	0.007	−0.005	−0.028	−0.014	0.027	0.018
	(0.001)	(0.001)	(0.016)	(0.012)	(0.019)	(0.013)	(0.021)	(0.020)
Literate	0.008	0.007	0.672	1.079**	2.554***	2.037***	−0.010	0.299*
	(0.020)	(0.018)	(0.468)	(0.490)	(0.814)	(0.676)	(0.129)	(0.179)
No. Dependent	0.012*	0.012	−0.108	−0.076	0.312	0.270	−0.021	0.004
	(0.007)	(0.007)	(0.103)	(0.093)	(0.221)	(0.234)	(0.101)	(0.112)
Household size	−0.007	−0.007	0.040	0.061	−0.037	−0.061	0.013	0.029
	(0.013)	(0.013)	(0.107)	(0.115)	(0.185)	(0.183)	(0.093)	(0.087)
Political party	0.014	0.015	0.290	0.307	0.477	0.449	−0.308***	−0.296***
	(0.011)	(0.012)	(0.243)	(0.241)	(0.355)	(0.340)	(0.111)	(0.104)
Land area	0.012	0.013	0.124	0.179	0.247	0.179	0.391***	0.433***
	(0.012)	(0.014)	(0.102)	(0.112)	(1.038)	(1.088)	(0.131)	(0.161)
Income per capita	0.010	0.011	0.199***	0.212***	−0.047	−0.058	0.151***	0.161***
	(0.008)	(0.007)	(0.037)	(0.036)	(0.258)	(0.265)	(0.030)	(0.032)
Saving	−0.081***	−0.081***						
	(0.020)	(0.020)						

(continued)

Table 10.3 (continued)

	Loan approve	*Loan approve*	*Interest (%)*	*Interest (%)*	*Duration*	*Duration*	*Collateral*	*Collateral*
Loan purpose			6.313***	6.314***	6.328***	6.330***	6.308***	6.311***
			(0.171)	(0.189)	(0.228)	(0.261)	(0.273)	(0.296)
Previously rejected Loan			−12.575***	−12.539***	−12.609***	−12.576***	−12.568***	−12.533***
			(0.270)	(0.269)	(0.260)	(0.259)	(0.256)	(0.258)
N	3,295	3,295	3,295	3,295	3,295	3,295	3,295	3,295

Notes Robust standard deviation is reported in parentheses. ***, **, *, respectively, denote statistical significance at 1, 5, 10%. Year and provincial fixed effects are included but not reported

Table 10.4 Impact of business characteristics on credit access in Thailand

	Loan approve	*Loan approve*	*Interest (%)*	*Interest (%)*	*Duration*	*Duration*	*Collateral*	*Collateral*
Household head	−0.031		−0.142		−1.014*		−0.518***	
	(0.036)		(0.199)		(0.559)		(0.073)	
Business head		0.010***		−0.125		−1.174***		−0.371
		(0.002)		(0.177)		(0.220)		(0.335)
Firm age	−0.001	−0.001*	−0.007	−0.007	−0.009	−0.007	−0.020*	−0.018*
	(0.001)	(0.000)	(0.012)	(0.012)	(0.032)	(0.031)	(0.010)	(0.010)
Total labour	0.001	0.001	−0.0348*	−0.0351**	0.057	0.054	0.050***	0.050***
	(0.002)	(0.002)	(0.018)	(0.018)	(0.054)	(0.055)	(0.008)	(0.010)
Revenue	0.007	0.007*	0.070***	0.069***	0.274**	0.271**	0.246***	0.245***
	(0.005)	(0.004)	(0.016)	(0.016)	(0.131)	(0.129)	(0.053)	(0.052)
Age of head	−0.001	−0.001***	0.000	0.000	−0.010	−0.012	−0.005	−0.007
	(0.001)	(0.000)	(0.003)	(0.004)	(0.017)	(0.021)	(0.007)	(0.008)
Literate	0.014	0.023	−0.155	−0.122	−0.601	−0.377	0.227	−0.103
	(0.040)	(0.045)	(0.138)	(0.134)	(1.670)	(1.550)	(0.615)	(0.667)
No. Dependent	−0.004	−0.004	0.023	0.026	−0.071	−0.041	0.072	0.083
	(0.014)	(0.012)	(0.066)	(0.063)	(0.277)	(0.269)	(0.064)	(0.065)
Household size	0.002	0.002	0.005	0.006	−0.015	−0.008	−0.132***	−0.128**
	(0.009)	(0.008)	(0.038)	(0.038)	(0.104)	(0.110)	(0.047)	(0.050)
Political party	0.032	0.028***	−0.204	−0.185	−0.482	−0.318	−0.224**	−0.159*
	(0.020)	(0.010)	(0.264)	(0.297)	(0.643)	(0.606)	(0.095)	(0.092)
Land area	0.034***	0.036***	0.400***	0.401***	0.513***	0.506***	0.903***	0.911***
	(0.012)	(0.012)	(0.049)	(0.047)	(0.160)	(0.143)	(0.245)	(0.221)
Income per capita	0.002	0.002	−0.100	−0.098	0.462**	0.477***	0.201***	0.207***
	(0.008)	(0.008)	(0.081)	(0.079)	(0.185)	(0.180)	(0.060)	(0.057)
Saving	−0.037***	−0.038***						
	(0.008)	(0.007)						

(continued)

Table 10.4 (continued)

	Loan approve	*Loan approve*	*Interest (%)*	*Interest (%)*	*Duration*	*Duration*	*Collateral*	*Collateral*
Loan purpose			6.270***	6.285***	6.616***	6.610***	6.329***	6.328***
			(0.217)	(0.247)	(0.132)	(0.140)	(0.144)	−0.146
Previously rejected Loan			−13.183***	−13.194***	−13.441***	−13.432***	−13.076***	−13.071***
			(0.356)	(0.369)	(0.244)	(0.241)	(0.283)	(0.270)
N	3091	3091	3091	3091	3091	3091	3091	3091

Notes Robust standard deviation is reported in parentheses. ***, **, *, respectively, denote statistical significance at 1, 5, 10 %. Year and provincial fixed effects are included but not reported

Blinder–Oaxaca Decomposition Test

Finally, to capture the mean difference in gender of the four loan determinants, the Blinder–Oaxaca decomposition test (Blinder, 1973; Oaxaca, 1973) is employed in our study to test the robustness of the first two statical techniques. Technically, this test is a statistical method that explains differences in dependent variable means between two groups. It decomposes the gap into two parts: one due to differences in independent variable means within groups (prediction 1, male only), and one due to differences in independent variable effects across groups (prediction 2, female only). Then, the results of two predictions shall be presented as differences (male–female), explained/unexplained, and the interaction between them.

The results obtained from the Blinder–Oaxaca decomposition test are presented in Table 10.5. The main difference (by gender) found is in loan collateral of both female headed households and enterprises in both Vietnam and Thailand, which is similar to the preliminary results of the mean difference t-tests. Besides, a statistically significant difference of 1% of woman-led households in loan approval is also identified in Thailand—which is also in line with the previous results.

Conclusion and Policy Implications

This study makes several key contributions to indigenous entrepreneurship scholarship. First, it contributes to decolonizing the field by providing an in-depth examination of rural entrepreneurship in Vietnam and Thailand through an indigenous lens. The context-specific results offer new perspectives beyond Western theories on entrepreneurial discrimination and financial access.

Second, the comparative analysis of two developing Southeast Asian countries addresses notable gaps in indigenous research identified by Padilla-Meléndez et al. (2022) and Salmon et al. (2022). The findings provide important insights into how gender impacts indigenous entrepreneurs in Vietnam and Thailand, advancing limited knowledge in this geographical area.

Third, the mixed-methods approach combining statistical tests, instrumental variables, and Heckman techniques rigorously investigates financial discrimination. This addresses calls for more empirical indigenous

Table 10.5 Blinder–Oaxaca decomposition

	Vietnam							
	Female household head				*Female manager*			
	Loan approve	Interest	Duration	Collateral	Loan approve	Interest	Duration	Collateral
Prediction 1	0.662***	5.355***	18.512***	1.893***	0.660***	5.418***	18.097***	1.994***
	(0.009)	(0.120)	(0.292)	(0.071)	(0.015)	(0.200)	(0.4653)	(0.116)
Prediction 2	0.649***	4.268***	18.359***	1.160***	0.660***	5.060***	18.669***	1.666***
	(0.020)	(0.258)	(0.659)	(0.128)	(0.010)	(0.130)	(0.326)	(0.074)
Difference	0.013	1.088***	0.152	0.733***	0.0003	0.358	−0.571	0.328**
	(0.022)	(0.285)	(0.721)	(0.146)	(0.018)	(0.238)	(0.568)	(0.138)
Explained	0.055***	0.528***	2.198***	0.197***	0.017***	0.215***	0.224	0.167***
	(0.011)	(0.136)	(0.353)	(0.072)	(0.005)	(0.071)	(0.197)	(0.045)
Unexplained	−0.042*	0.560*	−2.046***	0.536***	−0.016	0.143	−0.796	0.161
	(0.024)	(0.308)	(0.747)	(0.158)	(0.018)	(0.237)	(0.563)	(0.136)
Interaction	−0.216	−2.078	−3.915	−1.844	0.168	−2.530	−3.430	−1.013
	(0.205)	(2.653)	(6.600)	(1.227)	(0.199)	(2.514)	(5.339)	(1.277)

	Thailand							
	Female household head				*Female manager*			
	Loan Approve	Interest	Duration	Collateral	Loan Approve	Interest	Duration	Collateral
Prediction 1	0.769***	4.413***	16.507***	2.764***	0.765***	4.430***	16.802***	2.832***
	(0.009)	(0.089)	(0.253)	(0.091)	(0.011)	(0.113)	(0.330)	(0.118)
Prediction 2	0.712***	4.008***	14.692***	2.007***	0.745***	4.206***	15.401***	2.348***
	(0.016)	(0.151)	(0.421)	(0.135)	(0.011)	(0.105)	(0.287)	(0.099)
Difference	0.057***	0.405**	1.816***	0.757***	0.020	0.223	1.400***	0.484***
	(0.018)	(0.175)	(0.491)	(0.163)	(0.016)	(0.154)	(0.437)	(0.154)
Explained	0.038***	0.259***	0.930***	0.382***	0.010**	0.101***	0.188	0.154***
	(0.007)	(0.061)	(0.176)	(0.065)	(0.004)	(0.039)	(0.117)	(0.048)
Unexplained	0.019	0.146	0.886*	0.375**	0.010	0.123	1.212***	0.330**
	(0.019)	(0.181)	(0.497)	(0.167)	(0.015)	(0.152)	(0.431)	(0.150)
Interaction	0.227	3.448**	−0.853	0.654	0.188	1.464	5.309	−0.145
	(0.187)	(1.667)	(4.855)	(1.655)	(0.195)	(1.609)	(4.612)	(1.555)

Notes Standard deviation is reported in parenthesis. *, **, ***, respectively, denote the 10, 5, 1% statistical significance

scholarship by Bastien et al. (2022). The paper demonstrates how quantitative studies can complement qualitative methods dominating current literature.

For practitioners, the results suggest microfinance programs in Vietnam and Thailand to successfully serve female and male entrepreneurs equally. This is a model for other developing contexts seeking to uplift indigenous entrepreneurs through financial inclusion. However, female indigenous entrepreneurs with political connections in Thailand can further leverage these ties to improve access. Additionally, more initiatives are needed to raise awareness of updated gender norms in rural areas based on principles of decoloniality. Persistent colonial attitudes marginalizing indigenous women must be dismantled to empower female leadership. Focused trainings through community organizations and NGOs can transform traditional mindsets.

Future studies should explore informal financing among indigenous networks versus formal bank lending. More data on loan source preferences and rejection rates can reveal remaining gender discrepancies. Researchers can also conduct interviews and focus groups to understand nuanced discrimination experiences of indigenous female entrepreneurs accessing finance. Advanced analytical techniques from development economics and econometrics should be applied to expand the statistical robustness of findings. And expanded panels over longer timeframes can track progress on gender equality as indigenous entrepreneurship grows. Engagement with critical perspectives from Banerjee (2022) and Boussebaa (2022) can situate results within updated theories.

This study provides a useful foundation, but more indigenous scholarship is critical as called for by Filatotchev et al. (2022) and Bruton et al. (2022). Exploring entrepreneurship through local lenses reveals the precise support needed for vulnerable populations to equitably thrive in their traditional contexts.

References

Andrianova, S., Baltagi, B., Demetriades, P., & Fielding, D. (2015). Why do African banks lend so little? *Oxford Bulletin of Economics and Statistics, 77*(3), 339–359.

Aterido, R., Beck, T., & Iacovone, L. (2013). Access to finance in Sub-Saharan Africa: Is there a gender gap? *World Development, 47*, 102–120.

Banerjee, S. B. (2022). Decolonizing management theory: A critical perspective. *Journal of Management Studies, 59*(4), 1074–1087. https://doi.org/10.1111/joms.12756

Bastien, F., Coraiola, D. M., & Foster, W. M. (2022). Indigenous peoples and organization studies. *Organization Studies, 44*(4), 659–675. https://doi.org/10.1177/01708406221141545

Becker, G. S. (2010). *The economics of discrimination.* University of Chicago Press.

Bertrand, M., Chugh, D., & Mullainathan, S. (2005). Implicit discrimination. *American Economic Review, 95*(2), 94–98.

Blinder, A. S. (1973). Wage discrimination: Reduced form and structural estimates. *Journal of Human Resources, 8*(4), 436–455.

Boussebaa, M. (2022). Unsettling West-centrism in the study of professional service firms. *Human Relations*, 00187267221128262. https://doi.org/10.1177/00187267221128262

Brock, J. M., & De Haas, R. (2019). *Gender discrimination in small business lending: Evidence from a lab in the field experiment in Turkey.* European Bank for Reconstruction and Development.

Bruton, G. D., Zahra, S. A., Van de Ven, A. H., & Hitt, M. A. (2022). Indigenous theory uses, abuses, and future. *Journal of Management Studies, 59*(4), 1057–1073. https://doi.org/10.1111/joms.12755

Elborgh-Woytek, M. K., Newiak, M. M., Kochhar, M. K., Fabrizio, M. S., Kpodar, M. K., Wingender, M. P., Clements, M. B. J., & Schwartz, M. G. (2013). *Women, work, and the economy: Macroeconomic gains from gender equity.* International Monetary Fund.

Filatotchev, I., Ireland, R. D., & Stahl, G. K. (2022). Contextualizing management research: An open systems perspective. *Journal of Management Studies, 59*(4), 1036–1056. https://doi.org/10.1111/joms.12754

Galor, O., & Zeira, J. (1993). Income distribution and macroeconomics. *The Review of Economic Studies, 60*(1), 35–52.

Ghosh, J. (2004). *Informalisation and women's workforce participation: A consideration of recent trends in Asia.* Report on gender equality: Striving for justice in an unequal world, United Nations Research Institute for Social Development, Geneva.

Gugerty, M. K. (2007). You can't save alone: Commitment in rotating savings and credit associations in Kenya. *Economic Development and Cultural Change, 55*(2), 251–282.

Heckman, J. J. (1979). Sample selection bias as a specification error. *Econometrica: Journal of the Econometric Society, 47*, 153–161.

Hoff, K., & Stiglitz, J. E. (1997). Moneylenders and bankers: Price-increasing subsidies in a monopolistically competitive market. *Journal of Development Economics, 52*(2), 429–462.

Morgan, P. J., & Trinh, L. Q. (2020). *Fintech and financial literacy in Viet Nam* (ADBI Working Paper 1154). Asian Development Bank Institute, Tokyo.
Morsy, H., El-Shal, A., & Woldemichael, A. (2019). *Women self-selection out of the credit market in Africa* (Working Paper Series, No. 317). African Development Bank, Abidjan.
Myers, S. C. (2000). Outside equity. *The Journal of Finance, 55*(3), 1005–1037. https://doi.org/10.1111/0022-1082.00239
Oaxaca, R. (1973). Male-female wage differentials in urban labor markets. *International Economic Review, 14*(3), 693–709.
Padilla-Meléndez, A., Plaza-Angulo, J. J., Del-Aguila-Obra, A. R., & Ciruela-Lorenzo, A. M. (2022). Indigenous entrepreneurship. Current issues and future lines. *Entrepreneurship & Regional Development, 34*(1–2), 6–31. https://doi.org/10.1080/08985626.2021.2011962
Pham, T., & Talavera, O. (2018). Discrimination, social capital, and financial constraints: The case of Viet Nam. *World Development, 102*, 228–242. https://doi.org/10.1016/j.worlddev.2017.10.005
Phelps, E. S. (1972). The statistical theory of racism and sexism. *The American Economic Review, 62*(4), 659–661.
Salmon, E., Chavez, R. J. F., & Murphy, M. (2022). New perspectives and critical insights from Indigenous peoples' research: A systematic review of Indigenous management and organization literature. *Academy of Management Annals, 17*(2), 439–491. https://doi.org/10.5465/annals.2021.0132
Shoma, C. D. (2019). Financing female entrepreneurs in cottage, micro, small, and medium enterprises: Evidence from the financial sector in Bangladesh 2010–2018. *Asia & the Pacific Policy Studies, 6*(3), 397–416.
Stiglitz, J. E., & Weiss, A. (1981). Credit rationing in markets with imperfect information. *The American Economic Review, 71*(3), 393–410.
Witbooi, M., & Ukpere, W. (2011). Indigenous female entrepreneurship: Analytical study on access to finance for women entrepreneurs in South Africa. *African Journal of Business Management, 5*(14), 5646.

CHAPTER 11

How Does Business Owner's Employee-Centric Leadership Affect SME Employees' Work Engagement: The Mediating Role of "Diuwongke"

Endro Puspo Wiroko and Ade Iva Murty

Introduction

Small and medium-sized enterprises (SMEs) have significantly contributed to the growth of many countries worldwide. In Indonesia, the sentiment for the sector remains positive due to various investments poured into the country. SMEs in Indonesia absorb a substantial amount of labor, significantly contributing to the nation's economy. The role of human resources, especially leaders (entrepreneurs) and employees, is

E. P. Wiroko (✉)
Universitas Pancasila, South Jakarta, Indonesia
e-mail: endro.puspowiroko@univpancasila.ac.id

A. I. Murty
Sampoerna University, South Jakarta, Indonesia
e-mail: ade.wicaksono@sampoernauniversity.ac.id

E. L. Eijdenberg et al. (eds.), *Indigenous Entrepreneurship in Southeast Asia*, Palgrave Studies in Equity, Diversity, Inclusion, and Indigenization in Business, https://doi.org/10.1007/978-3-031-54457-6_11

crucial for business sustainability (Sulaeman et al., 2019). According to the Indonesia Statistics Bureau in 2020, 84% of SMEs in Indonesia experienced a revenue decrease due to market demand and supply changes impacted by the COVID-19 pandemic. SMEs in Indonesia need help in sustaining competition in the industry. Leadership has proven to be the key ingredient for the success of SME businesses. Therefore, business leaders must have a particular set of leadership skills that can be adopted according to the situation.

Compared to a large company, the most significant difference relates to how leadership is perceived and applied within a small or medium enterprise (SME). This is due to the direct influence of the owner on his/her employees (Mihai et al., 2017). In a large enterprise, leadership is layered in multiple hierarchical levels. In an SME, the owner (usually the manager) directly and personally influences his or her employees. This influence results from involvement in daily operations (Durham et al., 1997). In SMEs, the leader controls activities, including relationships with clients, suppliers, employees, long-term development plans, financial control, and accounting systems. As a result, leadership style is a crucial sign of the leader's predisposition to certain managerial behaviors and actions and is an essential contributor to success.

Researchers have studied how different leadership styles of small business managers affect survival, but research still needs to be done on which leadership strategies improve employee performance. Employee-centric and selfless leadership (known in business literature as servant leadership) shows promising signs of becoming the best practice for organizations in the time to come, including SMEs. In the context of SME businesses, owners play an integral role in the enterprises by engaging in closer work relationships with their employees. Employee-centric and selfless leadership are commonly described as going beyond one's self-interest and concerning people's growth and well-being within the organization (Greenleaf, 1995). A selfless leader is exceptional in a way that noble values are recognized as a vital component of the leadership process (Northouse, 2016). Selfless and employee-centered leadership has been shown to work well in small and medium-sized businesses (Amah & Oyetuunde, 2020; Cahyadi et al., 2022; Hisham et al., 2020; Maula-Bakhsh & Raziq, 2018).

Previous studies have proven a positive relationship between servant leadership and work engagement (Kaya & Karatepe, 2020; Wiroko,

2021). Work engagement can promote the excellence of an organization's ability to achieve its mission, an important matter that is required in present economic challenges (Hoole & Bonnema, 2015). Work engagement is relevant not only to employees in large companies but also in SMEs. Previous studies have shown that work engagement is central among SMEs employees (Ghani et al., 2019; Kusuma et al., 2021; Maden-Eyiusta, 2021; Utami & Sukmawati, 2019). Organizations can support their employees' work engagement using top-down and bottom-up approaches (Bakker & Albrecht, 2018). The first means involves leadership interventions and strategic human resources practices. The second means considered include individual efforts, such as crafting the job, self-help, using a solid personal point, and deploying ego capacities. Organizations can determine which strategy is excellent for supporting environmental and personal resources. This research uses a leader's servant leadership as the top-down approach to predict work engagement.

Although it is clear that servant leadership positively correlates with work engagement, this study argues that there is a mediating mechanism between perceived servant leadership and work engagement. A typical, indigenous Indonesian psychological phenomenon is included to explain the relationship between servant leadership and work engagement: *diuwongke*. This Javanese-Indonesian concept refers to treating people with dignity and respect. Since the current study is carried out in Indonesia, the mediating effect of *diuwongke* is investigated. This refers to being treated kindly and humanely, meaning that the person feels respected, their presence is recognized, their opinion heard, and their contribution considered. In essence, it signifies that the person is allowed to participate in decision-making even though they have less power in the social interaction. The meaning of *diuwongke* can also be inferred linguistically. *Uwong* in the Javanese language or orang in Bahasa Indonesia literally means man/human. Combined with the passive voice *di-kan/ke* (Javanese/Bahasa Indonesia), *di-uwong-ke* literally means "to be treated as human." In Javanese-Indonesian culture, people feel safe and happy when they experience a sense of humanness, that is when they feel treated as human in society (Prasetyo, 2016). Previously, *diuwongke* was examined among employees in a large company (Rahmadani & Schaufeli, 2022). The researchers argue that *diuwongke* will also have a positive impact among SME employees whose business owners are Javanese.

Javanese bosses are expected to have a more personal relationship with employees. Not only managing the employees for business reasons but Javanese bosses are also expected to help when the employees incur personal situations (financial problems and medical bills, for example). The employees also wait for gifts during religious holidays. These practices are common among SMEs whose bosses are Javanese. These bosses' behaviors will create a sense of respect for the employees. If the boss of a smaller firm neglects to do these things, employees will feel unhappy and disengaged from the workplace.

All business owners in this study are Javanese, although they live and open their stores in Jakarta and the surrounding cities. When the business owner displays an employee-centric and selfless leadership style, the SME employees will feel valued for their contributions. They will also feel treated with dignity and respect by the business owner. Instead of merely being treated as a job holder, they are likely to feel a sense of self-worth and be more willing to put effort into their job and contribute to their enterprise. All these feelings are called *diuwongke*. The self-determination theory's (SDT) basic psychological needs (Canavesi & Minelli, 2022) can support this dynamic. Higher levels of *diuwongke* are likely to fulfill employees' competence, relatedness, and autonomy, which, in turn, will increase work engagement. Employees will feel energized and are willing to invest extra energy, attention, and time in their work when their leaders fulfill their basic needs and when they simultaneously treat them kindly and humanely.

Based on previous findings, this research aims to investigate the mediating effect of *diuwongke* in the servant leadership–work engagement relationship. Finally, the authors stated the research problem: Can *diuwongke* mediate between servant leadership and work engagement?

The majority of work engagement studies use the Job Demands-Resources model (JD-R), which Demerouti, Bakker, Nachreiner, and Schaufeli introduced in 2001. The JD-R model supposes that risk factors associated with job-related stress do exist in any work (Barello et al., 2021; Frank et al., 2017). These factors are categorized into two general categories: job demands and resources (Nielsen et al., 2011). Accordingly, the JD-R model comprises an interaction between demands and resources.

The model benefits in alleviating roles, such as preventing oversupply by influencing the connection between depletion and needs. The authors use this JD-R model to contribute to the prevailing literature. The authors hypothesize (H1) that (1) employee-centric and selfless leadership shows a positive correlation with work engagement, (2) employee-centric and selfless leadership shows a positive correlation with *diuwongke*, (3) *diuwongke*

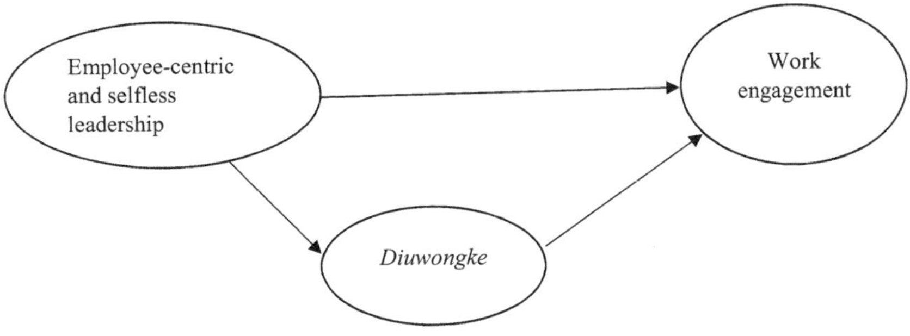

Fig. 11.1 Hypothesised model

shows a positive correlation with work engagement, and (4) ***diuwongke*** mediates employee-centric and selfless leadership and work engagement in the study sample, as shown in Fig. 11.1.

This study is important in several ways. First, it examines the business owner's servant leadership in the SME context. This effort is essential since there is a need to understand how different leadership styles work within the framework of small business enterprises (Howard et al., 2019). Second, we examine ***diuwongke*** as an indigenous psychological phenomenon in Indonesia. This addition is important because more research needs to be done on the different types of indigenous business situations (Croce, 2017). Third, this study is conducted in Indonesia, one of the developing countries. This effort answers the call to explore the dynamics that influence the social construction of indigenous concepts in developed and developing countries (Croce, 2019). Finally, the model that this study suggests becomes a fresh contribution to the body of literature.

Methods

A quantitative correlational study with a cross-sectional research design was employed for this study. Data on three variables were collected from a specific population at a single time. Research participants consisted of male and female employees working in various SMEs in Greater Jakarta and surrounding cities, with a minimum tenure of 6 months. Online questionnaires were distributed using convenience sampling as a non-probability technique. A research assistant supported the authors by contacting some SME owners to distribute the online questionnaire link. The research assistant also visited some SMEs to approach employees, informing them about the questionnaire link and requesting them to share it with their colleagues. Data collection took place from June to December 2022. All participants were informed that participation was voluntary and without any reward. The authors emphasized that all data would be confidential and used solely for academic purposes. The authors also try to comply with research ethics by putting an informed consent form on the front page of the questionnaire. To ensure quality, the authors selected 147 questionnaires for later analysis.

In this study, servant leadership serves as an independent variable, diuwongke acts as a mediating variable, and work engagement is the dependent variable. Three scales were used to collect data: the 9-item Utrecht Work Engagement Scale (UWES), the 6-item Servant Leadership Behavior Scale (SLBS-6) (Sendjaya et al., 2017), and the 10-item *Diuwongke* Scale (Rahmadani & Schaufeli, 2022). Two separate experts in organizational psychology facilitated the translation and back-translation process. Participants were instructed to respond to the given scales.

The Macro Process on SPSS from Hayes was utilized to test the mediation. This method is powerful for predicting path coefficients and generating bootstrap confidence intervals for the total and specific indirect effects of X on Y (Preacher & Hayes, 2008).

Results

Table 11.1 displays participants' demographic information, encompassing gender, age, location, job tenure, product, and education.

The correlation analyses in Table 11.2 elucidate our variables. Hypothesis 1 posited a positive relationship between servant leadership and work engagement. As indicated in Table 11.2, servant leadership is positively correlated with *diuwongke* ($r = 0.148$, $p < 0.05$). The data substantiate Hypothesis 1, suggesting that employees perceiving higher levels of servant leadership from their leaders tend to exhibit increased work engagement. Hypothesis 2 proposed a positive relationship between servant leadership and *diuwongke*. The data in Table 11.2 reveal a positive correlation between servant leadership and *diuwongke* ($r = 0.253$, $p < 0.01$), supporting Hypothesis 2. Employees who perceive a higher level of servant leadership from their leaders also tend to report a higher level of *diuwongke*. Hypothesis 3 predicted a positive relationship between

Table 11.1 Demographic of Participants (n = 147)

Category	*n (%)*
Gender	
Male	57 (40.0%)
Female	90 (60.0%)
Age (year)	
18–22	83 (55%)
23–27	45 (33%)
28–32	16 (10%)
33–37	3 (2%)
Location	
Bekasi	30 (21%)
Bogor	25 (18%)
Depok	21 (13%)
Jakarta	45 (33%)
Karawang	8 (5%)
Tangerang	16 (10%)
Job Tenure (year)	
1–2	77 (52%)
3–4	41 (28%)
5–6	25 (18%)
> 6	3 (2%)
Product	
Grocery	68 (47%)
Foods and Beverages	45 (33%)
Office & school tools	20 (12%)
Others	14 (8%)
Educational Level	
High School	122 (85%)
Diploma	20 (12%)
Bachelor	5 (3%)

diuwongke and work engagement. As depicted in Table 3, *diuwongke* is positively correlated with work engagement ($r = 0.344$, $p < 0.01$). The data validates Hypothesis 3, indicating that employees with a high level of *diuwongke* are more likely to exhibit elevated work engagement.

The results of the study include descriptive statistics such as frequency, mean, and standard deviations, as well as the outcomes of assumptions tests and hypotheses tests. These results were analyzed and presented sequentially. The results section provides an explanation of the data analysis findings.

Table 11.2 Means, Standard Deviations, and Correlations between Study Variables

Variable	*Mean*	*SD*	*1*	*2*	*3*
Perceived servant leadership	34.32	2.238	1		
Diuwongke	43.10	1.764	0.253**	1	
Work engagement	47.55	2.203	0.148*	0.344**	1

n = 147 ** $p < 0.01$ * $p < 0.05$

Discussion

It is hypothesized that ***diuwongke*** mediates between perceived leader's servant leadership and work engagement. The hypothesis (Ha) is supported by the results. This study contributes to the existing literature by revealing new mechanisms from perceived servant leadership to work engagement through the mediation of ***diuwongke***. The authors assert that ***diuwongke*** can mediate between servant leadership and work engagement. A perceived leader's servant leadership emerges as a crucial predictor of work engagement, as this variable proves relevant to employees in the SME context. In the SME setting, variables such as HR practices and other organizational factors may be less pertinent. The close relationship between business owners and employees makes the servant leadership style appropriate. Having a servant leader makes SME employees feel ***diuwongke***, a feeling that is particularly relevant given that their work does not require a sophisticated management style. Employee work engagement levels are elevated when their basic needs are fulfilled, and they feel valued as humans by their leaders. In contrast, when leaders focus solely on satisfying basic needs to motivate employees without treating them with a more profound sense of kindness and humanity, their impact on work engagement is likely to be less intense.

SME owners are looking for the best strategy to manage their employees. Based on this study, indigenous concepts can be taken advantage of in entrepreneurial practices. We can learn from the Javanese SME owners that applying ***diuwongke*** can positively impact their employees. SME owners from other parts of the world can also think of any indigenous concept in their region that will be fit for managing employees.

The authors encountered several limitations during the research process. First, the study sample is relatively small (n = 147) compared to the entire population, and participants were heterogeneous as they came from different workplaces. This condition calls for careful consideration before generalizing the results. Second, there is potential bias due to the self-administered and cross-sectional nature of the study. Third, common method variance (CMV) could still impact the results. Despite these limitations, this study underscores the importance of *diuwongke* as a mediating mechanism in explaining the relationship between perceived employee-centric leadership and work engagement.

Conclusion

This study aimed to contribute to the existing literature by examining leadership styles to predict work engagement. A cross-sectional quantitative approach was chosen to address the research question. It is concluded that *diuwongke* mediates the relationship between perceived employee-centric leadership and work engagement.

As a practical recommendation, SME owners may consider adjusting their leadership style to employee-centric leadership. Additionally, future research is encouraged to target a larger sample for improved generalization. Using multiple enterprises and probability sampling techniques is recommended over snowball sampling, especially with a larger sample size. Organizational studies may benefit from gathering longitudinal data.

Acknowledgements The authors thank the research assistant for assistance in data collection and technical matters.

Declaration The authors thank the research assistant for assistance in data collection and technical matters.

References

Amah, O. E., & Oyetuunde, K. (2020). The effect of servant leadership on employee turnover in SMEs in Nigeria: The role of career growth potential and employee voice. *Journal of Small Business and Enterprise Development, 27*(6), 885–904. https://doi.org/10.1108/JSBED-01-2019-0009

Bakker, A. B., & Albrecht, S. (2018). Work engagement: Current trends. *Career Development International, 23*(1), 4–11. https://doi.org/10.1108/CDI-11-2017-0207

Barello, S., Caruso, R., Palamenghi, L., Nania, T., Dellafiore, F., Bonetti, L., Silenzi, A., Marotta, C., & Graffigna, G. (2021). Factors associated with emotional exhaustion in healthcare professionals involved in the COVID-19 pandemic: An application of the job demands-resources model. *International Archives of Occupational and Environmental Health, 94*(8), 1751–1761. https://doi.org/10.1007/s00420-021-01669-z

Cahyadi, A., Marwa, T., Hágen, I., Siraj, M. N., Santati, P., Poór, J., & Szabó, K. (2022). Leadership styles, high-involvement human resource management practices, and individual employee performance in small and medium enterprises in the digital era. *Economies*, *10*(7). https://doi.org/10.3390/economies10070162

Canavesi, A., & Minelli, E. (2022). Servant leadership: A systematic literature review and network analysis. *Employee Responsibilities and Rights Journal, 34*(3), 267–289. https://doi.org/10.1007/s10672-021-09381-3

Croce, F. (2017). Contextualized indigenous entrepreneurial models: A systematic review of indigenous entrepreneurship literature. *Journal of Management and Organization, 23*(6), 886–906. https://doi.org/10.1017/jmo.2017.69

Croce, F. (2019). Indigenous entrepreneurship, society, and the dimensions of diversity: An overview of the canadian national context. *Advanced Series in Management, 21*, 359–371. https://doi.org/10.1108/S1877-636120190000021017

Durham, C. C., Knight, D., & Locke, E. A. (1997). Effects of leader role, team-set goal difficulty, efficacy, and tactics on team effectiveness. *Organizational Behavior and Human Decision Processes, 72*(2), 203–231.

Frank, J., Lambert, E. G., & Qureshi, H. (2017). Examining police officer work stress using the job demands-resources model. *Journal of Contemporary Criminal Justice, 33*(4), 348–367. https://doi.org/10.1177/1043986217724248

Ghani, A. B. A., Kaliappen, N., & Jermsittiparsert, K. (2019). Enhancing Malaysian SME employee work engagement: The mediating role of Job Crafting in the presence of task complexity, self-efficacy and autonomy. *International Journal of Innovation, Creativity and Change, 6*(11), 1–18.

Greenleaf, R. (1995). *Reflections on leadership: How Robert K. Greenleaf's theory of servant leadership influenced today's top management thinkers* (L. C. Spears (ed.)). John Wiley & Sons, Inc.

Hisham, R. R. I. R., Ismail, S. A., Manan, E. A., & Ramli, M. R. (2020). An empirical study of servant leadership on the performance of small and medium-sized enterprises in Malaysia. *Management and Accounting Review, 19*(2), 1–18.

Hoole, C., & Bonnema, J. (2015). Work engagement and meaningful work across generational cohorts. *SA Journal of Human Resource Management, 13*(1), 1–11. https://doi.org/10.4102/sajhrm.v13i1.681

Howard, T. L., Ulferts, G. W., & Hannon, J. (2019). Leadership styles of small business owners: linking theory to application. *Journal of Leadership, Accountability and Ethics*, *16*(2), 47–55. https://doi.org/10.33423/jlae.v16i2.2021

Kaya, B., & Karatepe, O. M. (2020). Does servant leadership better explain work engagement, career satisfaction and adaptive performance than authentic leadership? *International Journal of Contemporary Hospitality Management*, *32*(6), 2075–2095. https://doi.org/10.1108/IJCHM-05-2019-0438

Kusuma, N. T., Soni kurniawan, I., & Herawati, J. (2021). Mediasi work engagement pada perceived organizational support Yang Dirasakan Terhadap Job Satisfaction Dan organizational citizenship behavior. *Jurnal Ilmiah Ekonomi Dan Bisnis*, *18*(2), 128–136. https://doi.org/10.31849/jieb.v18i2.5664

Maden-Eyiusta, C. (2021). Role conflict, role ambiguity, and proactive behaviors: Does flexible role orientation moderate the mediating impact of engagement? *International Journal of Human Resource Management*, *32*(13), 2829–2855. https://doi.org/10.1080/09585192.2019.1616590

Maula-Bakhsh, R., & Raziq, A. (2018). Relationship between Servant Leadership and Subjective Well-Being: Evidence from manufacturing and services based SMEs in Pakistan. *Journal of Management Sciences*, *5*(1), 62–85. https://doi.org/10.20547/jms.2014.1805104

Mihai, L., Burlea Schiopoiu, A., & Mihai, M. (2017). Comparison of the leadership styles practiced by Romanian and Dutch SME owners. *International Journal of Organizational Leadership*, *6*(1), 4–16. https://doi.org/10.33844/ijol.2017.60262

Nielsen, M. B., Mearns, K., Matthiesen, S. B., & Eid, J. (2011). Using the job demands-resources model to investigate risk perception, safety climate and job satisfaction in safety critical organizations. *Scandinavian Journal of Psychology*, *52*(5), 465–475. https://doi.org/10.1111/j.1467-9450.2011.00885.x

Northouse, P. G. (2016). *Leadership: Theory and practice*. Sage Publications Ltd.

Prasetyo, W. (2016). Fraternal culture in build harmony selling price determination: Perspective of Kejawen Panunggalan Community. *The 1st International Conference on Business, Economics, Socio-Culture & Tourism: Managing Global Power*, *1*, 155–166. http://www.academia.edu/%0A32619652/ICBEST_Online_Proceedings

Preacher, K. J., & Hayes, A. F. (2008). Asymptotic and resampling strategies for assessing and comparing indirect effects in multiple mediator models. *Behavior Research Methods*, *40*(3), 879–891. https://doi.org/10.3758/BRM.40.3.879

Rahmadani, V. G., & Schaufeli, W. B. (2022). Engaging leadership and work engagement as moderated by "diuwongke": An Indonesian study. *International Journal of Human Resource Management*, *33*(7), 1267–1295. https://doi.org/10.1080/09585192.2020.1799234

Sendjaya, S., Eva, N., Butar, I., Robin, M., & Castles, S. (2017). SLBS-6: Validation of a Short Form of the Servant Leadership Behavior Scale. *Journal of Business Ethics, 156*(4), 941–956. https://doi.org/10.1007/s10551-017-3594-3

Sulaeman, A., Tisnawatisule, E., Hilmiana, H., & Cahyandito, M. F. (2019). Determining SMEs business sustainability: Human resources management for sustainability approach. *Advances in Economics, Business and Management Research*, *65*(Icebef 2018), 764–768. https://doi.org/10.2991/icebef-18.2019.160

Utami, A., & Sukmawati, A. (2019). Pengaruh Kompetensi terhadap Kepuasan Kerja dan Work Engagement Karyawan UKM Kluster Hasil Pengolahan Perikanan di Bogor. *Jurnal Manajemen Dan Organisasi*, *9*(1), 10–21. https://doi.org/10.29244/jmo.v1i1.25336

Wiroko, E. P. (2021). The role of servant leadership and resilience in predicting work engagement. *Journal of Resilient Economies*, *1*(1), 32–40. https://doi.org/10.25120/jre.1.1.2021.3821

CHAPTER 12

The Rise of Digital Technology and Indigenous Entrepreneurship in Southeast Asia

Stavros Sindakis and Sakshi Aggarwal

Introduction

Over time, the fundamentals of economic development have altered and moved in different ways. Development was fuelled by industrialization, modernization, and economic expansion following World War II. Until the 1970s, growth was characterized by increased labor productivity within structural transformation under technological advancement. The oil crisis and the liberalization of underdeveloped economies sparked the catch-up with advanced economies. From the 1980s through the 2000s, there was less inflation and growth volatility, leading decision-makers to

S. Sindakis (✉)
School of Social Sciences, Hellenic Open University, Patras, Greece
e-mail: sindakis.stavros@ac.eap.gr; s.sindakis@talient.education

S. Sindakis · S. Aggarwal
InnoLab Research, Talient Education, Athens, Greece
e-mail: s.aggarwal@talient.education

E. L. Eijdenberg et al. (eds.), *Indigenous Entrepreneurship in Southeast Asia*, Palgrave Studies in Equity, Diversity, Inclusion, and Indigenization in Business, https://doi.org/10.1007/978-3-031-54457-6_12

believe in the Washington Consensus's superior moderation. With the dot.com crash and Industry 4.0 (the fourth Industrial Revolution) at the turn of the millennium, the 2008 financial crisis prompted us to reevaluate development programs to become more goal-based. The main driving factor behind Industry 4.0, which directed economic progress in the twenty-first century, was digital technology (Retamal, 2019; Skare & Soriano, 2021).

The present situation is consistent with the fourth industrial revolution, which introduced a fresh movement known as digital transformation. The development of numerous supporting components, including leadership agility, strategy flexibility, and indigenous entrepreneurship, is required to realize digital transformation (Lee et al., 2020). Since the millennial generation is a nation's most significant source of human capital, digital technology must be used specifically for this generation. Widespread use of digital technology is possible, particularly in indigenous entrepreneurship (Muafi et al., 2021; Intarakumnerd & Korwatanasakul, 2020). Since indigenous entrepreneurship has been recognized as one of the dominant influences impacting economic growth, it is seen as a viable means of assisting developing nations in overcoming the severe obstacles faced by poverty. Prior studies have demonstrated that business venture development alone has little positive impact on economic growth. Small firms must act entrepreneurially if they want to make a significant and enduring positive impact on society and the economy in the future. But in developing nations, establishing a company is frequently difficult (Hisrich & Soltanifar, 2021; Soluk et al., 2021).

Around 476 million people, or 5–6% of the world's population, are indigenous and live in 90 different nations. The rights of indigenous people have improved over the past 20 years thanks to a variety of tools and mechanisms, including maintaining their communities' economic development and means of subsistence as well as implementing cultural preservation and development, which now also supports the Sustainable Development Goals (Padilla-Meléndez et al., 2022; Wadhwani et al., 2020). As a result, self-identification as a means of determining whether one is indigenous has recently gained recognition in literature. This implies that how indigenous people describe themselves today is considerably more significant than how any academic or governmental body defines indigeneity.

On the other hand, indigenous entrepreneurship covers any form of self-employment or entrepreneurial activity carried out by indigenous people using their own knowledge. According to Padilla-Meléndez et al. (2022), indigenous entrepreneurship is the capacity of indigenous communities to utilize the resources present in their environment in order to attain self-sufficiency and self-determination. Additionally, indigenous entrepreneurship is a distinct discipline within science that takes into account the development, management, and establishment of new businesses by indigenous people for the benefit of other indigenous people (Abubakre et al., 2021).

Therefore, the most significant barriers to indigenous entrepreneurship, particularly for newcomers, are connected to time and space constraints, a need for more networks, and restricted marketing mobility. Digital entrepreneurship can help with some of these issues. Digital entrepreneurship can generate business prospects with a much larger market and much lower cost. Technology-based indigenous entrepreneurship is also a trend in the modern world from the consumer's perspective (Rainnie & Dean, 2020; Tham et al., 2023). Consumers are always drawn to convenience, quickness, affordability, and high quality. Digital technology can help one do this and make it a reality. As a result, many offline firms are beginning to transition online. The conversion of an offline company to an online company shows that online companies have promising futures (Muafi et al., 2021; Retamal, 2019).

The main goal of indigenous and digital entrepreneurship is to build new company ventures and transform existing ones through innovative digital technologies. Digital technology has also facilitated the expansion of the sharing economy by bridging owners and users and upending the traditional dichotomy between businesses and consumers. All businesses in different economic areas will receive technological advancements from the digital economy. The topic is pertinent in this regard since it must investigate how digital technologies help in the growth of indigenous entrepreneurship, mainly in Southeast Asia, and can be used to generate anti-turbulent conditions in the mode of effective business activity and the economy in general (Gregorioa & Ancog, 2020; Fauzi et al., 2021; Rainnie & Dean, 2020). On the other hand, the global integration of economies, the advances in communication technology, the changes in social and demographic characteristics, and the environmental changes have affected business models significantly and led to a growing need for skilled labor in companies.

Since indigenous entrepreneurship has been recognized as one of the dominant influences impacting economic growth, it is seen as a viable means of assisting developing nations in overcoming the severe obstacles faced by poverty. Prior studies (e.g., Morton & Baird, 2019; Padilla-Meléndez et al., 2022; Wadhwani et al., 2020; Abubakre et al., 2021; Bruton et al., 2022; Muafi et al., 2021; Soluk et al., 2021) have demonstrated that business venture development (predominantly indigenous entrepreneurship) in Southeast Asia alone has little positive impact on economic growth. Small firms must act entrepreneurially if they want to make a significant and enduring positive impact on society and the economy in the future. But, in developing nations, establishing a company is frequently difficult. The most significant barriers to indigenous entrepreneurship, particularly for newcomers, are connected to time and space constraints, a need for more networks, and restricted marketing mobility (Sadiq et al., 2022; Khan et al., 2021; Kimuli et al., 2021). Therefore, in this chapter, we study the persistent problem of rural poverty in emerging nations, which is frequently seen as being best addressed via indigenous entrepreneurship. In particular, we look at how family, regional overview, community, and business partners can support one another to fill institutional gaps and promote indigenous entrepreneurship in Asian enterprises. We also examine how digital technology, such as smartphone apps, might improve these interactions. Further, we allow upcoming researchers and scholars to understand the challenges and benefits of digital and indigenous entrepreneurship. Lastly, we discuss digital technology adoption, indigenous entrepreneurship, and its impact on business processes.

Literature Review

Indigenous People of Southeast Asia and its Regional Overview

Only 8.7% of the territory in the area that indigenous peoples and local communities occupy is officially recognized. There are over 140.3 Mha of unrecognized indigenous and communal lands in just nine countries in South and Southeast Asia (AIPP, 2022; Bruton et al., 2022). Indigenous peoples lack secure tenure rights over their traditional territory across an area greater than Cambodia, Thailand, Laos, and the Philippines combined. There may be as many as 411 million indigenous peoples in Asia alone, according to the Asia Indigenous People Pact (AIPP) (Asia

Indigenous Peoples Pact, 2022). Indigenous peoples are significant to the preservation of biodiversity, and their territories share a great deal of space, with places still intact and vital to biodiversity protection. In Asia, the term "conservation" is associated with the oppression of indigenous peoples, elitist disrespect for institutions and customary knowledge, and marginalization of indigenous peoples (AIPP, 2022; Morton & Baird, 2019).

As of October 2021, protected areas in Asia spanned 478.5 million hectares or 15.37 percent of the continent. A total of 859.2 million people reside in places that are extremely important for preserving biodiversity in the area, in addition to the 150 million people who live in protected areas. These individuals are most likely Native Americans. The Post-2020 Global Biodiversity Framework (GBF) should decolonize conservation, according to the ICCA Consortium, and the mainstream conservation sector should be rid of all forms of colonialism, destructive capitalism, and systemic injustice and inequality (AIPP, 2022). Therefore, the 10 nations that make up the Association of Southeast Asian Nations are home to three of the world's megadiverse nations—Indonesia, Malaysia, and the Philippines—as well as almost 20% of the planet's biodiversity, 35% of its mangrove ecosystems, 30% of its coral reefs, over 2000 animal and plant species, and over 800 indigenous and ethnic local communities that serve as the biodiversity's de facto guardians (AIPP, 2022).

In Thailand, indigenous groups are claiming their cultural uniqueness as indigenous groups and their commonality with the Thai people (Morton & Baird, 2019). In this way, the Indigenous movement in Thailand is distinct from those found in "liberal democratic settler states" like New Zealand, Canada, Australia, and the United States. In those countries, Indigenous peoples "must execute their cultural distinction so as to retain political recognition." When they exercise their political rights, they are criticized for not being "culturally different enough." Thus, the indigenous movement in Thailand is gaining pace even as it continues to experience setbacks, and it is unclear if and how it will evolve in the upcoming years. Most importantly, activists from indigenous and non-indigenous communities are helping to gradually localize the idea of indigenousness in Thailand (Banerjee, 2022; Morton & Baird, 2019).

Indigenous People and Digital Technologies

Recent developments in mobile technology have facilitated the closing of the digital gap. Indigenous youth have embraced mobile technology quickly in Singapore, Vietnam, and Thailand, like Southeast Asian countries, according to synthesis research. In contrast, indigenous communities in Southeast Asia expressed a significant desire to use mobile technology for interacting (Frazer et al., 2022; Li et al., 2021). Communication via mobile phones has grown to standard as they are now more readily available and affordable for many indigenous youths. As a result, this has encouraged interest in various digital technologies, particularly among indigenous youth, who have deliberately incorporated information and communication technology (ICT) into their daily lives. Texting and social media are popular forms of communication among indigenous people, who utilize photography and video to make content to self-represent, forge their identities, and gain visibility both within and outside their communities (Li et al., 2021; van't Hooft, 2022). Research has noted that social media, particularly Facebook, has influenced Indigenous youths' daily conversations. Indigenous elders reportedly thought that the utilization of digital technology widened doors for young people, who consequently play an integral part in upholding cultural traditions and bringing modern innovations into the community (Van't Hooft, 2022). This, in turn, contributes to amplifying Indigenous voices across space and time. According to a previous study by Meighan (2021) and Kennedy (2020), many indigenous communities have welcomed modern technology.

Indigenous people have inadequate literacy and language skills, so efforts have been undertaken to establish teaching and learning methodologies that use digital technologies. A growing body of literature has demonstrated how digital technology has allowed indigenous adolescents with increased motivation to engage in literacy acquisition to engage in new types of textual communications and linguistic innovation in their businesses. Therefore, we conducted a thorough literature analysis investigating the usefulness of employing digital technology for indigenous people, the benefits and challenges of digital entrepreneurship, the growth of indigenous entrepreneurship in Southeast Asia, and trends in developing new business models in Southeast Asia (Frazer et al., 2022; Kennedy, 2020; Li et al., 2021).

Concludingly, indigenous people increasingly use digital technologies to connect, share their cultures, and advocate for their rights. There are now many online communities where indigenous people worldwide can connect and share their experiences. These communities can provide a sense of support and belonging for Indigenous people who may feel isolated in their own communities (Li et al., 2021; van't Hooft, 2022). Digital technologies are also being used to share indigenous cultures. For example, many indigenous people use social media to share their languages, music, and art with the world. This helps raise awareness of indigenous cultures and promotes preservation (Frazer et al., 2022).

The Role of Digital Technologies in the Growth of Indigenous Entrepreneurship in Southeast Asia

In 90 different countries around the world, according to the United Nations Permanent Forum on Indigenous Issues (2020), there are more than 370 million Indigenous people who practice distinctive traditions and retain social, cultural, economic, and political traits that are different from those of the settler societies in which they live. While not all Indigenous peoples have the same worldview, most have a land-based, relational, holistic, spiritual, and materially dual worldview. It is a manifestation of identity and culture that shapes the socioeconomic ideals of a community (Padilla-Meléndez et al., 2022; Parhankangas & Colbourne, 2022; Wadhwani et al., 2020). This worldview is based on the active recognition of the connections, interdependencies, and relationships between individuals, the natural world, and the spiritual world. As a result, Indigenous peoples have a strong sense of connection to their ancestral lands and a duty to take care of the land by acting as stewards and ensuring all actions and interactions are respectful and sustainable. In doing so, they are responsible for protecting, upholding, preserving, and advancing the welfare of everyone living in their community and on their grounds. Indigenous values are put into practice through traditions, laws, and practices that are based on their unique experience and worldview (Filatotchev et al., 2022; Parhankangas & Colbourne, 2022; Welter et al., 2019).

Indigenous entrepreneurship is an incipient and developing field, and early researchers concentrated on examining the dynamics of economic development in indigenous communities. They also recognized the tensions, problems, and challenges facing indigenous economic development as a distinctive activity that operates at the nexus of social and economic development. Indigenous and non-indigenous scholars have now built on the basis that these authors laid, establishing indigenous entrepreneurship as a viable field distinct from mainstream, ethnic, and social entrepreneurship studies (Padilla-Meléndez et al., 2022; Parhankangas & Colbourne, 2022; Wadhwani et al., 2020).

The dynamics of Indigenous digital entrepreneurship are, however, rarely studied. However, literature that does concentrate on indigenous people's digital experiences explores digital technology's adaptability, the tremendous impact on the growth of indigenous entrepreneurship, and new business models that help in the growth of indigenous entrepreneurship (see Fig. 12.1) (Filatotchev et al., 2022; Welter et al., 2019). The adaptability of digital technology has made it a considerable source of chances for business owners to launch new ventures and new indigenous entrepreneurs (see Fig. 12.1). Digital entrepreneurs develop innovative combinations of social and material resources to produce value for users by building on the specific characteristics of digital technologies. The ability of digital technology to connect various processes and provide platforms that create new opportunities for commercial and social interactions is often the foundation around which they build their business models (Abubakre et al., 2021; Croce, 2019).

Other studies suggested that certain mechanisms, including identification, may be used to explain how indigenous beliefs affect entrepreneurial endeavors. For instance, Abubakre et al. (2021) suggested that local factors, such as business norms of deliberation, supported the development of local identity, the "spirit of Gnosjö," which shaped the entrepreneurial behavior in the district, in a study of entrepreneurship within the industrial district of Gnosjö in Sweden. The importance of community norms and attitudes in determining an entrepreneur's capacity to launch new companies is highlighted by the function of indigenous values in molding entrepreneurial activity (Abubakre et al., 2021). Technology has had a tremendous impact on the growth of indigenous entrepreneurship, both in terms of facilitating the work that new indigenous entrepreneurs do and helping them reach new markets. Technology has allowed start-ups to increase and grow faster than ever before. This growth benefits everyone involved—from indigenous entrepreneurs to investors willing to support them to employees who can quickly and easily join these businesses (Sadiq et al., 2022; Tham et al., 2023; Vlassis, 2021). Consequently, as the world becomes increasingly digital, so too has the role of digital technologies in the growth of indigenous entrepreneurship.

Digital platforms and internet-based company models are examples of concepts where the principles of digital entrepreneurship can be used. Digital business models, entrepreneurship education, digital ecosystems, platform strategies, digital entrepreneurship processes, and social and digital entrepreneurship were the six research streams connected to digital entrepreneurship highlighted by Muafi et al. (2021) in their research. External investment from the public and private sectors can serve to launch and promote the development of digital-based entrepreneurship. Digital entrepreneurship helps promote innovative business models and the interchange, transfer, and acquisition of knowledge since web-based platforms make peer-to-peer transactions possible (Chen et al., 2021a, 2021b; Hisrich & Soltanifar, 2021; Soluk et al., 2021).

Additionally, a digital brand positioning strategy is necessary for any organization that operates online. Being digital refers to how something leverages its online presence, selects an audience, and establishes a presence. The first step of new business growth is the growing demand for digital-based firms, which will increase sales and necessitate hiring new staff (Muafi et al., 2021; Retamal, 2019). Consequently, a newly digital-based organization with strong sales or staff growth might be seen as a business using digital technology to survive this fast-paced period. Also, information and communication technology play four key roles in digital entrepreneurial operations, according to Muafi et al. (2021):

- It facilitates start-up operations by making them easier.
- It acts as a mediator for new venture operations.
- It is a result of entrepreneurial operations.
- It is a ubiquitous business model (see Fig. 12.1).

The application of digital technology in indigenous entrepreneurship is ideally suited for classroom use. Numerous university graduates in this situation should be more utilized while having excellent potential. This happens because students and undergraduates still have a relatively low level of entrepreneurial motivation (Tham et al., 2023; Wang et al., 2021). Digital technology for indigenous entrepreneurship is a chance that can improve students' and scholars' enthusiasm to become indigenous entrepreneurs due to its ease of use, the size of the market, and its market share, along with assistance from institutions and the government. Academics engaging in digital entrepreneurship, as well as indigenous entrepreneurship, will have more employment options, lowering the unemployment rate. Every scientific field can adopt digital and indigenous entrepreneurship as a practice and turn it into a profitable enterprise or venture (Hisrich & Soltanifar, 2021; Muafi et al., 2021; Soluk et al., 2021).

Additionally, digital technologies make it easier for indigenous entrepreneurs to track their progress and achievements. This information can help them measure the success of their businesses and identify areas in which they need to improve (George et al., 2021; Intarakumnerd & Korwatanasakul, 2020). Digital technologies allow indigenous entrepreneurs to access customer data through online databases. This information can be used to tailor the products or services companies offer to the needs and interests of particular consumers (Elia et al., 2020; Vlassis, 2021). Moreover, digital technologies allow indigenous companies in the Southeast Asian region (especially Thailand, Malaysia, Indonesia, Vietnam, and the Philippines) to aggregate this data into a comprehensive database that can be used for reference purposes (Nicoletti et al., 2020). For example, Southeast Asian e-commerce websites (like Shopee, Lazada, etc.) use customer databases for marketing purposes to provide consumers with a wider choice of products. Likewise, companies use these databases for research purposes to understand how different types of products are performed when placed in different markets. For instance, a company can use this data to ascertain the potential of a new product or service. This might open new markets or provide a platform on which a company can expand, such as the Southeast Asian companies' growth rate in 2022 was 20.6% and is expected to grow and cross the $100 billion mark in 2023 (Khan, 2019; Seo et al., 2021).

The conceptual framework (see Fig. 12.1) illustrates the role of technology in digital entrepreneurship and the qualities of indigenous people that help them connect to various processes and platforms provided through digital technology. Digital technology is a powerful tool that indigenous people can use to start and grow their own businesses. Using digital technology, indigenous entrepreneurs can reach a global audience, market their businesses effectively, and raise money to start or grow their businesses. The ability of digital technology to connect various processes and provide platforms that create new opportunities for commercial and social interactions is often the foundation around which they build their business models. Therefore, it indicates that when new opportunities are provided to indigenous people, they effectively concur with the platform provided and connect to various processes to form new ventures and create new entrepreneurs out of themselves. In addition, indigenous people are creating new enterprises in a variety of ways by utilizing digital technologies. Here are a few illustrations:

> E-commerce: Indigenous business owners are selling their goods and services to a worldwide clientele by utilizing e-commerce platforms. For instance, indigenous sellers can sell handmade goods, jewellery, and artwork in a special section of the website Etsy.
>
> Social media: Native American company owners use social media to communicate with customers and sell their brands. One Instagram account that promotes indigenous-owned businesses and their goods and services is @indigenousbusinessnet.
>
> Online education: To educate others about their cultures and customs, indigenous entrepreneurs develop online tutorials and courses. One website that provides a variety of courses on subjects, including indigenous history, language, and art, is indigenous online learning.

Indigenous company owners embrace crowdfunding sites to raise money to launch or expand their enterprises. For instance, there is a section for initiatives managed by indigenous people on the crowdsourcing website Indiegogo.

Trends in the Development of New Business Models in Southeast Asia

Digital technologies are changing how businesses operate while creating new opportunities for indigenous entrepreneurs to develop new business models. From freemium and subscription-based services to digital platforms, ecosystems, and asset-light business models, we explore the key directions to watch in developing new business models and discuss how these trends impact industries.

A growing trend in developing new business models is the freemium business model. The freemium model is where a primary product or service is provided free of charge with the option to buy additional features, services, or goods that add value to what is already being provided by the user (Panda, 2019; Rietveld, 2018; Vlassis, 2021). This

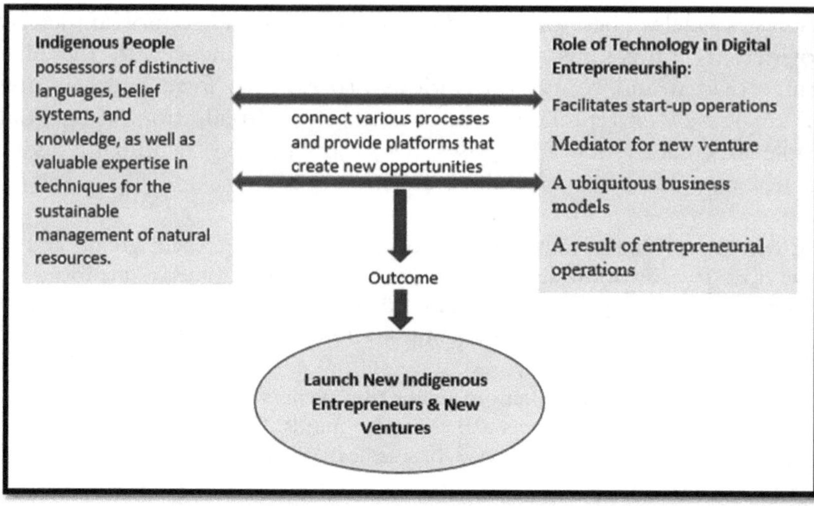

Fig. 12.1 The role of digital technologies in launching new Indigenous entrepreneurs

revenue model can be used to reach a broader audience and has been exceedingly popular for Web 2.0 companies in recent years. Examples of successful freemium companies include Flickr, YouSendIt, and Evernote. On the contrary, subscription-based services have emerged as a successful business model in recent years. This model allows customers to access a service or product regularly, typically with a monthly or yearly fee (Chun, 2019; Fauzi et al., 2021; Khan, 2019). Some popular examples of subscription-based services include Netflix, Hulu, and Spotify. Another trend in the development of new business models is that of the sharing economy. The sharing economy is a peer-to-peer business model that provides access to goods or services without ownership (Lee et al., 2020; Wirtz et al., 2019). The main feature of a sharing economy business model is the act of renting rather than buying. This means that the seeker is not responsible for owning the asset but is allowed access to it in exchange for money. A platform brings together owners and seekers and facilitates all processes involved. The sharing economy has affected many industries, including transportation with car-sharing (e.g., Liftshare), shared transport vehicles (e.g., Uber), housing with sharing among individuals (e.g., Airbnb), or house sharing (e.g., Home-Exchange), clothing with renting between individuals, selling or buying second-hand clothing (e.g., Vinted), and more.

Furthermore, platforms and ecosystems are other trends in developing new business models. These business models allow companies to share resources and collaborate with others to create a more efficient marketplace or ecosystem. Digital platforms enable indigenous entrepreneurs to develop their businesses more flexibly and cost-effectively than traditional business models (Ansong & Boateng, 2019; Khan, 2019; Yue et al., 2019). For example, such online platforms allow indigenous entrepreneurs to sell products and services online without investing in inventory or setting up a physical storefront. This has created new opportunities for individuals and small businesses to compete with larger companies by offering lower prices and more convenient customer service (Kenney & Zysman, 2016; Intarakumnerd & Korwatanasakul, 2020). Popular examples of platforms include Spotify, Facebook, Instagram, and YouTube. Likewise, e-commerce is growing exponentially due to the increasing popularity of online platforms like Amazon, eBay, and Shopify. These platforms allow indigenous entrepreneurs to sell products and services online without spending much time and money setting up a website (Li et al., 2018; Yue et al., 2019). This has led to a surge in the number of small businesses in Southeast Asian regions selling goods and services online.

Another business model trend is the asset-light model, which entails moving capabilities such as people, processes, and technology to other owners for organizations to migrate from a fixed cost structure to a variable cost structure (Fauzi et al., 2021; Linz et al., 2017; Mody et al., 2020). When carefully planned and executed, these techniques decrease complexity, provide new income streams, boost innovation, and contribute to a greater return on capital. Companies that use an asset-light model typically outsource assets such as customer service, manufacturing, information technology, real estate, research and development, and other functions to a network of vendors and service providers, allowing them to keep costs low while maintaining operations agile (Khan, 2019; Lee et al., 2020; Seo et al., 2021). Examples of the asset-light model include Instacart, DoorDash, and Verbling. Overall, these significant trends affect digital and indigenous entrepreneurship, creating new opportunities for indigenous entrepreneurs in Southeast Asia to develop new business models that are more flexible and cost-effective than traditional ones.

Benefits and Challenges of Digital Entrepreneurship

Digital entrepreneurship is a growing trend in business, offering new opportunities for businesses to grow and compete with other companies. However, there are challenges that digital entrepreneurs face when trying to start and run their businesses. The potential drawbacks of digitalization have received much less consideration. Digital technology, however, can have a wrong side and have an adverse effect on people, companies, and society as a whole, as reality shows demonstrate (Nosova & Norkina, 2021; Secundo et al., 2021; Soluk et al., 2021; von Briel et al., 2021). As is sometimes claimed, digital technologies do not unquestionably and necessarily democratize creativity and indigenous entrepreneurship. As an alternative, they might favor some actors while disadvantaging others. For instance, Indonesia and Malaysia are becoming increasingly concerned that the expanding digital divide between rich and emerging nations could widen the gap between the amount of value that different nations can generate and seize (Berger et al., 2021; Hisrich & Soltanifar, 2021; Rainnie & Dean, 2020; Gregorioa & Ancog, 2020).

Digital tools may also assist indigenous entrepreneurs in utilizing the advice and assistance they receive from their communities, particularly self-help organizations. For example, computer-based solutions may make it easier, more thorough, and more sustainable to incorporate community members' understanding of fundamental marketing best practices in microenterprises than paper-based methods (Berger et al., 2021; Kraus & Marchenko, 2021). Digital technologies can assist business owners in maximizing the benefits of financial support in this way. As a result, the (unfavorable) impacts of institutional gaps—particularly those associated with the absence of institutions in the fields of education, market research, and company development—will be further mitigated (Khan et al., 2021, 2022; Kimuli et al., 2021; Wang et al., 2021; Zahra, 2021; Purbasari et al., 2021). Digital technologies can also boost community members' interactions more frequently. Entrepreneurs can ask for and offer support anytime on platforms like WhatsApp and WeChat, and they can also "document" or save the advice they receive from others. Therefore, if communities embrace digital technology, the value of all such evaluations (along with the archives of information and input received) may be significantly improved. Institutions like established communication service providers or quality certification organizations, which are frequently missing in rural developing areas, are not involved in developing this area (Ciarli et al., 2021; Soluk et al., 2021).

Also, a start-up's establishment process has been shown to be supported and facilitated by digital technology. The fourth industrial revolution is brought up by digital technology. The advancement of the digital technology-related entrepreneurial research agenda is necessary for the fourth industrial revolution. One of the interesting topics resulting from the growth of study on digital-based entrepreneurship is that of academics. Universities and other academic settings have all the necessary resources and tools to assist the growth of digital-based entrepreneurship for indigenous people. The institution is well-equipped to assist the growth of digital-based entrepreneurship because it has qualified human resources, policies encouraging student invention and creativity, and sufficient funding (Boeker et al., 2021; Muafi et al., 2021).

Digital Technology Adoption and its Impact on Asian Business Processes

Digital technology adoption, which is defined as the business use of computer-based tools like smartphone apps, can help an organization in many ways, including lower costs, higher revenues, competitive advantages, and the chance to create new business models for indigenous entrepreneurship. In fact, irrespective of an organization's age, size, location, community, or industry, adopting digital technology is becoming increasingly crucial (Kraus & Marchenko, 2021; Soluk et al., 2021).

Companies can develop firm value and competitive advantages by utilizing digital technologies, which could encourage them to become more entrepreneurial. Therefore, underdeveloped nations (like Timor-Leste in Southeast Asia) may find it more important to adopt digital technologies for the growth of indigenous entrepreneurship. However, prior studies on the effects of utilizing digital technologies needed more empirical data. Although the deployment of digital technology can benefit organizations of any size, prior literature has recognized small- and medium-sized enterprises' unique adoption and commercialization patterns. For instance, the adoption of digital technology by smaller businesses or new ventures is influenced by variables like a relative advantage (i.e., the degree to which a firm outperforms its rivals), uncertainty, or geo-restrictions (Hisrich & Soltanifar, 2021; Nosova & Norkina, 2021; Soluk et al., 2021).

However, most people worldwide have yet to see much of an impact from the development of digital technologies. The reality is that many Southeast Asian enterprises, particularly those in the financial, public service, healthcare, and tourism sectors, already utilize digital technologies in their operations, particularly benefiting indigenous entrepreneurs. Artificial intelligence advancements, in particular, have drawn much interest from researchers and practitioners and created a variety of beneficial potential for usage in the public sector. Businesses today must aggressively advance the creation of automated technical systems (Kraus & Marchenko, 2021; Nosova & Norkina, 2021). Organizations must handle important data difficulties to successfully use digital technologies for the growth of new indigenous enterprises, such as developing effective data management, defining ontologies, structuring data around "channels" from data sources, and handling legal limitations. Given the high computing demands of deep learning, some businesses will keep their own data centers due to regulatory or security concerns. Still, the capital expenses can be high, particularly when using specialist gear. Organizations will need to employ cutting-edge software practices like Agile and DevOps and strong data maintenance and management methods. Efforts on the "first mile," or how to gather and organize data and efforts, as well as on the "final mile," or how to ensure that the fantastic ideas supplied by the DT are transformed into the behavior of people and processes of the firm, will need to be taken into consideration by businesses (Nosova & Norkina, 2021; Skare & Soriano, 2021; Khan et al., 2021).

On the other hand, digital technology implementation through "digital transformation" is a "systematic method," "overly complicated," and "companywide endeavor" that "may significantly influence a business and its operations." Through digital transformation, an organization can reconsider its customers' values to obtain a competitive edge and improve operational efficiency. By using digital technology as a lever, digital transformation aims to foster more harmony among organizational business areas to improve goods, services, and business models (Chen et al., 2021a; Nosova & Norkina, 2021).

Additionally, opportunities to improve the operational efficiency of any new enterprise, including profitability and new income growth, customer satisfaction, boosting operational efficiency, convenience, and high-quality technical standards, boosting business agility, and boosting employee productivity and competitive advantage, can also serve as a driving force behind digital transformation (Chen et al., 2021b; Jafari-Sadeghi et al., 2021; Skare & Soriano, 2021).

Conclusion and Recommendations

Indigenous entrepreneurship and digital technology together have emerged as a powerful force in the business world. However, it becomes imperative for businesses to be agile and adapt quickly to changing trends in today's economy. This is especially valid for new indigenous ventures and small companies relying on technology to stay competitive. Since a great deal of business innovation comes from innovative ideas and improvements, the people who run these companies must understand how technology influences their business. As the world becomes increasingly digital, it is no surprise that companies adapt and change to stay ahead of the curve. Therefore, indigenous entrepreneurs need to understand the impact of new technologies on their industry and explore how digital technologies can help them identify opportunities, develop innovative solutions, and address market needs to stay ahead of the competition. For instance, indigenous entrepreneurs must have a strong understanding of applying the latest technology to current problems and issues and comprehend the financial benefits, performance gains, and efficiency improvements that can be achieved using digital technologies. As well as being innovative, they must also be able to identify potential barriers that strategies involving digital technologies may encounter and explore how these barriers can be overcome to increase business success rates. Indigenous entrepreneurs must also understand how digital technologies impact consumer behavior and develop strategies that address consumer needs to increase sales revenue (Bican & Brem, 2020). Since more than half of global consumption happens online, indigenous companies must ensure their products are always available through all channels.

A company's digital transformation may impact a wide range of stakeholders and business units, including those involved in product development, IT, human resources, marketing, management, and strategy. According to earlier research, most firms implement digital transformation to enhance workflows and boost productivity, modify products, boost production efficiency, or exchange consumer data for servitization. According to numerous studies (e.g., Chen et al., 2021a, 2021b; Nosova & Norkina, 2021; Soluk et al., 2021), small service businesses and indigenous businesses in southeast Asia primarily use digital transformation to improve the customer experience, implement agile working practices, and foster more significant customer interaction and collaboration. These businesses can expect to increase client engagement, improve business performance, and experience business growth by implementing digital transformation technologies. Accordingly, the result suggests that a company should carefully select its priority area when implementing digital transformation to reap the greatest rewards, particularly when it has limited resources to implement it throughout its operations. This result is consistent with the fact that businesses must prioritize certain areas while engaging in digital transformation operations. Our study would suggest that when choosing a top-priority digital transformation sector, one should evaluate the nature and features of the industry.

Small indigenous enterprises need the government to offer funding programs to address finance and resource issues. To improve the digital capabilities of small indigenous businesses, it is also suggested that the government establish a digital learning platform. Additionally, small indigenous enterprises must cope with technological and human resource issues to successfully implement digital transformation. Accordingly (e.g., Nosova & Norkina, 2021; Chen et al., 2021b; Soluk et al., 2021; Skare & Soriano, 2021; Khan et al., 2021; Bican & Brem, 2020), there are at least four government positions that can help small indigenous Asian businesses undergo digital transformation. First, a small indigenous company needs more funds and limited digital capacity to create its platform.

Furthermore, a digital platform from a third party might not be offered since it is not as profitable. As a result, the government can assist small enterprises in creating a digital platform for their transition to the digital age. This platform allows small indigenous businesses to digitalize their operations internally and externally. The government might also advocate for the use of digital tools to assist small indigenous businesses in transforming their operations. E-commerce, official websites, social networking, smartphone applications, and other digital technologies are all readily available. Different digital technologies will be appropriate for particular goods/services and objectives. A small indigenous business must, therefore, identify one or two digital technologies that are appropriate for its purposes.

Second, the government must support mobile/digital payments to accelerate digital transformation for indigenous companies. Although they require a minimum number of customers and merchants, digital payment systems play a significant role in digital business ecosystems. When a large firm (like Alibaba with Alipay) introduces a digital payment system, they have the financial wherewithal and economic clout to encourage customers to utilize it until the payment system reaches an economical size (Nosova & Norkina, 2021; Skare & Soriano, 2021; Khan et al., 2021). Small indigenous businesses need more financial and organizational capacity to establish a business environment for a digital payment system. Therefore, the development of the Southeast Asian business ecosystem, the creation of a digital payment system, and the promotion of its use are all required by small indigenous businesses. Additionally, indigenous companies depend on the Asian government to make it easier for web pages and payment networks to interact. Customers' convenience will be increased through integrated e-commerce and payment systems, increasing transaction intention.

Third, the Asian government can assist small or large indigenous businesses in becoming more digitally capable by providing owners or managers with digital training or education. Indigenous business owners' and managers' digital understanding can be improved through training, impacting an organization's digital competence. The effectiveness of digital transformation in indigenous businesses depends on these business owners' and managers' increased digital competency. Owners and managers will be motivated to create a digital vision if they have sufficient knowledge of digital technology (Bican & Brem, 2020; Skare & Soriano, 2021; Yue et al., 2019). In addition, having solid digital competence will influence an organization's ability to generate new digital products that will satisfy the needs of new customers.

Fourth, the Southeast Asian governments can help indigenous enterprises by creating an ecosystem that encourages collaboration and allows them to expand their networks. Systems for collaboration will assist indigenous enterprises in connecting with other entities and fostering collaborative creativity. Collaboration enables small indigenous businesses to overcome resource constraints, human resource shortages, and knowledge gaps (Bican & Brem, 2020; Rainnie & Dean, 2020). Indigenous businesses can work together using the following four models: knowledge sharing, marketing innovation, resource sharing, and product/service innovation models. Even with limited resources, an indigenous business can boost performance and accomplish business growth through collaboration with partners.

Moreover, our results further highlight the significance of digital technology adoption for Southeast Asian indigenous businesses. By amplifying the aforementioned benefits of family and community support, digital technologies today encourage indigenous entrepreneurship (Fig. 12.1). We have seen many methods microbusiness owners employ to expand and improve their business models. Indigenous entrepreneurs in rural areas can escape the poverty trap by gaining access to new lucrative markets. Further, digital technologies provide the foundation for boosting commercial operations' effectiveness. Exogenous shocks in the form of emerging technologies are now more probable to be incorporated into company operations and expanded in the digital economy, which will facilitate people's perception of it, including politicians and indigenous entrepreneurs. This allows them to interact constantly, strengthening trust in the uncertain processes of related managerial and technological changes. Also, digital technologies enable new commercial and indigenous ventures and the interchange, transmission, and knowledge gain. Economic development should prioritize creating and integrating digital technology into corporate operations (Nosova & Norkina, 2021; Skare & Soriano, 2021; Khan et al., 2021). A strong digital sector, where digital technologies are proactively addressed, particularly in producing artificial intelligence technologies, is required for such progress, in addition to having competent IT workers.

References

Abubakre, M., Faik, I., & Mkansi, M. (2021). Digital entrepreneurship and indigenous value systems: An Ubuntu perspective. *Information Systems Journal, 31*(6), 838–862.

Ansong, E., & Boateng, R. (2019). Surviving in the digital era–business models of digital enterprises in a developing economy. *Digital Policy, Regulation and Governance, 21*(2), 164–178.

Asia Indigenous Peoples Pact. (2022, March 18). *Restoring indigenous sovereignty and creating alternative civic space and responsibilities in Asia—Asia Indigenous Peoples pact*. Asia Indigenous Peoples Pact. https://aippnet.org/restoring-indigenous-sovereignty-creating-alternative-civic-space-responsibilities-asia/

Banerjee, S. B. (2022). Decolonizing management theory: A critical perspective. *Journal of Management Studies, 59*(4), 1074–1087.

Berger, E. S., Von Briel, F., Davidsson, P., & Kuckertz, A. (2021). Digital or not–The future of entrepreneurship and innovation: Introduction to the special issue. *Journal of Business Research, 125*, 436–442.

Bican, P. M., & Brem, A. (2020). Digital business model, digital transformation, digital entrepreneurship: Is there a sustainable "digital"? *Sustainability, 12*(13), 5239.

Boeker, W., Howard, M. D., Basu, S., & Sahaym, A. (2021). Interpersonal relationships, digital technologies, and innovation in entrepreneurial ventures. *Journal of Business Research, 125*, 495–507.

Bruton, G. D., Zahra, S. A., Van de Ven, A. H., & Hitt, M. A. (2022). Indigenous theory uses, abuses, and future. *Journal of Management Studies, 59*(4), 1057–1073.

Chen, C. L., Lin, Y. C., Chen, W. H., Chao, C. F., & Pandia, H. (2021a). Role of government to enhance digital transformation in small service business. *Sustainability, 13*(3), 1028.

Chen, Y., Visnjic, I., Parida, V., & Zhang, Z. (2021b). On the road to digital servitization–The (dis) continuous interplay between business model and digital technology. *International Journal of Operations & Production Management, 41*(5), 694–722.

Chun, S. H. (2019). Cloud services and pricing strategies for sustainable business models: Analytical and numerical approaches. *Sustainability, 12*(1), 49.

Ciarli, T., Kenney, M., Massini, S., & Piscitello, L. (2021). Digital technologies, innovation, and skills: Emerging trajectories and challenges. *Research Policy, 50*(7), 104289.

Croce, F. (2019). Indigenous entrepreneurship, society, and the dimensions of diversity: An overview of the Canadian national context. *Diversity within Diversity Management, 21*, 359–371.

Elia, G., Margherita, A., & Passiante, G. (2020). Digital entrepreneurship ecosystem: How digital technologies and collective intelligence are reshaping the entrepreneurial process. *Technological Forecasting and Social Change, 150*, 119791.

Fauzi, F., Antoni, D., & Suwarni, E. (2021). Mapping potential sectors based on financial and digital literacy of women entrepreneurs: A study of the developing economy. *Journal of Governance and Regulation/Volume, 10*(2).

Filatotchev, I., Ireland, R. D., & Stahl, G. K. (2022). Contextualizing management research: An open systems perspective. *Journal of Management Studies, 59*(4), 1036–1056.

Frazer, R., Carlson, B., & Farrelly, T. (2022). Indigenous articulations of social media and digital assemblages of care. *Digital Geography and Society, 3*, 100038.

George, G., Merrill, R. K., & Schillebeeckx, S. J. (2021). Digital sustainability and entrepreneurship: How digital innovations are helping tackle climate change and sustainable development. *Entrepreneurship Theory and Practice, 45*(5), 999–1027.

Gregorioa, G. B., & Ancog, R. C. (2020). Assessing the impact of the COVID-19 pandemic on agricultural production in Southeast Asia: toward transformative change in agricultural food systems. *Asian Journal of Agriculture and Development*, *17*(1362–2020–1097), 1–13.

Hisrich, R. D., & Soltanifar, M. (2021). Unleashing the creativity of entrepreneurs with digital technologies. In *Digital Entrepreneurship* (pp. 23–49). Springer, Cham.

Intarakumnerd, P., & Korwatanasakul, U. (2020). Business impacts and government support for firms' upgrading and innovation under COVID-19 in Southeast Asia. 과학기술정책, *3*(2), 33–65.

Jafari-Sadeghi, V., Garcia-Perez, A., Candelo, E., & Couturier, J. (2021). Exploring the impact of digital transformation on technology entrepreneurship and technological market expansion: The role of technology readiness, exploration and exploitation. *Journal of Business Research, 124*, 100–111.

Kennedy, T. (2020). *Indigenous peoples' experiences of harmful content on social media*. Macquarie University.

Kenney, M., & Zysman, J. (2016). The rise of the platform economy. *Issues in Science and Technology, 32*(3), 61.

Khan, S. A. R. (2019). The nexus between carbon emissions, poverty, economic growth, and logistics operations-empirical evidence from Southeast Asian countries. *Environmental Science and Pollution Research, 26*(13), 13210–13220.

Khan, S. A. R., Godil, D. I., Yu, Z., Abbas, F., & Shamim, M. A. (2022). Adoption of renewable energy sources, low-carbon initiatives, and advanced logistical infrastructure—a step toward integrated global progress. *Sustainable Development, 30*(1), 275–288.

Khan, S. A. R., Yu, Z., Umar, M., de Sousa Jabbour, A. B. L., & Mor, R. S. (2021). Tackling post-pandemic challenges with digital technologies: an empirical study. *Journal of Enterprise Information Management*.

Kimuli, S. N. L., Sendawula, K., & Nagujja, S. (2021). Digital technologies in micro and small enterprise: Evidence from Uganda's informal sector during the COVID-19 pandemic. *World Journal of Science, Technology and Sustainable Development*.

Kraus, N., & Marchenko, O. (2021). Innovative-digital entrepreneurship as key link of Industry X. 0 formation in the conditions of virtual reality. *Baltic Journal of Economic Studies*, *7*(1), 47–56.

Lee, K., Wong, C. Y., Intarakumnerd, P., & Limapornvanich, C. (2020). Is the Fourth Industrial Revolution a window of opportunity for upgrading or reinforcing the middle-income trap? Asian model of development in Southeast Asia. *Journal of Economic Policy Reform, 23*(4), 408–425.

Li, J., Brar, A., & Roihan, N. (2021). The use of digital technology to enhance language and literacy skills for Indigenous people: A systematic literature review. *Computers and Education Open, 2*, 100035.

Li, L., Su, F., Zhang, W., & Mao, J. Y. (2018). Digital transformation by SME entrepreneurs: A capability perspective. *Information Systems Journal, 28*(6), 1129–1157.

Linz, C., Müller-Stewens, G., & Zimmermann, A. (2017). *Radical business model transformation: Gaining the competitive edge in a disruptive world*. Kogan Page Publishers.

Meighan, P. J. (2021). Decolonizing the digital landscape: The role of technology in Indigenous language revitalization. *AlterNative: An International Journal of Indigenous Peoples, 17*(3), 397–405.

Mody, M., Wirtz, J., So, K. K. F., Chun, H. H., & Liu, S. Q. (2020). Two-directional convergence of platform and pipeline business models. *Journal of Service Management, 31*(4), 693–721.

Morton, M. F., & Baird, I. G. (2019). From Hill tribes to Indigenous Peoples: The localisation of a global movement in Thailand. *Journal of Southeast Asian Studies, 50*(1), 7–31.

Muafi, M., Syafri, W., Prabowo, H., & Nur, S. A. (2021). Digital entrepreneurship in Indonesia: A human capital perspective. *The Journal of Asian Finance, Economics and Business, 8*(3), 351–359.

Nicoletti, G., von Rueden, C., & Andrews, D. (2020). Digital technology diffusion: A matter of capabilities, incentives or both? *European Economic Review, 128*, 103513.

Nosova, S., & Norkina, A. (2021). Digital technologies as a new component of the business process. *Procedia Computer Science, 190*, 651–656.

Padilla-Meléndez, A., Plaza-Angulo, J. J., Del-Aguila-Obra, A. R., & Ciruela-Lorenzo, A. M. (2022). Indigenous entrepreneurship. Current issues and future lines. *Entrepreneurship & Regional Development, 34*(1–2), 6–31.

Panda, B. K. (2019). Application of business model innovation for new enterprises: A case study of digital business using a freemium business model. *Journal of Management Development, 39*(4), 517–524.

Parhankangas, A., & Colbourne, R. (2022). Indigenous entrepreneurship and venture creation: A typology of indigenous crowdfunding campaigns. *Entrepreneurship Theory and Practice*, 10422587221096907.

Purbasari, R., Muttaqin, Z., & Sari, D. S. (2021). Digital entrepreneurship in pandemic Covid 19 Era: The digital entrepreneurial ecosystem framework. *Review of Integrative Business and Economics Research, 10*, 114–135.

Rainnie, A., & Dean, M. (2020). Industry 4.0 and the future of quality work in the global digital economy. *Labour & Industry: A Journal of the Social and Economic Relations of Work, 30*(1), 16–33.

Retamal, M. (2019). Collaborative consumption practices in Southeast Asian cities: Prospects for growth and sustainability. *Journal of Cleaner Production, 222*, 143–152.

Rietveld, J. (2018). Creating and capturing value from freemium business models: A demand-side perspective. *Strategic Entrepreneurship Journal, 12*(2), 171–193.

Sadiq, M., Nonthapot, S., Mohamad, S., Chee Keong, O., Ehsanullah, S., & Iqbal, N. (2022). Does green finance matter for sustainable entrepreneurship and environmental corporate social responsibility during COVID-19? *China Finance Review International, 12*(2), 317–333.

Secundo, G., Gioconda, M. E. L. E., Del Vecchio, P., Gianluca, E., Margherita, A., & Valentina, N. (2021). Threat or opportunity? A case study of digital-enabled redesign of entrepreneurship education in the COVID-19 emergency. *Technological Forecasting and Social Change, 166*, 120565.

Seo, K., Woo, L., Mun, S. G., & Soh, J. (2021). The asset-light business model and firm performance in complex and dynamic environments: The dynamic capabilities view. *Tourism Management, 85*, 104311.

Skare, M., & Soriano, D. R. (2021). How globalization is changing digital technology adoption: An international perspective. *Journal of Innovation & Knowledge, 6*(4), 222–233.

Soluk, J., Kammerlander, N., & Darwin, S. (2021). Digital entrepreneurship in developing countries: The role of institutional voids. *Technological Forecasting and Social Change, 170*, 120876.

Tham, K. W., Abdul Ghani, R., Cua, S. C., Deerochanawong, C., Fojas, M., Hocking, S., … & Oldfield, B. (2023). Obesity in South and Southeast Asia—A new consensus on care and management. *Obesity Reviews*, *24*(2), e13520.

Van't Hooft, A. (2022). Connecting the old and the new. Identities, Indigenous literacies, and the creation of digital learning materials in Mexico. In *Multilingualism, Identity and Interculturality in Education* (pp. 67–88). Singapore: Springer Nature Singapore.

Vlassis, A. (2021). Global online platforms, COVID-19, and culture: The global pandemic, an accelerator towards which direction? *Media, Culture & Society, 43*(5), 957–969.

von Briel, F., Recker, J., Selander, L., Jarvenpaa, S. L., Hukal, P., Yoo, Y., … & Wurm, B. (2021). Researching digital entrepreneurship: Current issues and suggestions for future directions. *Communications of the Association for Information Systems*, *48*(1), 33.

Wadhwani, R. D., Kirsch, D., Welter, F., Gartner, W. B., & Jones, G. G. (2020). Context, time, and change: Historical approaches to entrepreneurship research. *Strategic Entrepreneurship Journal, 14*(1), 3–19.

Wang, C., Wang, D., Abbas, J., Duan, K., & Mubeen, R. (2021). Global financial crisis, smart lockdown strategies, and the COVID-19 spillover impacts:

A global perspective implications from Southeast Asia. *Frontiers in Psychiatry, 12*, 643783.

Welter, F., Baker, T., & Wirsching, K. (2019). Three waves and counting: The rising tide of contextualization in entrepreneurship research. *Small Business Economics, 52*, 319–330.

Wirtz, J., So, K. K. F., Mody, M. A., Liu, S. Q., & Chun, H. H. (2019). Platforms in the peer-to-peer sharing economy. *Journal of Service Management, 30*(4), 452–483.

Yue, A., Nekmat, E., & Beta, A. R. (2019). Digital literacy through digital citizenship: Online civic participation and public opinion evaluation of youth minorities in Southeast Asia. *Media and Communication, 7*(2), 100.

Zahra, S. A. (2021). International entrepreneurship in the post Covid world. *Journal of World Business, 56*(1), 101143.

CHAPTER 13

Reflections on Contributions, Inspiration for the Future: Ideas for Research and Practice of Indigenous Entrepreneurship in Southeast Asia and Beyond

Caroline Wong, Pengji Wang, Thirumaran K, and Emiel L. Eijdenberg

Introduction

Southeast Asia is a region of dynamic growth and transformation. Giving substance and context to the changing environment, the various chapters address how indigenous individuals and communities are coalescing limited resources with challenging reach to make a difference through market opportunities. Most of the governments in the region are in favour of shouldering indigenous entrepreneurship, although the actual support is sometimes limited. Based on the chapter contributions and literature, this chapter outlines areas for future research trajectories in the field of

C. Wong (✉) · P. Wang · T. K · E. L. Eijdenberg
James Cook University, Singapore, Singapore
e-mail: caroline.wong@jcu.edu.au

E. L. Eijdenberg et al. (eds.), *Indigenous Entrepreneurship in Southeast Asia*, Palgrave Studies in Equity, Diversity, Inclusion, and Indigenization in Business, https://doi.org/10.1007/978-3-031-54457-6_13

indigenous entrepreneurship. Apart from an academic discourse, we also hope to distil and identify lessons that could be useful for entrepreneurs and practitioners when contextualizing the participation of indigenous individuals and communities in stimulating business activities.

The opening chapter in this volume was an excellent stock-taking by Maheshwari and Nguyen. The chapter highlights the dearth of research on indigenous entrepreneurship in Southeast Asia with approximately only 24% of 171 articles published from 2006 to 2022 focusing on indigenous entrepreneurship in Southeast Asia. Furthermore, the other chapters shed more light on some of the pertinent areas and issues related to indigenous entrepreneurship through studies in Indonesia, Malaysia, Thailand, and Vietnam, among others. In drawing on specific cases of the Torajans and Bugis in Sulawesi (Indonesia), the Malay-Bumiputeras in Malaysia, the Lumad people in the Philippines, and the rural entrepreneurs in Northeastern Thailand and North Central Coast Vietnam, this book has addressed some of the nuances, sensitivities, and intricacies involved in indigenous entrepreneurship—especially regarding the role of indigenous wisdom, values, and attitudes—in contributing to resilience of small-scale entrepreneurial activities in the broader Southeast Asia region.

In many instances, the role of policy makers and governmental decision-makers to support indigenous entrepreneurship in education, economic stimulus packages and other resources are key solutions to the challenges faced. The contributions in our book provide several illustrations and directions for future research in this area. The scholarship on these cases also highlights the significance of approaching indigenous entrepreneurs from a community or group perspective even though generally they have a high level of individual and collective resilience. The chapters showcase that indigenous culture is greatly associated with mutual help, the maintenance and development of the culture of their communities as a means of support.

Reflections and Contributions

In the past decades, entrepreneurship has grown into a well-investigated research field that includes dozens of subdisciplines such as entrepreneurship education (Kuratko, 2005; Macmullan & Long, 1987; Nabi et al., 2017), international entrepreneurship (Jones et al., 2011; Keupp & Gassmann, 2009; Terjesen et al., 2016), and social entrepreneurship

(Certo & Miller, 2008; Peredo & McLean, 2006; Saebi et al., 2019). Many of these subdisciplines are largely inspired by and connected to "mainstream business and management" understanding and ideas, usually taking place in the West or industrialized world (e.g., Europe, Japan, United States) in which value creation is defined by profit-making and, in case of social and ecological purposes, caretaking of people and our planet. It is in this spirit of Western "mainstream business and management" ideology, researchers and practitioners look at entrepreneurial activities, but tend to be oblivious to alternative, critical, and non-Western views (Banerjee, 2022). Against the conventional setting of entrepreneurship research, a growing body of research emerges and takes a different route, i.e., the direction in which the values of the indigenous peoples are not ignored, but prevailed and well-integrated in entrepreneurial activities (Bastien et al., 2023; Dana, 2015; Dana & Anderson, 2007; Hindle & Moroz, 2010). This growing field of indigenous entrepreneurship research, which is somewhat strongly connected with interests in people and planet besides only profit, could potentially "teach" mainstream business and management studies, especially along the lines of safeguarding values regarding peoples (e.g., communities, families, tribes) and nature (e.g., conservation, protection, and considerate use). Such lessons learnt from *indigenous entrepreneurship to the world* are largely the point of departure of this book.

Inspiration for Future Research

It goes without saying that this book does not cover everything about indigenous entrepreneurship in Southeast Asia. As a matter of fact, from a geographic perspective, the volume lacks contributions from several Southeast Asian countries such as Cambodia, Laos, and Singapore. Without doubt these countries have many shapes and forms of indigenous entrepreneurship for which we call upon future researchers to address. As noted in the Introduction, Southeast Asia is a vast and highly populated region, inhabited by many indigenous peoples. Therefore, stories and voices from all corners in this region would be much appreciated. In the same vein, future researchers could address indigenous entrepreneurship in other places of the world that are largely overlooked hitherto, for instance South Asia, Sub-Saharan Africa, or the Tropics. While plenty of studies exist on small business owners and micro-entrepreneurship in these regions (e.g., Eijdenberg & Van Montfort, 2017; Eijdenberg et al., 2023; Paas et al., 2021), the "indigenous lens" is generally not adopted.

Future entrepreneurship research could particularly benefit from studies *by* and *for* indigenous peoples. Often studies are done by researchers who are not indigenous, but who are sometimes foreigners doing research about indigenous entrepreneurship—this partly holds true in this book. We believe better scholarship could be achieved by those who are indigenous, "Sons of the Soil", and/or those who practice indigenous entrepreneurial activities. Their voices are genuine and only they could bring in knowledge that others would never know. As we have learned that indigenous wisdom is often generational and anecdotical, indigenous researchers and authors who take the opportunity to write down their personal experiences and insights can greatly contribute and enrich the research field of indigenous entrepreneurship.

In addition to geographic scope and indigenization of academic contributors, we would like to illustrate a few emerging themes or areas of interest in association with indigenous entrepreneurship that could benefit from further investigation. These themes and areas are inspired by this volume's contributors. For instance, at the strategic level, many indigenous entrepreneurs, particularly those remote indigenous entrepreneurs, traditionally operate in solo, i.e., their operation is limited in their own communities, with little or no engagement with non-indigenous communities (Croce, 2017; Dana & Anderson, 2011). This has been clearly elucidated in a few chapters in this volume, where indigenous entrepreneurial activity consisted of subsistence activities based on local natural resources. With an increasing number of large companies engaging in Corporate Social Responsibility (CSR) initiatives and seeking to integrate societal well-being into their business frameworks, there is potential for indigenous enterprises to collaborate with these corporations and become integral parts of their supply chains. In this aspect, Porter and Kramer's (2011) model, proposing the design and implementation of CSR to create shared value for both companies and society, becomes relevant. Their model has received attention from scholars and practitioners and numerous studies were published showing cases of how the large companies integrate the communities into their business model. However, the cases gave little coverage about how large companies integrate the indigenous people and communities into their business models, and create more opportunities and positive spillover effects, such as transfer of knowledge and skills for indigenous entrepreneurs. Given the distinctive nature of indigenous entrepreneurs, delving into this topic presents an intriguing avenue for exploration.

The next area is the impact of technology on indigenous entrepreneurship. Traditionally, most indigenous entrepreneurs operate at a relatively small scale, due to their staying in the remote area (Scheyvens et al., 2017). The challenges stem from the difficulty of accessing expansive markets due to their geographical isolation. This has become even more severe during COVID-19-pandemic, as Idris et al.'s study shows. Additionally, these enterprises often contend with restricted production capacity, mainly attributable to the absence of modern production facilities. With the deeper penetration of latest technology, particularly digital technology, into the indigenous community, it is worth examining how new technologies reshape their business models and how they integrate the new technology with their unique cultures and values. It is also imperative to understand how the government plays a role in equipping the indigenous entrepreneurs with the necessary technological tools to better their well-beings.

Regarding the relatively small scale operations of indigenous entrepreneurs, future research could focus on directions to scale up and spillover effects. Scaled indigenous enterprises would have a broader socio-economic reach, thereby influencing and inspiring other indigenous entrepreneurs as well. As a result, a greater ecosystem of connected indigenous entrepreneurs could be created (e.g., through suppliers, stakeholders, customers), which can bring about greater societal impact where indigenous entrepreneurship is deeply integrated in different parts of society (e.g., education, government, multinational corporations). For instance, imagine how a group of indigenous entrepreneurs (e.g., educators of generational wisdom, medicine men) collaborate to make a society's education and healthcare at national level more holistic by the integration of indigenous knowledge and practices. Such an example could be a source of inspiration for future researchers.

The chapter authored by Wiroko and Murty highlights an unexplored area warranting further investigation—the adoption of a micro-level approach to examine the operations of informal economies. While existing studies on informal economies predominantly focus on identifying success factors and challenges at the strategic level, there has been comparatively less emphasis on understanding how informal economies manage their personnel and day-to-day operations. For instance, is there a divergence in leadership styles between indigenous and non-indigenous entrepreneurs within the realm of informal economies? Do employees harbour distinct expectations regarding leadership, personal development, and work methods when compared to those in non-indigenous entrepreneurial settings? These important questions, among many others, remain largely unaddressed and require further investigation.

On the practice side, the reach to capital and investment schemes appears as important for the survival of entrepreneurs starting their street cart shop to a posh established retail outlet in a shopping mall or factory establishment and to the digital world. While this edited volume delves into the experiences of ethnic and micro-entrepreneurs, there are few success stories of indigenous individuals who played pivotal roles in forming major business conglomerates, such as those in Thailand (e.g., Charoen Pokphand Group multi-industry company), Indonesia (PT Bakrie and Brothers TBK—multi-industry company), and Cambodia (e.g., Sokimex Investment Group—huge presence in the hospitality business), to name a few. Although, in some instances, the assimilated Chinese populace may be traced in these achievers' lineage, it is important to note that the success of these individuals cannot be solely judged by their ethnicity. Rather, it is a testament to their heightened awareness and the struggles they overcame within the negotiated strata. McVey (1992) highlights that indigenous entrepreneurship was dominated by global capitalism in much of Southeast Asia. From the contributions of the chapters in this book, it is indeed notable that the focus remains on the subterranean entrepreneurs and not much about how the competition is faced off with the larger local conglomerates and presence of multinational businesses. While the political and business elites may avail themselves to huge capital outlays for economic activities and business opportunities, the micro-entrepreneurs are often the ones that need the seed funding to catapult their business beyond the pushcart in many of the emerging and rural community regions (Prabhugaonkar et al., 2020). In this context, banks and financial institutions have an important role to play in stimulating and supporting such indigenous entrepreneurial entities. Tipton had written in 2008 about the debilitating effects of historical structures and institutional frameworks that impede the growth of indigenous businesses. In 2020, a team of scholars (Amiruddin et al., 2020) found that other than a lack of financial help, indigenous entrepreneurs also face the deficit in technical knowledge of markets, technology, and generic skills such as networking and management know-how. Herein lies another fertile ground for further investigation to review if much of these strong structures and frameworks have given way in the contemporary Southeast Asian business environment and contributed to the success of indigenous entrepreneurship activities.

This collection of chapter contributions clearly highlights the need for policy makers to reaffirm their recognition of institutional ease and strengthen support for indigenous enterprises with seed funding, market introduction, and importantly education for generic skills. The continuous nurturing of small and medium indigenous enterprises will go a long way to validate contributions of indigenous driven economic growth as much as the global capital stimulants.

Concluding Remarks

The chapters in this book have provided a flavour of different shapes and forms of indigenous entrepreneurship in Southeast Asia. Yet, much more scholarship and hands-on takeaways about indigenous entrepreneurship are needed. Highly cognizant of the book's limitations, we encourage future researchers to delve deeper in the phenomenon of indigenous entrepreneurship in general and in Southeast Asia in specific. It is our hope that indigenous entrepreneurship will be a great source of inspiration for both researchers and practitioners and that people around the world will be enlightened by refreshed ways of entrepreneuring that remain to be unearthed.

References

Amiruddin, M. H., Sumarwati, S., Madar, A. R., Abdullah, N. S., & Suib, S. N. (2020). Understanding the factors that inhibit the success of indigenous entrepreneurs in Malaysia. *International Journal of Research and Innovation in Social Science, 14*(10), 19–23.

Banerjee, S. B. (2022). Decolonizing management theory: A critical perspective. *Journal of Management Studies, 59*(4), 1074–1087.

Bastien, F., Coraiola, D. M., & Foster, W. M. (2023). Indigenous Peoples and organization studies. *Organization Studies, 44*(4), 659–675.

Certo, S. T., & Miller, T. (2008). Social entrepreneurship: Key issues and concepts. *Business Horizons, 51*(4), 267–271.

Croce, F. (2017). Contextualized indigenous entrepreneurial models: A systematic review of indigenous entrepreneurship literature. *Journal of Management & Organization, 23*(6), 886–906.

Dana, L. P. (2015). Indigenous entrepreneurship: An emerging field of research. *International Journal of Business and Globalisation, 14*(2), 158–169.

Dana, L. P., & Anderson, R. B. (2007). *International handbook of research on indigenous entrepreneurship*. Edward Elgar.

Dana, L. P., & Anderson, R. B. (2011). The evolution of entrepreneurship in Arviat: The southernmost community of mainland Nunavut. *International Journal of Entrepreneurship and Small Business, 14*(4), 509–532.

Chawla, T., Eijdenberg, E. L. & Wood, J. (2021). Environmental resilience of Bottom of the Pyramid strategies towards single-use plastics: A recipe from an emerging economy. In Chaiechi, T. (Ed.), *Economic effects of natural disasters* (pp. 161–178). Elsevier.

Eijdenberg, E. L., & van Montfort, K. (2017). Explaining firm performance in african least developed countries: Evidence from Burundi and Tanzania. *International Review of Entrepreneurship, 15*(3), 375–394.

Eijdenberg, E. L., Mukherjee, M., & Wood, J. (2023). *Innovation-driven business and sustainability in the tropics*. Springer.

Hindle, K., & Moroz, P. (2010). Indigenous entrepreneurship as a research field: Developing a definitional framework from the emerging canon. *International Entrepreneurship and Management Journal, 6*, 357–385.

Jones, M. V., Coviello, N., & Tang, Y. K. (2011). International entrepreneurship research (1989–2009): A domain ontology and thematic analysis. *Journal of Business Venturing, 26*(6), 632–659.

Kuratko, D. F. (2005). The emergence of entrepreneurship education: Development, trends, and challenges. *Entrepreneurship Theory and Practice, 29*(5), 577–597.

Keupp, M. M., & Gassmann, O. (2009). The past and the future of international entrepreneurship: A review and suggestions for developing the field. *Journal of Management, 35*(3), 600–633.

Mcmullan, W. E., & Long, W. A. (1987). Entrepreneurship education in the nineties. *Journal of Business Venturing, 2*(3), 261–275.

McVey, R. (1992). The materialization of the Southeast Asian entrepreneur. In Ampalavanar, B. (Ed.), *Chinese business enterprise: Critical perspectives on business and management* (pp. 335–365). Routlegde.

Nabi, G., Liñán, F., Fayolle, A., Krueger, N., & Walmsley, A. (2017). The impact of entrepreneurship education in higher education: A systematic review and research agenda. *Academy of Management Learning & Education, 16*(2), 277–299.

Paas, L. J., Eijdenberg, E. L., & Masurel, E. (2021). Adoption of services and apps on mobile phones by micro-entrepreneurs in Sub-Saharan Africa. *International Journal of Market Research, 63*(1), 27–42.

Porter, M. E., & Kramer, M. R. (2011). Creating shared value: Redefining capitalism and the role of the corporation in society. *Harvard Business Review, 89*(1/2), 62–77.

Peredo, A. M., & McLean, M. (2006). Social entrepreneurship: A critical review of the concept. *Journal of World Business, 41*(1), 56–65.

Prabhugaonkar, Y. B., Minh, D. X., Thirumaran, K., Sim, K. S., Pruhtpahon, S., & Raghav, M. (2020). Asian entrepreneurship in tourism and hospitality: Financial support, business sustainability. *Entrepreneurial development and innovation in family businesses and SMEs*, 1–21.

Saebi, T., Foss, N. J., & Linder, S. (2019). Social entrepreneurship research: Past achievements and future promises. *Journal of Management, 45*(1), 70–95.

Scheyvens, R., Banks, G., Meo-Sewabu, L., & Decena, T. (2017). Indigenous entrepreneurship on customary land in the Pacific: Measuring sustainability. *Journal of Management & Organization, 23*(6), 774–785.

Terjesen, S., Hessels, J., & Li, D. (2016). Comparative international entrepreneurship: A review and research agenda. *Journal of Management, 42*(1), 299–344.

Tipton, F. B. (2009). Southeast Asian capitalism: History, institutions, states, and firms. *Asia Pacific Journal of Management, 26*, 401–434.

Index

E. L. Eijdenberg et al. (eds.), *Indigenous Entrepreneurship in Southeast Asia*, Palgrave Studies in Equity, Diversity, Inclusion, and Indigenization in Business, https://doi.org/10.1007/978-3-031-54457-6

FSC
www.fsc.org
MIX
Papier | Fördert gute Waldnutzung
FSC® C083411

Kolibri 360 GmbH
Ferdinand-Jühlke-Straße 7
99095 Erfurt, Deutschland
produktsicherheit@kolibri360.de